Gail,

Thanks for opening up your lovely home. March 200?

Margie

Julie

Kiss
Susan ♡

Thank you!
Michelle ☺

NEW ALBANY

Cooking with Friends

A SIGNATURE COLLECTION

NEW ALBANY, OHIO

ISBN-10: 0-9790015-0-1
ISBN-13: 978-0-9790015-0-5

Published by New Albany Cooking with Friends
PO Box 741, New Albany, Ohio 43054
info@nacookingwithfriends.com   www.nacookingwithfriends.com

Watercolor paintings: George W. Acock
Cover photos (left to right): Original New Albany School House (courtesy E. Gibbs); Cooking with Friends food spread (courtesy Daniel W. Floss & Associates Photography); New Albany residence (New Albany Classic Signature Series photos courtesy Daniel W. Floss & Associates Photography)

10 9 8 7 6 5 4 3 2 1

Printed in China.

Callawind
Custom Cookbooks

Produced by Callawind Custom Cookbooks
A division of Callawind Publications Inc.
3551 St. Charles Boulevard, Suite 179, Kirkland, Quebec H9H 3C4
E-mail: info@callawind.com   Website: www.callawind.com
Cover and text design: Marcy Claman
Copy editing: Shaun Oakey
Indexing: Heather Ebbs

Note from the Cookbook Co-chairs

New Albany Cooking with Friends is proud to welcome you to *A Signature Collection*. This culinary labor of love is a compilation of the best recipes from our club's first five years of cooking.

Left to right: Mia Johansson-Strench, Marilu Faber, Diane Forrest LaHowchic

Recipes were collected from our friends and families, from exotic fare encountered in our travels around the world, from our varied ethnic and cultural heritage, and most of all, from our own inspired experimentation. Members enthusiastically dug into family treasure troves, and recipes that have been "in the family for generations" were generously shared for the sheer pleasure of participating in this special project. The recipes that follow have been tested multiple times by club members and their relatives and friends. Most were tried out in our homes, others at potluck parties, and still others were sent to former members now living in other regions or abroad. Out of the recipes selected for the book, we crafted a variety of menu suggestions to make planning for that special dinner, cocktail party, or family get-together a breeze. An added bonus is a primer filled with advice and tips on how to form a cooking club from a group that has successfully done it and has greatly enjoyed the experience.

A Signature Collection was also designed to give you a glimpse into the special character of this place we call home, the village of New Albany, Ohio. Each of the food chapters includes a short essay and a corresponding picture depicting life in our unique and gorgeous Georgian-inspired community. Sprinkled throughout the pages are historical commentaries and articles that introduce you to various aspects of the township and the areas around it. These features highlight the strong sense of community that exists in New Albany and why organizations like New Albany Cooking with Friends thrive and feel strongly committed to giving back to the community.

As you read our book, we hope you will be inspired to try one of our menus at your next party, discover new recipes to add to your "favorites" collection, and enjoy a leisurely stroll through New Albany's history and present.

We are grateful for your support. Ultimately, the families and children serviced by the Mid-Ohio FoodBank, New Albany Special Connections, and New Albany Safety Town are the beneficiaries of your purchase of *A Signature Collection*. On their behalf, as well as on behalf of New Albany Cooking with Friends, we thank you.

— *Marilu Faber, Diane Forrest LaHowchic, and Mia Johansson-Strench, Cookbook Co-chairs*

New Albany scenes

Contents

Note from The New Albany Company vi

About George W. Acock — The Artist vii

Acknowledgments viii

Sponsors ix

INTRODUCTION 11

New Albany Cooking with Friends 13

History 14

Cooking Club Primer: A Simple Recipe 17

Menu Selections 21

BEVERAGES 25

APPETIZERS 43

SOUPS 85

SALADS 105

VEGETABLES AND SIDE DISHES 127

MAIN COURSES 159

DESSERTS, COOKIES, AND CAKES 205

INDEX 241

COOKBOOK ORDER FORM 248

Note from The New Albany Company

DEAR NEIGHBORS,

It is with great pride that I congratulate New Albany Cooking with Friends on the publication of *A Signature Collection,* the organization's inaugural cookbook.

I'm particularly proud of this book because it so poignantly reflects the spirit of New Albany and its people. New Albany residents for generations have combined social events with support of worthy philanthropic causes. From the village's earliest days, New Albany neighbors supported each other and the greater good through events such as ice cream socials and community celebrations. That spirit is alive and well today as groups such as Cooking with Friends, the New Albany Women's Network, the New Albany Community Foundation, the New Albany Chamber of Commerce, and the New Albany Classic Signature Series continue to build community through their good work.

This book contains beautiful images of the community, but it also serves as a wonderful illustration of what can happen when neighbors gather to enjoy a shared passion. Through Cooking with Friends, neighbors have developed lasting friendships. Moreover, they have built on their love of cooking and used it to enrich the lives of others by designating the cookbook proceeds to benefit local charity organizations and non-profits.

The New Albany Company and New Albany Realty are pleased to support this wonderful cookbook, this worthy cause, and this extraordinary community organization. We hope you enjoy *A Signature Collection* and that it becomes a treasured part of your own cookbook collection.

Sincerely,

John W. Kessler
Chairman
The New Albany Company

About George W. Acock—The Artist

A GRADUATE OF THE OHIO STATE UNIVERSITY, GEORGE ACOCK RECEIVED HIS DEGREE IN ARCHITECTURE IN 1963.

He is professionally registered in Arizona, Florida, Georgia, Iowa, Maryland, Massachusetts, Michigan, New Jersey, New York, Ohio, Texas, and Utah. George has taught architecture at the Ohio State University and is a 1999 Distinguished Alumni Award Recipient from the Austin E. Knowlton School of Architecture. Families throughout New Albany neighborhoods are enjoying the style and detail of Acock's residential designs. The New Albany Library and the Tween Brands headquarters are perfect examples of the diversity of his architectural portfolio.

In the spring of 2001, George accompanied the Study Abroad program from the Knowlton School of Architecture to Italy, where he taught watercolor painting classes.

Acock's passion for watercolors commenced at the early age of five. His mother, a schoolteacher, encouraged him by providing all the necessary paints, brushes, and paper. George's father, an engineer, added math and the sciences to his skills that later led to his decision to study architecture. His architecture has received many public awards and acknowledgments, and at the same time his watercolors have adorned the walls of his many clients' homes and offices since 1980.

George is a member of the Central Ohio Watercolor Society, an associate of the American Watercolor Society, and a member of the National Watercolor Society. Since 1992, George has been sharing his watercolors in an annual desktop calendar that clients, friends, and colleagues treasure and display with great pleasure.

Over the years, George has graciously donated his work to numerous organizations throughout the area in support of their fundraising efforts. His watercolors have been exhibited in one-person shows at the Ohio State University Faculty Club and the Ohio State University Humanities Institute.

Acknowledgements

New Albany Cooking with Friends
A Signature Collection
Cookbook Committee

Editorial and Executive Board
Marilu Faber, Diane Forrest LaHowchic, Mia Johansson-Strench

Food Features and Recipes
Marilu Faber

Community Features
Diane Forrest LaHowchic and Mia Johansson-Strench

Book Production and Finance
Diane Forrest LaHowchic

Marketing and Media Relations
Mia Johansson-Strench

Book Launch Event
Rhonda Koulermos and Sheryl Zangardi

Logo Design
Tonya Petrucci

Website
Patrice Douglas

Recipe Testing Coordination

Jakki Allen   Kathleen Gaydos
Jody Altschule   Lindy Turnbull
Patrice Douglas   Carline Weddington
Jan Espersen   Stella Woo
Sally Farber   Sheryl Zangardi

Recipe Proofreading

Melissa Baginski   Colleen O'Dell
Lori Griffith   Ginger Sluder
Josie Harris

Sponsors

We wish to acknowledge our sponsors without whom this project would not have been possible. Thank you for your generous support.

PREMIER PARTNER

NEW ALBANY REALTY, LTD.

THE NEW ALBANY CLASSIC
SIGNATURE SERIES

SUPPORTING SPONSOR

Abercrombie & Fitch

BENEFACTOR

PATRONS

Marilu and Tim Faber

Sally and Sandy Farber

Diane Forrest and Nick LaHowchic

Ellen and David Ryan

Lynne and Stephen Smith

Budros, Ruhlin & Roe

Vorys, Sater, Seymour and Pease LLP

ASSOCIATES
Jody and Joel Altschule
Linda and Tom Hellman
Mia Johansson-Strench and Don Strench
Jennie and Mark Wilson
Bob Evans Farms
Fifth Third Bank
Genesis Audio Ltd
Giant Eagle
Limited Brands Foundation

FRIENDS
Veronica and Walter Casey • Anne Bramman and Scott Davis • Patrice, Vince and Alyx Douglas
Leslie and Gilbert Faust • Kathleen and Ed Gaydos • Janet and Michael Grafton • Lori and Scott Griffith
Josie and Jim Harris • Marci and Bill Ingram • Penny and Rick Jackson • Dana and Mike Kramer
Eileen and Bill Leuby Family • Gloria and Bill May • Cindy and Tom McFadden • Tracy and Tom Myers
Colleen and Tim O'Dell • Sandy Raines • Ed Razek • Dr. Karen A. Riccio • Phyllis and Len Schlesinger
Eleanor and Marty Sedluk • Kate and Tony Thomas • Marianne and George Troutman • Lindy and Gary Turnbull
Laura and Adam Weiser • Ellen and Ed Yen • Roy Gottlieb, DDS • Huntington Bank New Albany
Insurance Office of Central Ohio • Mark Levy, DDS of StoneRidge Dental Care
McCullough's Landscape and Nursery LLC • New Albany Women's Network • The Raines Group • Salon Therapy

TALENT AND RESOURCE DONATIONS

Book Production Contract Analysis
Connie Resanovich

Digital Production of Watercolors
Stingray Studios

Marketing Materials Design
Palladia House Ltd

Warehousing and Shipping
New World Van Lines

Cooking with Friends Membership Photographs
Dan W. Floss & Associates

Legal Services
Jerry O. Allen, Esq., Bricker & Eckler, LLP

Sponsor Presentation Pamphlet
Icon Group

Web Master
Scott Freeman

GIFT CERTIFICATES
Giant Eagle
Limited Brands Foundation
Tween Brands Inc
Woodhaven Farms – The Cooking Connection

We sincerely hope that no one involved with this cookbook has been inadvertently overlooked.

Introduction

Cooking with Friends Membership

Back row (left to right): Jakki Allen, Ellen Yen, Stella Woo, Susan Fortner, Josie Harris, Sheryl Zangardi, Chris Gehr, Jan Espersen, Jody Altschule, Lindy Turnbull

Middle row: Patrice Douglas, Susan Milne, Tonya Petrucci, Kate Thomas, Ginger Sluder, Susan Corley, Laura Weiser, Sally Farber, Rhonda Koulermos, Kathleen Gaydos, Colleen O'Dell

Front row: Carline Weddington, Diane Forrest LaHowchic, Marilu Faber, Mia Johansson-Strench

Not in picture: Melissa Baginski, Lori Griffith, Ronda Hobart, Pat Huddle, Dana Kramer, Gloria May, Lisette McVey, Tracy Myers, and Nimfa Stewart

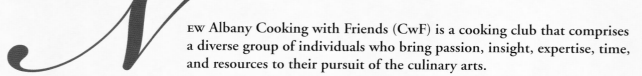

New Albany Cooking with Friends

NEW Albany Cooking with Friends (CwF) is a cooking club that comprises a diverse group of individuals who bring passion, insight, expertise, time, and resources to their pursuit of the culinary arts.

- CwF was established in January 2001. Since then, members have met each month (with a break during the summer) to explore new and time-tested menus from all over the world.

- CwF has been featured in the *Columbus Dispatch, This Week in New Albany*, and *New Albany News*.

- CwF was granted a 501c(3) tax-exempt status in March 2006.

OUR MEMBERS

From its inception, Cooking with Friends has maintained an open membership available to individuals interested in the activities of a cooking club.

ACTIVE MEMBERSHIP ROSTER

Jakki Allen, Jody Altschule, Melissa Baginski, Susan Corley, Patrice Douglas, Jan Espersen, Marilu Faber, Sally Farber, Diane Forrest LaHowchic, Susan Fortner, Kathleen Gaydos, Chris Gehr, Lori Griffith, Josie Harris, Ronda Hobart, Pat Huddle, Mia Johansson-Strench, Rhonda Koulermos, Dana Kramer, Gloria May, Lisette McVey, Susan Milne, Tracy Myers, Colleen O'Dell, Tonya Petrucci, Ginger Sluder, Nimfa Stewart, Kate Thomas, Lindy Turnbull, Carline Weddington, Laura Weiser, Stella Woo, Ellen Yen, Sheryl Zangardi

ASSOCIATE MEMBERS

Robin Bishop, Zsuzsa Bocsardy, Ronni Casey, Paula Ewell, Melissa Fata, Michelle Flaks, Fiona Gauntlett, Lynn Hanon, Linda Hellman, Laura Hill, Lisa Kehoe, Kim Moreland, Eileen Pewitt, Sandy Raines-Cadieux, Kim Richardson, Phyllis Schlesinger, Eleanor Sedluk, Kim Tarnapoll, Jana Torchia, Sats Tripathy

History

NEW ALBANY COOKING WITH FRIENDS IS A NON-PROFIT ORGANIZATION COMPRISING A DIVERSE GROUP OF WOMEN WHO BRING PASSION, INSIGHT, EXPERTISE, TIME, AND RESOURCES TO THEIR PURSUIT OF ANYTHING CULINARY. AS WE CELEBRATED OUR FIFTH ANNIVERSARY IN JANUARY 2006, WE DECIDED TO SHARE OUR EXPERIENCES AND OUR RECIPE COLLECTION BY PUBLISHING *A Signature Collection.*

New Albany Cooking with Friends is the story of a group of women coming together to share meals, recipes, and friendships. Our inspiration grew out of a desire to foster connections with others in our community. Many had recently moved to New Albany and were searching for new friends and ways to connect with others who had similar interests. Marilu Faber established the club in January 2001 when she invited seven friends to get together for a cooking demo followed by lunch. The theme of the inaugural lunch was "East/West Fusion," reflecting the diversity of the invitees. Two of the women were from the United States, two from the Philippines, one from Hungary, one from Malaysia, one from

Left to right: Stella Woo, Carline Weddington, Sally Farber, Kathleen Gaydos

Sweden, and one from South Africa. Pure serendipity had brought them together, whether it was residing in the same neighborhood, having husbands who shared a common employer, or having children in the same playgroup.

Over the next five years the group continued to get together, attracted new members, and saw some original members move away. Since the club's inception more than 50 women have participated in the cooking sessions and celebrations. In addition to varied cultural backgrounds, our members represent a wide range of age, life experiences, occupations, and culinary skills. This diverse mix creates an interesting and fun group of women who constantly learn from each other and about each other.

As we look back, the success of Cooking with Friends seems almost inevitable. We were guaranteed to thrive in a community such as New Albany, where the large number of new residents makes it easier to connect with other newcomers who are not yet established in a social group. Unlike gourmet groups or food and wine societies where culinary credentials are required to join, we have maintained an open membership, with the only requirements for admission being an enthusiasm to meet new friends, an adventurous spirit to experiment with new cuisines, and an ability to laugh when a dish turns out to be a failure. The club has become a home where individuals share meals and cooking secrets and catch up on each other's lives. It has become a support group, a venue for making lasting friendships, and a vehicle for community sharing.

Editorial and Executive Board Members with Recipe Captains (seated left to right)—First row: Jakki Allen, Mia Johansson-Strench, Marilu Faber, Diane Forrest LaHowchic, Carline Weddington; Second row: Stella Woo, Lindy Turnbull, Sally Farber (seated), Jan Espersen, Jody Altschule, Sheryl Zangardi (seated), Patrice Douglas, Kathleen Gaydos

A SIGNATURE COLLECTION: THE JOURNEY

After four years of successful cooking events, our members started talking about publishing a Cooking with Friends cookbook. Having accumulated a rich collection of recipes covering a wide range of themes, cuisines, and regions of the world, it made sense to collate the recipes in a book so we could share them beyond the group and preserve them for posterity. We brainstormed and came up with the concept of a cookbook that featured the "best of Cooking with Friends recipes" and at the same time showcased the uniqueness of our wonderful community of New Albany. The fascination with this exciting idea began to take hold, and a few months before our fifth anniversary, Diane Forrest LaHowchic committed to researching the different aspects of publishing a cookbook.

Over coffee one afternoon in fall 2005, with a dozen members in the same dining room where we had our inaugural lunch five years before, we started to make the cookbook a reality. Mia Johansson-Strench, an active community leader, signed on with Marilu and Diane to form the Executive Committee that has steered the project to completion. Ten members later agreed to be "food captains" and led the effort of selecting, testing, and evaluating the recipes. The rest of the membership participated by testing recipes and volunteering for the myriad tasks involved in putting together a book—proofreading recipes, creating a logo, designing marketing materials, developing a website, calling on sponsors, stuffing envelopes, and so on. We invited guest authors to contribute articles that celebrated New Albany and the areas surrounding it.

We reached out to photographers and artists to add color and texture to the book. We also enlisted spouses, friends, and members of the community for support and talent.

From the very beginning our members decided that proceeds from sponsorships and the sale of the cookbook will go back to the community, specifically to projects supporting women's and children's causes. We evaluated many deserving organizations, and the group chose the Mid-Ohio FoodBank as well as local organizations including New Albany Special Connections and New Albany Safety Town and Adventure Playground as beneficiaries.

One of the many pleasurable aspects of putting together this cookbook was the recipe testing. It gave our group countless hours doing what we love and prompted the scheduling of enjoyable get-togethers where we could provide feedback on the recipes. We are grateful for the commitment of our members who made this all possible and the many friends and family who tasted our cooking and gave their honest critiques.

Putting this book together has been a real adventure. As soon as we committed to creating the cookbook, we discovered how much effort was really going to be needed to accomplish this project with our small group in a short time. But we were determined to do it and are thankful for this great learning experience. Our Premier Partner, the New Albany Company, has provided invaluable resources and guidance along the way. We thank them deeply for that. We also thank the many sponsors, individuals, and friends who believed in our cause and provided the support and resources that made publication of this book possible.

— *Marilu Faber*

Proceeds from sponsorships and the sale of the cookbook will go back to the community

Cooking Club Primer: A Simple Recipe

We HAVE BEEN VERY HAPPY WITH OUR COOKING CLUB AND ARE NATURALLY EAGER TO SHARE THIS WONDERFUL RECIPE OF FRIENDSHIP. HERE IS A STEP-BY-STEP GUIDE FOR HOW TO GET A COOKING CLUB OFF THE GROUND AND RUNNING:

INGREDIENTS:

Loads of enthusiasm about meeting new people

Pounds of adventurous spirit

Cupful of ability to work with a team

Pinch of innovation

4 good cooks (preferably with a few cooking classes under their belt)

4 natural cooks (typically self-taught or kept their moms or grandmothers company in the kitchen)

4 apprentices, thrown in for good measure

1 dedicated event coordinator

Extra sense of humor for garnish

PROCEDURE:

Send out feelers in your community via the neighborhood grapevine; established groups such as book clubs, tennis teams, and aerobics classes; the workplace bulletin board; and on-line posting. The goal is to identify a core group of at least eight willing and enthusiastic members. (It is important to choose members that have compatible personalities and enjoy each other's company.)

Gather the core group at your home or the local coffee shop to brainstorm. At the end of this meeting you should have established some basic ground rules that include:

COURTESY DANIEL W. FLOSS & ASSOCIATES PHOTOGRAPHY

Left to right: Marilu Faber, Jody Altschule, Rhonda Koulermos, Jan Esperson, Josie Harris

• When and how often the group should meet

Establish how often you want to meet without making the gatherings feel like a chore. If most of your members have heavy work and volunteer commitments, pick a standing date and time (e.g., every first Monday at 6 p.m. every other month). In our club, we pick meeting dates based on the hosts-of-the-month's availability. Our members have a variety of commitments on their calendars, so picking a standing date would not have worked for us.

• *Meeting format*

We have tried three formats, all of which work for different occasions. The first is hands-on cooking. A pair (in some cases a trio) of members come up with a cooking theme based on a cuisine (e.g., Mediterranean, Tex-Mex, or Chinese) or occasion (e.g., Weekend Brunch or Fourth of July Picnic). The hosts research recipes for a complete menu, prepare a menu booklet for distribution to attendees, and shop for ingredients. The whole group convenes at a member's home to cook together and eat afterwards. Kitchen limitations in the average home make this format ideal for no more than 12 participants.

The second format is the progressive dinner. The hosts plan the theme and menu, but the various courses are prepared in two or more kitchens, after which the whole group meets in one home for the meal. This format accommodates more participants and makes it possible to do hands-on cooking in several smaller kitchens.

The third format is the potluck. The hosts decide the theme, come up with an extensive menu, and assign recipes that are prepared by members at home and brought to a host's home for the meal. A potluck variation has the hosts announcing a theme and assigning participants a food category (be it hors d'oeuvre, entrée, or dessert). Each participant then does her own research to come up with a recipe. Potlucks work well for occasions that call for a large number of participants. For instance, our club held a potluck on the occasion of a Fall Wine-Tasting Evening, where we invited members and their spouses.

Any of these formats can be adapted. It is important to plan a calendar of events at least six months ahead to ensure a good balance of formats and themes.

During the meals we discuss the recipes we prepared, highlighting the peculiarities of certain ingredients and methods, sharing new techniques learned, and on occasion analyzing why the recipe failed. Additionally, we share table presentation tips, a very important component of entertaining.

• *Membership policy*

Although it is important to choose members whom you will want to spend time with on a regular basis, it is also important to have a good mix of people with some common interests beyond food. Having a diverse membership has allowed our club to feature an interesting array of monthly menus that has run the gamut from Cajun/Creole, to Southeast Asian, to French provincial cooking. With adventurous members, we have featured innovative spa cuisine and aphrodisiac dinner fare. A club will only be as interesting as the types of people you include. The ideal number depends on your preferred format and comfort level. A hands-on session will be chaotic if there are more than 12 cooks in a regular home kitchen, but if you go with potluck you will be able to accommodate more. Our club has regular members who host and organize monthly events, and we maintain a list of "subs" or members who pitch in for the inevitable last-minute cancellation.

An issue to address is whether to make it a women-only club or allow both men and women to join. Decide this in light of the group's objectives. Our club's decision to go women-only was dictated by the time we agreed to meet, typically midday on Wednesdays and Thursdays.

• Event coordination

With busy lives and inattention by some members to the calendar, all the good intentions as well as the plans made at the last organizational meeting can easily fall by the wayside. The group will need a point person (and ideally a backup) to be overall coordinator to ensure that events get scheduled and members remember their assignments. E-mail and website postings are helpful communication tools.

Chef Tips:

Start with simple sessions for your first few meetings. As you gain confidence, attempt full-course dinners or fancy buffets. Our first session was a four-item menu and it was enough to whet the appetite without making participation in the cooking club intimidating.

Share the cost of events across the board and immediately collect the dues. We require no-shows to pay their contribution but we send them a plateful of treats. Cost sharing is easy when the hosts do all the food shopping and there is a total bill for the ingredients (plus wines) that can be divided equally. During potlucks, there will be variations on what individuals end up spending. There is no easy solution to making costs equitable in this case. The event coordinator may assign wines to the person making the salad course to even things out, but this solution is not perfect—salads aren't necessarily inexpensive! Just let the members know that costs will even out during the year and make every effort to be fair with assignments.

NEW ALBANY
SPECIAL CONNECTIONS

*N*ew Albany Special Connections is a non-profit organization founded in 2002 with a simple but ambitious mission: to better serve children with special needs through education, resources, and support. By strengthening the links between home, school, and community, New Albany Special Connections is working to improve the lives of children with special needs and their families.

Created by parents of children with special needs, New Albany Special Connections strives to build positive, productive, and collaborative partnerships among families, educators of the New Albany–Plain Local School District, and the greater New Albany community. Through these partnerships, New Albany Special Connections offers a wide range of innovative programs and services. The organization researches best practices and progressive models for education, socialization, and extracurricular activities.

New Albany Special Connections is fulfilling its mission by providing educational programs for parents and professionals featuring local and national experts, publishing a resource guide, developing children's programs in the arts, and advancing socialization for children with special needs through creative programs such as peer buddies. Complete information can be found by visiting www.naspecialconnections.org.
— *New Albany Special Connections*

Although we do not have an official course-rotation policy, we take turns doing different parts of the meal. Do not always assign the presumed "master baker" to desserts and breads, or the "grillmeister" to the meat, so that members continue to learn new things. If someone is not confident about making an unfamiliar recipe, encourage her to try. If the thing flops, you can all laugh about it. The venerable Julia Child was known to have dropped omelets to the floor as she did demos on national television. The goal is not perfection but to have FUN and learn along the way! If the daunting recipe works, celebrate the great feeling of accomplishment with some back-slapping and high-fives!

Clean-up after cooking must be addressed from the onset. Our club agreed early on that everybody helps out in the clean-up. This rule has to be reinforced frequently, as it is easy to forget when one has had a wonderful meal and the next appointment for the day beckons. One alternative is to hire cleaning help, with everyone pitching in to defray the cost of the service.

Keep business out of it. People join cooking clubs to have a special time when they can relax, bond as they broil kabobs or chop tomatoes, savor good food and wine, and engage in scintillating conversations. This camaraderie can easily be broken and awkward situations ensue if somebody, say, begins pushing her financial services on other members.

Finally, do not lose sight of the cooking club's objectives. The goal, first and foremost, is to have fun while expanding your food horizons and honing your cooking prowess. In our club, using our culinary talents to do something for our community imbued us with a sense of purpose and accomplishment. Be sensitive to everybody's idiosyncracies and remember to boost the cooking confidence in one another as much as possible. Mutual support and respect is the name of the game. It is what keeps a cooking club—or any organization for that matter—going.

SERVES: at least a dozen food lovers, their families and friends, and the community at large

PS: Take lots of pictures. Several years down the road, you can aspire to publishing your cooking club's cookbook. If you do not want to sweat it out, simply distribute copies of *A Signature Collection* to all your members and have extra copies available to hand out to friends and families whenever you have to dispense advice on how to run a successful cooking club. — *Marilu Faber*

Menu Selections

CELEBRATIONS FROM AROUND THE WORLD

East Meets West

Green Cardamom Chai 41

Fried Spring Rolls *(Lumpia Shanghai)* 76

Mixed Greens with Oriental Vinaigrette 112

Chicken Paprikash 180

Crème Caramel Filipino Style *(Leche Flan)* 224

A Jaunt Through Southeast Asia

Grilled Beef, Chicken, or Pork on Skewers (Satays) 81

Vietnamese Fresh Summer Rolls *(Goi Cuon)* 74

Corn and Crab Soup, Thai Style
(Kaeng Poo Kab Kao Phod) 103

Broccoli with Ginger 133

Thai Fried Noodles *(Pad Thai)* 168

Coconut Flan 225

"Gong Hei Fat Choi!" Chinese New Year Banquet

Pork and Vegetable Potstickers with
Soy Dipping Sauce 78

Bon Bon Chicken Salad 125

Roasted Pepper Pasta 140

Stir-fried Snow Peas with Shrimp 145

Kung Pao Chicken 176

Cantonese Pork Tenderloin *(Char Siu)* 200

Ginger and Vanilla Crème Brûlée 226

Exotic Indian Excursion

Spicy Chicken Drummettes 80

Lentil Soup *(Masoor Dal)* 99

Green Beans Poriyal 137

Fragrant Beef Curry 193

Mango Lassi 31

A Scandinavian Soiree

Creamy Beet and Apple Salad *(Rödbetssallad)* 116

Mia's Berry Glazed Asparagus 132

Lemon Rice 148

Pork Medallions in Crème Fraîche 201

Mormor's Meringue and Cream Torte 232

"La Dolce Vita" Italian Dinner

Bruschetta with Pesto and Tomatoes 54

Hearty Minestrone Soup 101

Asparagus and Red Pepper Salad
(Insalata di Asparagi e Peperoni Rossi) 109

Osso Buco (Braised Veal Shanks) 197

Tiramisù with Kahlua and Amaretto 231

Under the Tuscan Sun

Tomato and Eggplant Gratin Soup 95

Flatbread with Goat Cheese, Caramelized Onions,
and Rosemary 55

Arugula and Figs with Warm Shallot Vinaigrette 114

Citrus Angel Hair Pasta with Mint 163

Veal Braciola 196

Biscotti di Prato
(Bite-sized Almond Biscotti from Prato) 212

Dining à la Provence

Roasted Mushroom Soup (*Potage aux Champignons Rôtis*) 100

Gruyère Cheese Puffs (*Gougères*) 64

Beet, Pear, and Bitter Leaf Salad 111

French Green Bean "Kindling" (*Fagotins des Haricots Verts*) 136

Goat Cheese and Potato Pie (*Tarte au Fromage de Chèvre et aux Pommes de Terre*) 156

Pork Tenderloin in Baguette (*Porc en Baguette*) 202

Apple Clafoutis 227

Meandering Through the Mediterranean

Black Pepper and Herb–crusted Rack of Lamb 184

Feta Herb Dip 52

Braised Leeks and Tomatoes, Greek Style (*Prasa*) 137

Mediterranean Seafood Stew 172

Sally's Orange Almond Cake 236

A Moroccan Repast

Pearl Couscous with Olives and Roasted Tomatoes 147

Spinach with Chickpeas (*Espinacas con Garbanzos*) 146

Moroccan Meat-filled Phyllo Pastry (*Briouat Bil Kefta*) 195

Moorish Pork Kabobs (*Pinchos Morunos*) 83

Peach Currant Rugelach 218

Caribbean Cruising

Summer Tropical Fruit Soup 90

Cranberry Cashew Salad 110

Pork and Red Pepper Mini Skewers with Mango Salsa 84

Vegetable Kabobs with Balsamic Vinegar Toss 153

Flank Steak with Papaya-Kiwi Marinade 188

Bananas Foster 223

Mexican Fiesta

Jalapeño-spiked Deviled Eggs 65

Cowboy Caviar with "Homemade" Tortilla Chips 53

South-of-the-Border Corn Chowder 102

Spanish Potato Omelet (*Tortilla Española*) 68

Spicy Grilled Pork Tenderloin 204

Mexican Truffles 220

An International Buffet

Virgin Strawberry Daiquiri 32

Cauliflower and Black Pepper Hummus 50

Piquant Portuguese Shrimp 71

Couscous and Shrimp Salad 123

French Bean "Kindling" (*Fagotins des Haricots Verts*) 136

Greek Shrimp with Feta 166

Chicken Adobo (*Adobong Manok*) 181

Korean Barbecued Beef with Asian Pear Dipping Sauce (*Bulgogi*) 191

Golda's Hungarian King's Cake 234

Scandinavian Almond Wedges with Cointreau 210

CELEBRATIONS AT HOME

Tex-Mex Cookout

Lake Austin Iced Tea 30

White Gazpacho 91

Tex-Mex Salad 122

Barbecued Ribs with Spicy Lime Sauce 198

Mexican Sundae with Tortilla Crisps 228

Mardi Gras Fête

Cajun Party Punch 38

Blue Crab Stuffed Mushrooms 66

Sautéed Collard Greens 134

Shrimp Étouffée 167

Chicken Clemenceau 178

White Chocolate Bread Pudding with
White Chocolate Sauce 229

Winter Fireside Dinner

Spiced Hot Punch 42

Roasted Mushroom Soup *(Potage aux Champignons Rôtis)* 100

Palmiers with Honey Mustard and Prosciutto 62

Lemon and Roasted Garlic Risotto 151

Stuffed Flank Steak 189

Chocolate and Port Gâteau with Chocolate Icing 239

Rite-of-Spring Brunch

Bellini 33

Creamy Asparagus Tarragon Soup 93

Blue Cheese Popovers 63

Roasted Asparagus with Goat Cheese and Bacon 131

Grilled Plum Chicken 175

Flourless Chocolate Torte with Toffee
and Amaretto Cream 240

Summer's Harvest Luncheon

Luscious Slush Punch 38

Dilled Summer Soup 92

Oven-roasted Tomatoes with Goat Cheese 67

Summer Squash and Zucchini 144

Grilled Chicken Provençal 174

Blueberry and Nectarine Crisp 230

An Autumn Feast

Strawberry and Peach Sangría 35

Basil Spinach Cheese Spread 48

Sweet Potato Vichyssoise 97

Cranberry Cashew Salad 110

Pork Tenderloin with Shallot Sauce 203

Black Russian Cake 235

A Thanksgiving Dinner

Mulled Apple Cider 42

Roasted Mushroom Soup *(Potage aux Champignons Rôtis)* 100

Spinach Salad with Cranberry Vinaigrette, Walnuts, and Goat Cheese 112

French Green Bean "Kindling" *(Fagotins des Haricots Verts)* 136

Sweet Potato Purée with Bourbon and Buttered Pecans 143

Deep-fried Turkey 183

Raspberry-topped Chocolate Tart with Pecan Crust 221

Christmas or Holiday Dinner

Cranberry Wassail 41

Baked Brie with Caramel Sauce 65

Fire and Spice Nuts 47

Minted Sweet Pea and Spinach Soup 96

Mélange of Roasted Root Vegetables
with Herb Vinaigrette 152

Christmas or Holiday Dinner (continued)

Rolled Stuffed Beef, Calabrian Style
(Braciole di Manzo alla Calabrese) 190

White Chocolate Bread Pudding with
White Chocolate Sauce 229

Easter Celebration

Kir Royale 32

Blue Cheese Popovers 63

Caraway Cabbage Salad 118

Potato Parmesan au Gratin 144

Rum-glazed Smoked Easter Ham 204

Black Forest Cupcakes 238

Pre-Theater Tapas

Sangría 35

Green Olive, Almond, and Brandy Tapenade 49

Sautéed Mushrooms 138

Spinach with Chickpeas *(Espinacas con Garbanzos)* 146

Spanish Potato Omelet *(Tortilla Española)* 68

Spicy Fried Calamari 72

Piquant Portuguese Shrimp 71

Chocolate and Port Gâteau with Chocolate Icing 239

Dinner for Dear Friends by the Relaxed Hostess

Portobello Mushroom Herb Crostini 56

Cranberry Cashew Salad 110

Mia's Berry Glazed Asparagus 132

Roasted Potatoes with Herbs and Parmesan Cheese 142

Pork Medallions in Crème Fraîche 201

Fresh Berry Cake with Raspberry Glaze 233

Potluck Potpourri

Pepperoni and Asiago Cheese Pinwheels 60

Mini Crab Cakes with Lemon Dill Sauce 73

Five-Onion Bisque 94

Bon Bon Chicken Salad 125

Potluck Potpourri (continued)

Oriental Coleslaw 117

Lemon and Roasted Garlic Risotto 151

Chicken Clemenceau 178

Beef Tenderloin with Mustard Peppercorn Sauce 185

Chicken Mediterranean *(Pollo Mediterraneo)* 182

Grand Marnier Madeleines 217

Dried Cranberry Biscotti 213

Terrific Buckeye Tailgate

Cranberry Slush 37

Blue Crab Stuffed Mushrooms 66

Spicy Chicken Drummettes 80

Shrimp Rémoulade 70

Roasted Peppers and Potatoes with Rosemary 141

Chopped Salad with Russian Dressing 121

Grilled Beef Tenderloin with Oriental Seasonings 186

Grilled Flank Steak with Far East Seasonings 188

Mint Chocolate Chip Cookies 216

Chocolate Almond Pound Cake 237

Market Day Al Fresco Lunch

Lemongrass Tea 30

Vietnamese Fresh Summer Rolls *(Goi Cuon)* 74

Dilled Summer Soup 92

Caramelized Onion and Tomato Galette 155

Veal Braciola 196

Strawberry Cream Tart 222

Not Just for Kids

Virgin Strawberry Daiquiri 32

Gruyère Cheese Puffs *(Gougères)* 64

Summer Tropical Fruit Soup 90

Macaroni with Five Cheeses 154

Vanilla Cream Wafers 209

Grand Marnier Madeleines 217

Beverages

G W ACOCK 06

New Albany residence

Appreciation for Planning and Design

W HEN approaching the village of New Albany, visitors often feel they are stepping back in time. They see a community where Old World design and careful planning are evident in every aspect. Walking to the Georgian-style library on tree-lined Market Street or enjoying a concert on the high school lawn with the Monticello-inspired dome in the foreground, residents are surrounded by a tranquil sense of timeless beauty. Having coffee in Market Square while looking over at brownstone homes or riding bicycles around the Jack Nicklaus championship golf course may be something that locals take for granted, but the village of New Albany is truly unique and continues to attract and awe visitors and new residents alike.

Georgian architecture is a hallmark of New Albany's homes, schools, and business campuses, where Palladian details showcase windows, doors, and brickwork. New Albany's landscape features majestic columned structures creating a community reminiscent of the towns that grew up along the Eastern Seaboard of the United States such as Richmond, Virginia, towns that were themselves inspired by English villages and cities of the Georgian era, in turn built in classical Greek and Roman style. No other style of architecture is more enduring or more welcoming at the end of the day.

New Albany is not huge tracts of homes but rather a collection of neighborhoods, each with its own distinctive characteristics, yet connected by common threads—signature white fencing, an extensive leisure path system, and, of course, Georgian architecture. From the spectacular homes on the golf course along Yantis Drive, to the cottage homes of Ashton Grove, to the grand estate homes of the New Albany Farms, there is a neighborhood to suit every lifestyle.

Sprinkled throughout the community are dedicated green spaces and athletic parks that provide the perfect backdrop for leisure pursuits, be it an afternoon stroll to the nearby playground or cheering on the team at a rousing game of Saturday lacrosse. New Albany has nearly 200 acres of dedicated parkland, and that number continues to grow as new acreage is added annually through the New Albany Joint Parks District.

New Albany is truly a one-of-a-kind village built with a careful master plan, a plan that ensures excellence in every detail, quality craftsmanship, and a sense of style that only gets better with age. It continues to be a relaxing and welcoming place for those who are fortunate to call it home.

— *New Albany Classic Signature Series*

Avocado Milkshake 29

Lake Austin Iced Tea 30

Lemongrass Tea 30

Mango Lassi 31

Virgin Strawberry Daiquiri 32

Kir Royale 32

Bellini 33

Margarita 33

Mimosa 34

Sangría 35

Strawberry and Peach Sangría 35

White Sangría 36

Tropical Fruit Sparkler 36

Cranberry Slush 37

Sea Breeze Punch 37

Luscious Slush Punch 38

Cajun Party Punch 38

Cranberry Pineapple Punch 39

Ginger Tea *(Salabat)* 40

Green Cardamom Chai 41

Cranberry Wassail 41

Mulled Apple Cider 42

Spiced Hot Punch 42

Avocado Milkshake

THIS MILKSHAKE COMES AS A SURPRISE TO MANY AMERICANS WHO NEVER THINK OF AVOCADO AS AN INGREDIENT FOR A SWEET DRINK OR DESSERT. IN SOUTHEAST ASIA, SWEETENED AVOCADO IS FREQUENTLY EATEN FOR DESSERT AND IS A POPULAR ICE CREAM FLAVOR.

1 Scoop the avocado flesh into a blender. Add the ice cubes, condensed milk, and evaporated milk. Purée until completely smooth, about 1 minute. Taste and adjust sweetness with more condensed milk. Add the coffee powder, if desired, and a scoop or two of ice cream. Blend again until smooth. You can adjust the thickness of the drink by varying the amount of milk.

SERVES: 4

CHEF TIP: It is important to use fully ripened avocados; an avocado that has not ripened has a bitter taste to it and will mar the flavor of the milkshake. Most ripened avocados have a dark, pimply skin that yields if you press it gently with your finger.

2 large ripe avocados, preferably Haas

2 cups ice cubes or crushed ice

¾ cup sweetened condensed milk

¾ cup evaporated or whole milk

1 teaspoon instant coffee powder (optional)

1 or 2 scoops vanilla ice cream

Original New Albany School House

Lake Austin Iced Tea

THIS CONCOCTION IS ALWAYS A TERRIFIC HIT, WHETHER ON A HOT SUMMER NIGHT ON THE PATIO OR AT A HOLIDAY PARTY IN THE WINTER COLD. IT CAN BE SERVED IN A PUNCH BOWL WITH FLOATING FROZEN RINGS OF SLICED LEMONS AND ORANGES OR IN INDIVIDUAL GLASSES OVER CRUSHED ICE.

1   Stir together well all the ingredients except the garnish. Pour over crushed ice in individual glasses, or serve in a punch bowl. Garnish with sliced oranges and/or lemons.

SERVES: 10

CHEF TIPS: Do not thaw or reconstitute the frozen lemonade or orange juice; the concentrate goes right from the can into the mix.

Use above "well-grade" bourbon, but not top-shelf. You may add much more than the recipe calls for according to your own taste.

To make strong tea, brew 2 cups using 4 teabags. Let steep until a dark color. Let cool before using.

The mix can be made in advance, but add the bourbon closer to serving time.

2 (6-ounce) cans frozen lemonade concentrate

1 (6-ounce) can frozen orange juice concentrate

6 cups water

2 cups strong tea (see Chef Tips)

1½ cups bourbon

1 cup superfine sugar

Sliced oranges and/or lemons for garnish

Lemongrass Tea

THIS LIGHTLY SWEETENED AND FRAGRANT DRINK, SERVED WITH BOTH LUNCH AND DINNER IN THAILAND, IS VERY COOLING WITH SPICY FOODS.

1   Cut off and discard all but the bottom 6 inches of the lemongrass. Smash the stalks with the side of a cleaver to release the flavor. In a saucepan, combine the lemongrass and the water. Boil for 20 minutes. Add sugar to taste and stir to dissolve. Let cool. Refrigerate for at least 4 hours. Strain. Add jasmine extract to taste, if desired. Serve with ice in a tall glass.

YIELD: 4 cups

CHEF TIP: Use the freshest (never dried) lemongrass to get the most flavor.

8 stalks lemongrass*

4 cups water

1 to 2 tablespoons sugar, or to taste

3 to 4 drops jasmine extract (optional)

*herb with long, thin, gray-green leaves and a scallion-like base; found in most Asian groceries and large supermarkets

Mango Lassi

THIS FAMOUS INDIAN DRINK IS A CROSS BETWEEN AN ICE CREAM SODA AND A YOGURT SHAKE. AT INDIAN RESTAURANTS IT IS SERVED WITH THE MEAL, BUT IT CAN BE A REFRESHING DRINK BY ITSELF ON A HOT SUMMER DAY.

1 In a blender, blend everything but the ice cubes until the sugar is dissolved. Add the ice and blend until frothy.

SERVES: 2

1¼ cups plain yogurt

½ cup fresh ripe mango pulp*

⅓ cup cold water

¼ cup liquid honey

½ teaspoon fresh lemon juice

9 to 10 ice cubes

*may use canned Alphonso mango pulp

COURTESY NEW ALBANY COUNTRY CLUB

Clubhouse at the New Albany Country Club

A BRIEF HISTORY OF NEW ALBANY

New Albany's beginnings date back to 1837, when William Yantis and Noble Landon laid out 72 lots on land they owned on both sides of High Street. The configuration of 50 by 100-foot lots is still discernible in the old town center.

The founders established the town where roads connecting early population centers—Granville, Worthington, Johnstown, and Delaware—intersected. On the southeast corner of today's Main and High Street intersection, Landon built a hotel and tavern probably in 1835, the year he first obtained a liquor license.

The town experienced steady growth and was incorporated in 1856. Store owners, doctors, carpenters, a lawyer, a dressmaker, and a wagon maker were among those who bought the Landon and Yantis lots. A columnist for the *Westerville Public Opinion* in 1883 reported the town's population as 350 inhabitants and described it as a "pleasant village inhabited by a pleasant people."

Why call the town New Albany? It seems clear that Noble Landon named the town in memory of Albany, New York, an important city where he and his relatives lived before settling in Ohio. Noble's brother William was proprietor of the Congress Hall in Albany, New York, the same time Noble was building his own hotel in soon-to-be New Albany, Ohio.

— *John E. Saveson on behalf of New Albany Historical Society*

Virgin Strawberry Daiquiri

*T*HIS FROZEN DRINK LOOKS SO FESTIVE, CHILDREN LOVE IT!

1 Combine all the ingredients except the 2 whole strawberries in a blender and blend at high speed until smooth. Pour into chilled Collins glasses and garnish each glass with a strawberry. Serve with a thick straw.

SERVES: 2

1 cup sliced strawberries

1 cup orange juice

3 tablespoons apple juice concentrate

1 teaspoon fresh lemon juice

1 teaspoon superfine sugar

6 to 8 ice cubes

2 whole strawberries for garnish

Kir Royale

*T*HIS COCKTAIL IS NAMED AFTER FÉLIX KIR (1876–1968), THE MAYOR OF DIJON IN BURGUNDY, WHO IN THE AFTERMATH OF THE SECOND WORLD WAR POPULARIZED THE DRINK BY OFFERING IT AT RECEPTIONS FOR VISITING DELEGATIONS. AN EXQUISITE TREAT BEFORE SITTING DOWN TO DINNER.

1 Place the sugar cube in a champagne flute. Pour the crème de cassis into the glass and gently pour champagne on top.

SERVES: 1

1 sugar cube

1 part crème de cassis

5 parts champagne

Bellini

This fruity cocktail drink was invented at Harry's Bar in Venice, Italy. This recipe with homemade peach purée is far superior to many Bellini cocktails in bars, which usually use a manufactured peach purée.

1 Stir together the peach chunks, sugar, and lemon juice in a saucepan. Let rest for 30 minutes. Bring the mixture to a boil, stirring until the sugar has dissolved. Reduce the heat to low; cover and simmer for 15 minutes. Let cool. Pour through a sieve, pressing on the solids to extract flavor and juices. Discard any solids and chill the purée.

2 To serve, place 1 teaspoon peach purée in each flute and fill with champagne. Garnish with a peach slice and mint sprig.

SERVES: 6

CHEF TIP: Asti Spumante, an Italian sparkling wine, is a relatively inexpensive champagne substitute.

2 large ripe white peaches, pitted and cut into chunks

½ cup sugar

2 teaspoons fresh lemon juice

1 bottle champagne or sparkling white wine

Garnish:

6 slices white peach

6 mint sprigs

Margarita

This internationally popular cocktail was invented sometime between 1930 and 1950, most likely in Mexico. This version was adapted from the famous Frontera Grill in Chicago.

1 In a pitcher, stir the tequila, orange liqueur, lime juice, lime zest, sugar, and water until the sugar dissolves. Cover and refrigerate at least 2 hours (but no more than 24). Strain into another pitcher.

2 Rub the rims of 8 martini or other 6 to 8-ounce glasses with a lime wedge, then dip the rims in a dish of coarse salt. Refrigerate the glasses if desired.

3 Serve the margaritas in the prepared glasses either straight up or on the rocks.

SERVES: 8

1⅔ cups Cuervo Especial gold tequila

¼ cup Grand Marnier

½ cup plus 1 tablespoon fresh lime juice (from about 2 large limes)

Finely grated zest of 1½ limes (about 1 teaspoon)

⅓ cup sugar

1 cup water

Lime wedges

Coarse salt

Mimosa

A SPLENDID WAY TO BEGIN THE DAY, THIS COCKTAIL DRINK IS A FAVORITE FOR FANCY BRUNCHES OR ROMANTIC BREAKFASTS IN BED. THIS COCKTAIL WAS CREATED AT THE RITZ HOTEL IN PARIS.

THE EALY HOMESTEAD

The Ealy homestead vividly appears on Plain Township maps as early as 1856. Near the corner of Dublin-Granville Road and Market Street, its wizened brick still carves out space against the trees. Although it is now empty, it is loud in its silence. For several generations, it housed the Ealy family, who bought nearly 75 acres of land from the Doran family in the early nineteenth century. Now, the Ealy home sits on one-third of the original property. Inside, six wooden fireplaces are empty of wood, but filled with the stories of the hands that carved each one individually.

The house was pieced together by careful hands, its bricks red and windows painted white. It was built in an America on the brink of civil war, and, as the country divided, it stood to watch. This house and the land surrounding it is spirit in and of itself. Its windows are eyes that have watched one civil war and two world wars, the Great Depression, and an era of great prosperity. It is history's observer, but just as much so, it is history.

Members of the New Albany community have sought to preserve this observer by both protection and restoration. Its restoration began early in 2005 in the hope that it becomes a space where history is taught and where history takes place.

— *Rachel Welty, 2004 Graduate of New Albany High School*

1 Fill a champagne flute one-third full with orange juice. Top off with champagne and garnish with a mint leaf or a slice of orange attached to the rim of the flute. A mimosa is not stirred.

SERVES: 1

VARIATION: Add ½ ounce of Grand Marnier to the drink. This is popularly known as a Grand Mimosa.

Champagne

Freshly squeezed orange juice

Fresh mint leaves or a slice of orange for garnish

Ealy Homestead

COURTESY E. GIBBS

Sangría

THIS POPULAR PARTY DRINK IS ESSENTIALLY A RED WINE PUNCH. SANGRÍA IS BEST SERVED CHILLED (OVERNIGHT, IF POSSIBLE), AND GOES WELL WITH JUST ABOUT ANYTHING!

1 Pour the wine into a pitcher over the ice cubes. Add the remaining ingredients. Stir well, pour into chilled glasses and sip slowly to beat the heat of a summer day!

SERVES: 6 to 8

1 (750-ml) bottle fruity full-bodied red wine

6 to 8 ice cubes

½ cup brandy

2 tablespoons sugar

2 lemons, sliced paper thin, seeded

2 oranges, sliced paper thin, seeded

3 cups sparkling water

Strawberry and Peach Sangría

A DIFFERENT TWIST ON AN OLD CLASSIC.

1 Gently crush the orange and lemon slices in a large pitcher. Add the remaining ingredients and stir well. Let stand at room temperature at least 2 hours or chill up to 4 hours.

2 Serve sangría over ice.

SERVES: 8

CHEF TIP: Strawberry syrup can be found in the beverage section of the grocery or with the maple syrup.

1 large orange, cut crosswise into 6 slices, seeded

1 large lemon, cut crosswise into 6 slices, seeded

1½ cups sliced strawberries

3 ripe peaches, each cut into 12 slices

1 (750-ml) bottle dry white wine

1½ cups Essensia*

1 cup peach liqueur

¼ cup strawberry syrup (optional)

*orange Muscat, a sweet dessert wine

White Sangría

*P*ERFECT FOR A SUMMER EVENING ON THE PATIO!

1   Combine the wine, Cointreau, and sugar in a large glass pitcher.
Mix well until the sugar dissolves. Stir in the fruits. Chill until ready
to serve. Before serving, add the club soda. Pour the sangría and fruits
over ice in oversized wine glasses.

YIELD: 1½ quarts

CHEF TIP: In addition to the fruits listed in the recipe, you may use
peaches, nectarines, or strawberries.

1 (750-ml) bottle dry white wine,
chilled

½ cup Cointreau

¼ cup superfine sugar

1 orange, sliced and seeded

1 lemon, sliced and seeded

1 lime, cut into wedges

1 (12-ounce) can club soda, chilled

Tray of ice cubes

Tropical Fruit Sparkler

*G*UARANTEED TO WHISK YOU AWAY TO WARM TROPICAL ISLANDS.

1   Finely chop papaya, pineapple, and ginger in a food processor.
With the machine running, add ½ cup of the juice and process
until smooth. Pour into a large pitcher. Stir in the remaining juice.
(Can be made to this point 4 hours ahead. Refrigerate.) Stir in crushed
ice. Gradually pour in sparkling water. Stir until blended and serve.

SERVES: 4

1 cup chopped, seeded, peeled ripe
papaya (about 1 pound Hawaiian
papaya)

1 cup cubed peeled fresh pineapple
cubes

1 teaspoon grated fresh ginger

2 cups chilled tropical fruit juice
blend (such as pineapple, orange,
and banana)

1 cup crushed ice

1 cup chilled sparkling water

Cranberry Slush

THE DESIGNATED DRIVERS WILL THANK YOU FOR SERVING THIS MARVELOUS REFRESHER AT A COCKTAIL PARTY.

1 In a large bowl and using an electric mixer, beat the cranberry sauce until smooth. Add the cranberry apple juice concentrate, lemonade concentrate, allspice, and cinnamon. Mix on low speed until well blended and smooth. Pour the mixture into a large freezer-safe, nonreactive container. (A 6-quart ice cream container will work well.) Add the water and stir well. Cover and freeze for 2 hours. Stir again. Cover and freeze for 8 hours or overnight. (The slush will keep, frozen, for several weeks.)

2 To serve, thaw slush until it can be easily scooped. For individual servings, mix ½ cup slush and ½ cup lemon-lime soda in a glass. Stir gently to blend. For serving in a punch bowl, combine one-third of the slush with 1 liter of lemon-lime soda at a time and stir gently to blend.

YIELD: 20 (1-cup) servings

CHEF TIP: For a festive touch, add cranberries and cinnamon sticks for a holiday party or sliced oranges, lemons, and limes for a tropical-themed party.

3 (8-ounce) cans jellied cranberry sauce

1 (12-ounce) can frozen cranberry-apple juice concentrate, partially thawed

2 (12-ounce) cans frozen lemonade concentrate, partially thawed

1 teaspoon ground allspice

1 teaspoon cinnamon

4 cups water

3 (1-liter) bottles lemon-lime soda

Sea Breeze Punch

A GREAT SUMMERTIME PARTY DRINK!

1 In a 2-quart pitcher or punch bowl (see Chef Tip), combine the cranberry juice, grapefruit juice, vodka, lime juice, and sugar; stir until the sugar is dissolved. Add the sparkling wine; stir briefly to mix. Garnish with the lime slices, if desired.

YIELD: 16 (½-cup) servings

CHEF TIP: Double the recipe to fill a standard 4-quart punch bowl.

2 cups chilled cranberry juice

1 cup chilled grapefruit juice

1 cup chilled vodka

Juice of 1 lime

1 tablespoon superfine sugar, or to taste

1 (750-ml) bottle sparkling white wine, chilled

Lime slices for garnish

Luscious Slush Punch

THIS FRUITY CONCOCTION IS FROZEN INTO A SLUSH AND THEN PLACED IN A PUNCH BOWL WITH SODA. THIS RECIPE MAKES ENOUGH FOR TWO STANDARD-SIZED PUNCH BOWLS.

1 In a large saucepan, boil the water with the sugar for 3 minutes or until the sugar is dissolved. Let cool. Stir in the orange juice, lemonade, pineapple juice, and bananas. Blend well. Freeze the mixture in 2 separate containers.

2 When ready to serve, place the frozen contents of one container in a punch bowl and pour in 1 bottle of 7Up or Sprite; stir until slushy. Repeat with a second punch bowl.

YIELD: 30 (12-ounce) glasses

6 cups water

4 cups sugar

1 (12-ounce) can frozen orange juice concentrate

1 (12-ounce) can frozen lemonade concentrate

1 (46-ounce) can unsweetened pineapple juice

5 ripe bananas, mashed

2 (2-liter) bottles 7Up or Sprite

Cajun Party Punch

LET THE GOOD TIMES ROLL . . . NEW ORLEANS STYLE!

1 In a 3-quart heavy saucepan, combine the tea, sugar, mint, cinnamon sticks, and cloves. Cook over medium heat, stirring until the sugar dissolves. Cool slightly; refrigerate until cold.

2 Strain the tea into a punch bowl; discard the spices. Add the rum, pineapple juice, lime juice, and club soda. Stir until blended. Add ice and fruit slices.

YIELD: About 5 quarts

CHEF TIP: To make strong tea, brew 4 cups using 8 teabags. Let steep until a dark color.

1 quart strong tea

1½ cups sugar

10 mint sprigs

4 (3-inch) cinnamon sticks

1 teaspoon whole cloves

1 quart dark rum

2 cups unsweetened pineapple juice

1 cup fresh lime juice

2 (1-quart) bottles club soda

Ice ring or large block of ice

1 lemon, sliced

1 lime, sliced

1 orange, sliced

Cranberry Pineapple Punch

*E*ASY AND FESTIVE!

1 In a large punch bowl, combine the cranberry juice cocktail, pineapple juice, ginger ale, and seltzer. Add an ice block and serve garnished with the pineapple.

YIELD: 3½ quarts

2 (1-quart) bottles cranberry juice cocktail, chilled

1 (46-ounce) can unsweetened pineapple juice, chilled

2 cups chilled ginger ale

2 cups chilled seltzer or soda water

Ice block

Fresh pineapple spears for garnish

New Albany street scene

COURTESY E. GIBBS

STREET NAMES PRESERVE MEMORIES OF THE EARLIEST SETTLERS

*P*ermanent settlement in New Albany began soon after 1802, when John Hoffman bought 4,000 acres of the township from Dudley Woodbridge for 4,000 gallons of whiskey. Closely related German farming families—Hoffmans, Baughmans, Swickards, and Dagues—soon moved here, some of them suspect in the "Whiskey Rebellion" in Pennsylvania in the late 1790s. Hoffman's daughter Priscilla married Adam Baughman. A New Albany street bears the Baughman name. Swickard Woods preserves another.

All of Plain Township at that time was reserved for veterans in a "Military District." After 1812, the Federal Government opened the land for sale to all comers causing great excitement. The Clouses, Kitzmillers, and Smith families settled here beginning in 1813. Archibald Smith, self-taught carpenter, engineer, and surveyor, operated a sawmill on Blacklick Creek from the 1830s to the 1850s, as commemorated in "Smith's Mill Road."

The 1820s introduced Bevelhymers, Dorans, Ranneys, Goodriches, Taylors, and Trumbos. Pike Taylor wrote that his mother, "among the best of old women," carried him as a baby "from the headwaters of the Potomac in Virginia in her lap on horseback."

Street signs and historical markers commemorate Noble Landon and William Yantis laying out New Albany in the 1830s. That same decade, the Ealy and Neiswander families immigrated. In 1860 George Ealy built the Ealy House on Dublin-Granville Road; it was restored by the New Albany Historical Society in 2005–2006.
— John E. Saveson on behalf of New Albany Historical Society

Ginger Tea (Salabat)

Ginger tea in some form or other is drunk nearly everywhere in the Far East. It is very soothing when you have a cough or a cold and it is also a digestive. In the Philippines, it is often served at breakfast and with midday snacks called merienda.

WEXNER COMMUNITY PARK

Nestled between the Georgian-inspired New Albany Primary School building and the Plain Township Aquatic Center, Wexner Community Park is a green oasis. Children, teens, and adults alike enjoy this "Central Park" of the village of New Albany.

The park, established in 2003 and named in honor of the Wexner family who graciously donated the 45-acre land parcel to the community, is a wonderful center of activity and leisure for residents and visitors. The lacrosse and soccer fields are frequented by middle- and high-school teams. The Wexner Pavilion offers residents a covered shelter house complete with a kitchen and open fireplace to enjoy a family cook-out or a Girl Scout outing. The Eagles Nest playground, built by funds raised by the New Albany Women's Network and other community groups, offers the youngest residents a place to play and have fun.

The park has grown to be a center of activity throughout the year for family relaxation as well as the venue for large-scale community events like the annual Spring Fest, a community-wide celebration of spring organized by New Albany's Community Events Board. The Wexner Community Park will also be the site of the permanent New Albany Safety Town and Adventure Playground.

— Mia Johansson-Strench

1 Peel the ginger, cut it into three pieces and lightly smash with a mallet or the side of a cleaver. Put it into a saucepan with the water and honey. Bring to a boil. Reduce the heat to low, cover and simmer gently for 20 minutes. Strain and serve. You may also serve this tea cold.

YIELD: 4 cups

1 (5-inch) piece fresh ginger

5 cups water

5 teaspoons honey or light brown sugar, or to taste

COURTESY DANIEL W. FLOSS & ASSOCIATES PHOTOGRAPHY

Abigail and Leslie Wexner at the Wexner Community Park Dedication

Green Cardamom Chai

Chai is the Indian term for tea, and it is typically a sweetened spiced milk tea. Chai has become very popular in the United States in the last decade, and coffee outlets like Starbucks and many large groceries now offer the beverage in various forms. The following is an easy and very aromatic chai.

1 In a saucepan, bring the water and milk almost to a boil. Add the cardamom and steep for 3 minutes, uncovered. Add the sugar and tea. Stir lightly. Steep 2 minutes more, uncovered. Strain and enjoy.

SERVES: 2

2¼ cups water

¾ cup milk

2 green cardamom pods, split

2 tablespoons sugar, or to taste

2 teaspoons loose green tea leaves

Cranberry Wassail

This traditional holiday libation is so soothing to have on a cold night while relaxing next to the fireplace.

1 Combine the honey, water, cloves, and cinnamon sticks in a small saucepan. Bring to a boil, reduce heat and simmer for 20 minutes. Remove cloves and cinnamon sticks.

2 In a 5-quart saucepan combine the cranberry juice, cider, orange juice, and honey mixture. Simmer for 1 hour. Add the cranberries. Serve hot.

SERVES: 12

½ cup honey

½ cup water

12 whole cloves

2 cinnamon sticks

48 ounces cranberry juice

32 ounces fresh apple cider

3 cups orange juice

Fresh cranberries for garnish

Mulled Apple Cider

THIS CLASSIC AUTUMN BEVERAGE IS ALWAYS GOOD TO HAVE AT THANKSGIVING CELEBRATIONS. KEEP IT WARM ALL DAY LONG IN AN ELECTRIC URN WITH A SPIGOT—SOMETHING MOST FOLKS WOULD ONLY THINK OF USING FOR COFFEE.

1   In a large saucepan, combine the cider, sugar, lemon juice, and nutmeg. Tie the cinnamon stick and cloves in a cheesecloth bag and place in the pan. Simmer over medium-high heat for 10 minutes. Remove the bag of spices and serve hot.

SERVES: 8

8 cups fresh apple cider

1 cup packed light brown sugar

½ cup lemon juice

½ teaspoon grated nutmeg

1 cinnamon stick

8 whole cloves

Spiced Hot Punch

IMAGINE YOURSELF SITTING IN FRONT OF A ROARING FIREPLACE DURING THE COLD MONTHS OF WINTER WITH A WARM CUP OF SPICED HOT PUNCH IN YOUR HANDS AND LISTENING TO YOUR FAVORITE MUSIC. THIS PUNCH IS ALSO DELIGHTFUL TO SIP WHILE PLAYING BRIDGE OR DOING PUZZLES WITH THE FAMILY.

1   Combine all the ingredients in a large saucepan. Bring to a boil, reduce heat and simmer for 10 minutes. (Your house will smell wonderful!) Serve hot.

SERVES: 8

3 cups orange juice

3 cups cranberry-apple juice

3 cups apple juice

½ lemon, thinly sliced crosswise

½ orange, thinly sliced crosswise

2 cinnamon sticks

2 whole cloves

Appetizers

G.W. Acock 06

The New Albany Classic Invitational Grand Prix & Family Day

Belief in Active Community Stewardship

ENRICHING lives for the greater good is a shared community value in New Albany. It plays out daily throughout New Albany neighborhoods as people gather to learn more about issues, discuss ways to help, and, ultimately, take action to improve lives in the immediate and broader community. Local stewardship opportunities are too varied and numerous to list, but anyone with a passion for volunteering will easily find others of like mind in New Albany.

Village of New Albany Community Events Board members volunteer time and effort to put on a community-wide Independence Day parade, festival, and fireworks display, and the annual Spring Fest. Parent Teacher Organization volunteers raise funds for the schools and assist with school programs. Historical Society members devote time to archive New Albany's history in articles and artifacts and to contribute to building restorations. The New Albany Women's Network focuses its energy on reaching out to neighbors in need and supporting initiatives that improve the lives of women and children. New Albany Cooking with Friends uses its culinary skills to raise funds to feed the hungry and supports local children's causes.

But perhaps no group better exemplifies this commitment to stewardship than the New Albany Community Foundation, which brings together many of these organizations and individuals to achieve shared aspirations. The Foundation is best known for its ongoing presentation of the New Albany Classic Signature Series, featuring an array of lectures, concerts, and fundraisers. The Signature Series was born out of the success of the New Albany Classic Invitational Grand Prix & Family Day, a world-class equestrian competition and country fair conceived and hosted by Abigail Wexner. The Classic draws nearly 20,000 people to the grounds of the Wexner home to witness expert competition among the riders and their mounts and enjoy an afternoon of family fun, all with the goal of raising money to support the Columbus Coalition Against Family Violence. Annual proceeds have consistently exceeded $1 million, making the work of the coalition possible and forever changing the way Central Ohio responds to domestic violence.

It is this spirit of engagement that continues to shape New Albany and creates deep, lasting bonds within our community.

— *New Albany Classic Signature Series*

Fire and Spice Nuts 47

Basil Spinach Cheese Spread 48

Green Olive, Almond, and Brandy Tapenade 49

Cauliflower and Black Pepper Hummus 50

Swiss and Cream Cheese Dip 51

Feta Herb Dip 52

Cowboy Caviar with "Homemade" Tortilla Chips 53

Bruschetta with Pesto and Tomatoes 54

Flatbread with Goat Cheese, Caramelized Onions,
and Rosemary 55

Portobello Mushroom Herb Crostini 56

Curried Shrimp Crostini 57

Smoked Salmon and Trout Roulade
on Pumpernickel 58

Mamma Mia's Pesto Pinwheels 59

Pepperoni and Asiago Cheese Pinwheels 60

Spinach and Artichoke Puff Pastry Rolls 61

Palmiers with Honey Mustard and Prosciutto 62

Blue Cheese Popovers 63

Gruyère Cheese Puffs *(Gougères)* 64

Jalapeño-spiked Deviled Eggs 65

Baked Brie with Caramel Sauce 65

Blue Crab Stuffed Mushrooms 66

Oven-roasted Tomatoes with Goat Cheese 67

Spanish Potato Omelet *(Tortilla Española)* 68

Shrimp Rémoulade 70

Piquant Portuguese Shrimp 71

Spicy Fried Calamari 72

Mini Crab Cakes with Lemon Dill Sauce 73

Vietnamese Fresh Summer Rolls *(Goi Cuon)* 74

Fried Spring Rolls *(Lumpia Shanghai)* 76

Cashew Chicken Bites with Apricot Dipping Sauce 77

Pork and Vegetable Potstickers with
Soy Dipping Sauce 78

Spicy Chicken Drummettes 80

Grilled Beef, Chicken, or Pork on Skewers (Satays) 81

Moorish Pork Kabobs *(Pinchos Morunos)* 83

Pork and Red Pepper Mini Skewers with Mango Salsa 84

Fire and Spice Nuts

A GREAT COCKTAIL SNACK TO HAVE ON HAND; YOUR GUESTS WILL KEEP COMING BACK FOR MORE OF THESE UNUSUALLY FLAVORED MUNCHIES.

1 Position racks in top third and center of oven; preheat the oven to 225°F. Line two large, heavy baking sheets with parchment paper.

2 In a small bowl, stir together the five-spice powder, ground ginger, cumin, salt, cinnamon, chili powder, and garlic powder. In a separate large bowl, whisk the egg whites until foamy. Whisk in the spice mixture. Add pecans, walnuts, and cashews; toss to coat completely. Sprinkle with the sugar and toss again.

3 Divide the nuts between prepared baking sheets and spread them in a single layer. Bake, stirring every 20 minutes, until the nuts are toasted and the coating is dry, about 1 hour 20 minutes. Sprinkle nuts with salt to taste, if desired. Transfer nuts to a large bowl. Stir in the crystallized ginger. Cool completely. The nuts will keep in an airtight container at room temperature for at least 3 weeks.

YIELD: 6 cups

CHEF TIP: Purchase good-quality nuts from specialty nut stores or produce markets with a high turnover. Salted and roasted nuts are not suitable for this recipe.

2 teaspoons Chinese five-spice powder

2 teaspoons ground ginger

2 teaspoons ground cumin

2 teaspoons salt

1½ teaspoons ground cinnamon

1 teaspoon Mexican chili powder

½ teaspoon garlic powder

2 large egg whites

2 cups pecan halves

2 cups walnut halves and pieces

2 cups raw cashews, preferably halves

¼ cup sugar

Salt to taste (optional)

½ cup minced crystallized ginger

Basil Spinach Cheese Spread

THIS VERY EASY TO ASSEMBLE SPREAD MAKES A DRAMATIC PRESENTATION WHEN MOLDED IN A MINI BUNDT PAN OR DECORATIVE MOLDS SUCH AS THOSE MADE FAMOUS BY NORDIC WARE.

1 Put the cream cheese and Roquefort in a bowl. Using an electric mixer, beat until well combined. Set aside.

2 Combine the spinach, parsley, basil, and garlic in the bowl of a food processor and process to a rough paste. With the motor running, drizzle the oil through the feed tube; continue processing until smooth. Transfer the pesto to a bowl, add the walnuts and Parmesan, and stir thoroughly.

3 Line a 5½ by 3-inch loaf pan with plastic wrap, leaving a few inches of extra wrap hanging over the sides. Lightly spray with olive oil.

4 Spread one-third of the cheese mixture evenly over the bottom of the pan. Top with half the pesto mixture, spreading evenly. Arrange half the sun-dried tomatoes on top. Repeat the cheese, pesto, and tomato layers. Finish with the remaining third of the cheese mixture. Cover with the overhanging plastic wrap and refrigerate for at least 24 hours.

5 Half an hour before serving, take the loaf out of the refrigerator to come just to room temperature. Peel back the plastic and invert the loaf onto a platter. Remove the plastic. Serve with crackers.

SERVES: 6 to 8

8 ounces cream cheese, at room temperature

4 ounces Roquefort cheese, at room temperature

1 cup loosely packed fresh spinach leaves, rinsed and thoroughly dried

¾ cup loosely packed fresh flat-leaf parsley leaves

¼ cup loosely packed fresh basil leaves

1 teaspoon minced garlic

¼ cup vegetable oil

¼ cup finely chopped walnuts

1 cup freshly grated Parmesan cheese

¼ cup slivered oil-packed sun-dried tomatoes, patted dry

Water crackers for serving

Green Olive, Almond, and Brandy Tapenade

*N*OTHING CONJURES A LEISURELY PROVENCE REPAST MORE THAN THIS SIMPLE AND DELICIOUS SPREAD.

1 Place the olives, almonds, capers, anchovies, garlic, and brandy in a food processor and process until coarsely ground. With the machine running, slowly pour the olive oil through the feed tube to bind the mixture into a cohesive yet textured spread. Be careful not to over-process the mixture to a paste. Add the basil and pulse to combine. Season the tapenade with pepper. Transfer the tapenade to a decorative crock or bowl, cover and let mellow in the refrigerator for a few hours before serving.

2 Serve the tapenade at room temperature surrounded by toasted slices of French bread. Leftover tapenade will keep in the refrigerator for several weeks.

YIELD: 1½ cups

1 cup pitted imported green olives, such as picholine

⅓ cup lightly toasted slivered almonds

1½ tablespoons capers, drained

3 anchovy fillets, drained

1 clove garlic, coarsely chopped

¼ cup brandy

¼ cup olive oil

¼ cup slivered fresh basil

Freshly ground black pepper to taste

Toasted slices of French bread

COURTESY DON STRENCH

Children enjoying safety lessons in New Albany Safety Town

Cauliflower and Black Pepper Hummus

THIS HUMMUS IS LIGHT TEXTURED, FLAVORFUL, AND VERY EASY TO MAKE. EVEN THOUGH IT TASTES RICH, IT IS ACTUALLY LOW IN FAT. SERVE WITH PITA OR OTHER FLATBREAD OR AS A DIPPING SAUCE FOR CRUDITÉS.

1 In a large saucepan fitted with a steaming basket, bring 1 to 2 inches of water to a boil. Add the cauliflower, cover and steam until tender when pierced with a fork, 5 to 8 minutes. Remove from the pan and let cool. (Alternatively, drop cauliflower into a pan of boiling salted water and boil until tender; the timing will be almost the same. Drain and let cool.)

2 Place cauliflower in a food processor with the garbanzo beans, garlic, lemon juice, olive oil, and pepper. Process until smooth. Transfer to a bowl, cover and chill well. Before serving, garnish with a drizzle of olive oil and a dusting of paprika.

YIELD: 2 cups

1½ cups cauliflower florets

1 (15½-ounce) can garbanzo beans, drained and rinsed

3 cloves garlic, coarsely chopped

¼ cup freshly squeezed lemon juice

1 tablespoon extra virgin olive oil

1½ teaspoons freshly ground black pepper (medium grind)

Drizzle of olive oil and a dusting of paprika for garnish

COURTESY ABERCROMBIE & FITCH

Abercrombie & Fitch interior firepit

Swiss and Cream Cheese Dip

THIS DIP HAS BEEN MAKING THE ROUNDS OF POTLUCK PARTIES IN NEW ALBANY, SOMETIMES SHOWING UP TWICE AT THE SAME PARTY; NO HOSTS MINDED BECAUSE INEVITABLY THE DIPS DISAPPEAR FROM THE TABLE.

1 Preheat the oven to 350°F.

2 In a bowl, stir together until well blended the cream cheese, Swiss cheese, mayonnaise, onions, nutmeg, pepper, and half of the almonds. Spread evenly in a 9-inch pie pan. Bake for 15 minutes. Sprinkle with the remaining almonds and bake for an additional 12 minutes.

3 Serve warm with cocktail crackers like water biscuits, sliced French bread or as a dip for crudités.

YIELD: 2 cups

CHEF TIP: If you double the recipe, add 10 to 15 minutes of baking time if baking in one pan or bake in 2 9-inch pie pans for the prescribed time in the recipe.

8 ounces cream cheese, softened

1½ cups shredded Swiss cheese

⅓ cup low-fat mayonnaise

2 tablespoons minced onions

⅛ teaspoon nutmeg

⅛ teaspoon black pepper

⅓ cup toasted sliced almonds

Cocktail crackers, sliced French bread or crudités

Feta Herb Dip

THIS IS THE HORS D'OEUVRE TO MAKE WHEN YOU'RE TIGHT FOR TIME. SERVE WITH STURDY CHIPS OR CRACKERS.

A&F CHALLENGE

Abercrombie & Fitch has made New Albany its home since the spring of 2001. As Abercrombie & Fitch has grown during this time, so too has the company's commitment to reinvest in Central Ohio communities and beyond. Complementing the company's philanthropy program, Abercrombie & Fitch introduced an annual fundraiser, the A&F Challenge, shortly after moving "on campus." The company's fundraising effort, led by A&F associates, culminates on a late-summer evening with this company-hosted celebration.

In the five years since its inception, the A&F Challenge has provided major support to non-profit organizations; the event now generates more than $1 million each year. The A&F Challenge beneficiaries include the Columbus Coalition Against Family Violence, the New Albany Community Foundation, Columbus Children's Hospital, and the Ohio State University Medical Center.

Driven by teamwork, the A&F Challenge has become hugely successful because of the partnerships developed between Abercrombie & Fitch associates, the company's valued business partners, and the community.
— *Abercrombie & Fitch*

1 Finely crumble the feta and spread on the bottom of an 8-inch round serving dish with sides. Sprinkle the cheese with the thyme, oregano, garlic powder, and ginger. Layer the green onions, bell pepper, and tomato on top. Drizzle with the olive oil.

YIELD: 3 cups

8 ounces feta cheese, drained

2 teaspoons dried thyme

2 teaspoons dried oregano

2 teaspoons garlic powder

2 teaspoons ground ginger

2 to 3 green onions, thinly sliced

1 small orange or yellow bell pepper, diced

1 small tomato, chopped

¼ cup olive oil

A&F Challenge

COURTESY ABERCROMBIE & FITCH

Cowboy Caviar with "Homemade" Tortilla Chips

Take this to your next tailgate party!

1 In a bowl, combine the beans, olives, peppers, and onion. In a separate bowl, whisk together all the dressing ingredients. Pour the dressing over the bean mixture and toss. Cover and refrigerate overnight. Serve with "homemade" tortilla chips (see below).

SERVES: 10

2 (15-ounce) cans black beans, drained and rinsed

1 (4½-ounce) can chopped black olives

½ cup chopped red bell pepper

½ cup chopped green bell pepper

½ cup chopped yellow bell pepper

½ cup minced onion

Dressing:

½ cup vegetable oil

½ cup fresh lime juice

2 teaspoons minced garlic

1 teaspoon salt

1 teaspoon red pepper flakes

1 teaspoon ground cumin

½ teaspoon black pepper

"HOMEMADE" TORTILLA CHIPS

1 Cut each tortilla into 8 wedges. Pour about 1 inch vegetable oil in a large skillet and heat over medium-high heat until the oil begins to simmer. Carefully slide 6 to 8 tortilla wedges into the hot oil. When the tortillas begin to puff and are lightly brown around the edges, about 2 minutes, turn over and cook 1 minute more. Drain on paper towels. Salt immediately. Repeat with the remaining tortilla wedges. (Tortilla chips can be made 4 hours ahead.)

1 (17.5-ounce) package flour tortillas (10 tortillas)

Vegetable oil for frying

Kosher salt to taste

Bruschetta with Pesto and Tomatoes

*N*O ANTIPASTI PLATTER SHOULD BE WITHOUT THIS CLASSIC OFFERING. THE BRUSCHETTA ALSO MAKES A GREAT BASE FOR AN OPEN-FACED STEAK SANDWICH.

1 Preheat the oven to 400°F.

2 To make the pesto, in a food processor, blend the basil and garlic to a fine paste, scraping down the sides of the bowl as necessary. Add the pine nuts, cheese, olive oil, salt, and pepper; process until smooth. Taste and adjust seasonings. Set aside.

3 Stir together the tomatoes and parsley. Sprinkle with balsamic vinegar and toss.

4 Cut bread diagonally into 18 slices about ¾ inch thick. Arrange slices in one layer on a baking sheet and lightly brush tops with olive oil. Toast in oven until golden brown.

5 Spread pesto on the untoasted side of each bread slice. Top with tomato mixture. Sprinkle with Parmesan cheese and serve immediately.

YIELD: 18 pieces

Pesto:

2 cups packed fresh basil leaves

2 large cloves garlic

½ cup pine nuts

¾ cup freshly grated Parmesan or Romano cheese

⅔ cup olive oil

½ teaspoon salt

½ teaspoon pepper

8 to 10 Roma tomatoes, seeded and diced

¼ cup chopped fresh flat-leaf parsley

1½ tablespoons balsamic vinegar

1 (1-pound) loaf Italian bread

Olive oil for brushing on bread

¼ cup grated Parmesan cheese

COURTESY DON STRENCH

New Albany scene

Flatbread with Goat Cheese, Caramelized Onions, and Rosemary

WOW YOUR FRIENDS WITH THIS INCREDIBLY DELICIOUS APPETIZER.

1   Halve the onions lengthwise, then cut into very thin slices. (A mandoline or V-slicer would be very helpful here.) Melt 1½ tablespoons of the butter in a large, heavy skillet over medium-high heat. Add the onions, sugar, vinegar, and a few grinds of black pepper. Stir well, then cook, stirring constantly, until the liquid has evaporated, about 15 minutes. As the onions start to brown, reduce heat to very low and add the remaining 1½ tablespoons butter. Cook over very low heat for another 20 to 30 minutes, stirring occasionally, until the onions begin to turn deep brown. The exact cooking time depends on the moisture content of the onions. Taste and season with a little salt if desired. (Onions can be prepared 24 hours ahead and refrigerated until needed.)

2   Put a pizza stone in the oven, if using, and preheat the oven to 450°F.

3   Spread the goat cheese over the pizza shell or focaccia. Spread the caramelized onions over the cheese. Sprinkle with the rosemary and dust with more pepper. Drizzle with olive oil. Bake on a pizza stone or in a pizza pan for 10 minutes or until toppings are hot. To serve, cut into small wedges. Serve hot or just warm.

SERVES: 6

CHEF TIP: Boboli pizza crust, widely available in the Italian section of grocery stores, works well in this recipe.

2 large yellow onions (about 1½ pounds)

3 tablespoons butter

¼ cup dark brown sugar

1 tablespoon balsamic vinegar

Freshly ground pepper

6 ounces goat cheese, at room temperature

1 (12-inch) pizza crust (not thin) or plain focaccia

2 tablespoons minced fresh rosemary

Olive oil

Portobello Mushroom Herb Crostini

THIS DO-AHEAD APPETIZER DREW RAVES FROM OUR TESTERS.

1   Preheat the oven to 400°F. Spread ¼ cup of the olive oil on a baking sheet. Arrange the mushrooms over the oil in one layer and sprinkle with salt, pepper, and 2 teaspoons of the garlic; drizzle with the remaining ¼ cup oil. Roast mushrooms for 12 minutes. Remove mushrooms from the oven and let cool in the pan.

2   Preheat the oven to 350°F.

3   Pulse the mushrooms in a food processor just until diced, being careful not to over-process into a paste. Transfer mushrooms to a medium bowl. Wipe the baking sheet clean.

4   In the food processor, combine the mayonnaise, cheese, parsley, basil, and remaining 1 teaspoon garlic; process until mixed. Pour over the mushrooms and fold to blend.

5   Spread a heaping tablespoon of the mushroom mixture on each slice of bread and arrange in a single layer on the baking sheet. Warm in the oven for 8 to 10 minutes.

YIELD: 40 to 60 pieces

CHEF TIP: After they are baked and cooled, the crostini may be frozen in resealable plastic bags or airtight plastic containers. Take out as many as you need from the freezer and reheat them at 350°F for 5 to 8 minutes until heated through.

½ cup extra virgin olive oil

½ pound sliced portobello mushrooms

Coarse salt and freshly ground black pepper to taste

3 teaspoons finely chopped garlic

2 cups mayonnaise

1 cup grated Parmesan or Romano cheese

½ cup chopped flat-leaf parsley

½ cup shredded basil leaves

2½ (1-pound) loaves French bread, cut straight across in ½-inch slices

Curried Shrimp Crostini

Sweet curry gives this savory appetizer an intriguing depth of flavor not typically associated with an Italian antipasto.

1 In a bowl, combine the cream cheese, cheddar, Parmesan, and mayonnaise. Stir in the olives, onion, chives, curry powder and shrimp.

2 Preheat the broiler.

3 Cut the French bread into ½-inch slices, arrange on a baking sheet and broil on one side until toasted. Spread the shrimp mixture on the untoasted side and broil for a few minutes until hot and the edges are starting to brown. Sprinkle with minced parsley and serve immediately.

YIELD: 18 pieces

3 ounces cream cheese, softened

½ cup shredded sharp cheddar cheese

½ cup grated fresh Parmesan cheese

½ cup mayonnaise

¼ cup diced pitted green olives

2 tablespoons grated onion

2 tablespoons snipped chives

1 teaspoon curry powder

¼ pound cooked shrimp (medium to large is more succulent), finely chopped

1 (1-pound) French baguette

1 tablespoon minced fresh parsley

THE COLUMBUS COALITION AGAINST FAMILY VIOLENCE

Founded in 1998 by New Albany resident Abigail Wexner, the Columbus Coalition Against Family Violence was created to improve the way individuals and institutions in Central Ohio respond to family violence. As a young mother with children of her own, Abigail knew that, heartbreakingly, many children and women are not safe, even in their own homes. She founded the coalition in an effort to stop the violence here in Central Ohio. Domestic violence often spans generations, and the organization's vision is to break the cycle of family violence in homes, schools, workplaces, and neighborhoods throughout the community.

To support the work of the coalition, Abigail combined her love of horses with the desire to increase community awareness and understanding about domestic violence, and thus, the New Albany Classic Invitational Grand Prix & Family Day was born. Every year the Classic draws nearly 20,000 people to the Wexner home for a day of fun featuring a world-class equestrian competition and family fair. Through the proceeds from ticket sales and sponsorship dollars, the event consistently raises more than $1 million to support the critical work of the coalition.

— *The New Albany Classic Invitational Grand Prix & Family Day*

COURTESY CURTIS WALLS PHOTOGRAPHY, INC.

The New Albany Classic Invitational Grand Prix & Family Day

Smoked Salmon and Trout Roulade on Pumpernickel

Dress up a party with this sophisticated offering.

1 Remove any skin and bones from the trout and place trout in a food processor with 3 ounces of the cream cheese. Process until smooth, then season with salt and pepper. Add the lemon juice and pulse to combine.

2 On a piece of plastic wrap, arrange the smoked salmon slices, slightly overlapping, in an 8 by 6-inch rectangle. Carefully spread an even layer of the smoked trout mixture onto the salmon, then roll up the slices from a long side, like a jelly roll, using the plastic wrap to help lift as you roll. Wrap the roulade in plastic wrap and place it in the freezer overnight to firm up.

3 Remove the roulade from the freezer and let sit for 30 minutes before slicing. Using a 2-inch cookie cutter, cut out 20 rounds from the pumpernickel. Spread the remaining 1 ounce cream cheese on the pumpernickel rounds. Unwrap the roulade and, using a very sharp knife, cut about 20 slices. Top each piece of pumpernickel with a roulade slice and decorate with a sprig of chervil or parsley. Cover with plastic wrap and keep chilled until ready to serve.

YIELD: 20 rolls

4 ounces smoked trout fillet

4 ounces cream cheese

Salt and pepper to taste

1 tablespoon lemon juice

8 ounces smoked salmon slices

20 slices pumpernickel

Sprigs of fresh chervil or parsley for garnish

Mamma Mia's Pesto Pinwheels

THESE COLORFUL PINWHEELS ARE GREAT PARTY APPETIZERS THAT CAN BE MADE AHEAD AND BAKED RIGHT BEFORE GUESTS ARRIVE. MIA JOHANSSON-STRENCH CREATED THE RECIPE WITH FAVORITE ITEMS SHE HAD AVAILABLE IN THE KITCHEN. YOU CAN REPLACE THE VEGETABLES WITH YOUR FAVORITE TYPES. A CHILLED MARGARITA IS THE PERFECT MATCH FOR THESE HEARTY TREATS.

1   In a bowl, combine the mushrooms, red pepper, olives, green onions, thyme, and black pepper. Stir in the mayonnaise.

2   Unfold the pastry on a sheet of wax paper. (Use a rolling pin if needed to even out the pastry.) Spread a thin layer of tomato pesto over the pastry, leaving a small border around the edges. Spread half of the vegetable mixture on top of the pesto. Sprinkle with half of the feta cheese and half the pine nuts. Roll up the pastry, pinching the seam to seal. Wrap in wax paper. Repeat with the second pastry sheet. Freeze the rolls for 30 minutes.

3   Meanwhile, preheat the oven to 350°F.

4   Remove the wax paper and cut the rolls into ½-inch slices. Place on a cookie sheet and bake for 15 to 20 minutes or until golden brown. (Cover with foil if the wheels are coloring too quickly.) Serve hot.

SERVES: 10

1 cup finely chopped mushrooms

⅓ cup finely diced red bell pepper

⅓ cup halved green olives with pimientos

¼ cup chopped green onions

1 teaspoon ground thyme

½ teaspoon black pepper

⅓ cup mayonnaise

1 (17.3-ounce) package frozen puff pastry (2 sheets), thawed

3 to 4 tablespoons tomato pesto

1 (4-ounce) package crumbled feta cheese

⅓ cup pine nuts

Pepperoni and Asiago Cheese Pinwheels

THESE HORS D'OEUVRES ARE LIGHT, FLAKY, AND ABSOLUTELY ADDICTIVE—PERFECT FOR A PARTY.

1   In a bowl, stir together the Asiago, thyme, oregano, and pepper. Cut the puff pastry crosswise in half to form 2 rectangles. Place 1 rectangle on a sheet of plastic wrap. Spread 1 tablespoon of the mustard over the pastry, leaving a 1-inch border at one long edge. Place half of the pepperoni in a single layer atop the mustard. Top the pepperoni with half of the cheese mixture. Brush the plain border with the egg. Starting at the side opposite the plain border, roll up the pastry, sealing at the egg-coated edge. Wrap the roll in plastic wrap. Repeat with the remaining pastry, mustard, pepperoni, and cheese mixture. Chill the rolls until firm, at least 1 hour or up to 1 day.

2   Preheat the oven to 400°F. Line 2 baking sheets with foil. Lightly brush the rolls with the melted butter. Cut each roll into about thirty ¼-inch-thick rounds and transfer the pinwheels to the baking sheets. Bake until golden, about 15 minutes. Transfer to a platter; serve warm or at room temperature.

YIELD: 60 pinwheels

CHEF TIP: If you cannot find Asiago, use Parmesan or Romano cheese.

½ cup grated Asiago cheese

¾ teaspoon dried thyme

¾ teaspoon dried oregano

¼ teaspoon black pepper

1 sheet frozen puff pastry (half a 17.3-ounce package), thawed

2 tablespoons honey-Dijon mustard

2 ounces sliced pepperoni (1½-inch-diameter slices)

1 large egg, lightly beaten

2 tablespoons butter, melted

Spinach and Artichoke Puff Pastry Rolls

Paula Ewell serves this hors d'oeuvre at all her parties, and friends always ask for the recipe.

1 Thaw the puff pastry at room temperature for 30 minutes. Meanwhile, drain the spinach well, then press it between layers of paper towel to remove as much moisture as possible. Stir together spinach, artichoke hearts, mayonnaise, Parmesan, onion powder, garlic powder, and pepper.

2 Unfold one of the pastry sheets on a lightly floured surface or plastic wrap. Spread half of the spinach mixture evenly over the pastry, leaving a ½-inch border on all sides. Roll up the pastry, jelly-roll fashion, and press the seam to seal. Wrap in plastic wrap. Repeat with the remaining pastry and spinach mixture. Freeze the spinach rolls 30 minutes to firm them up (see Chef Tip).

3 Before serving, preheat the oven to 400°F. Remove the rolls from the freezer and cut into ½-inch-thick slices. Place the slices 2 inches apart on 2 cookie sheets. Bake for 25 minutes or until golden brown. Serve immediately.

YIELD: 2 dozen rolls

CHEF TIP: Rolls may be frozen, wrapped in heavy-duty plastic wrap, for up to 3 months.

1 (17.3-ounce) package frozen puff pastry (2 sheets)

1 (10-ounce) package frozen chopped spinach, thawed

1 (14-ounce) can artichoke hearts, drained and finely chopped

½ cup mayonnaise

½ cup grated Parmesan cheese

1 teaspoon onion powder

½ teaspoon garlic powder

½ teaspoon pepper

Palmiers with Honey Mustard and Prosciutto

YOU CAN'T GO WRONG SERVING THESE PRETTY PALMIERS AT A COCKTAIL PARTY.

1 Line 2 baking sheets with parchment paper. Place 1 sheet of the puff pastry on a floured work surface; using a rolling pin, roll out 3 to 4 inches more in each direction. Spread 3 tablespoons of the mustard over the pastry. Arrange half of the prosciutto over the mustard to cover all the pastry, and then sprinkle with ½ cup of the Parmesan. Lightly press the cheese into the prosciutto with the rolling pin.

2 Starting at one long edge, roll up the puff pastry like a jelly roll just to the middle of the dough; then roll up the other side in the same fashion, making two rolls that meet in the center. Using a serrated knife, cut the rolls crosswise into ½-inch slices. Place the slices on the baking sheets and press lightly with your hands to flatten to about ¼ inch. Refrigerate for 15 minutes. Repeat with the second sheet of puff pastry and the other half of the ingredients.

3 Preheat the oven to 400°F.

4 Beat the egg and water in a small bowl. Brush the top of each palmier with the egg wash. Bake until puffed and lightly golden, about 10 minutes. These are best served warm but may be served at room temperature.

YIELD: 2 dozen palmiers

CHEF TIPS: Use more or less mustard or prosciutto than the recipe calls for, if you prefer.

The palmiers can be prepared several hours in advance without baking. Keep well covered so they don't dry out in the refrigerator.

1 (17.3-ounce) package frozen puff pastry (2 sheets), thawed

6 tablespoons honey mustard

6 ounces very thinly sliced prosciutto

1 cup freshly grated Parmesan cheese

1 egg

2 teaspoons water

Blue Cheese Popovers

THIS BATTER MUST BE COLD BEFORE IT IS POURED INTO THE MUFFIN TINS, SO IT HELPS TO MAKE IT ONE DAY IN ADVANCE. THE PETITE SIZE IS PERFECT FOR HORS D'OEUVRES.

1 In a large bowl, combine the eggs, milk, melted butter, flour, salt, and pepper. Whisk together until all the lumps have disappeared. Whisk in the cheese and thyme. Transfer the batter to an airtight container and refrigerate for at least 3 hours or up to 1 day.

2 Preheat the oven to 425°F. Generously butter two mini muffin pans (see Chef Tip). Working with one pan, fill each cup to the top with the chilled batter. Bake the popovers until golden and puffed, 15 to 18 minutes. Serve immediately. Using the other muffin pan, repeat until all the batter is used.

YIELD: 32 popovers

CHEF TIP: The yield in this recipe is for mini muffin pans that measure 1⅞ inches across the top, the most common size. The ideal size for perfect one-bite hors d'oeuvres measures about 1¼ inches across the top, but it is very hard to find; it will yield at least 5 dozen.

4 large eggs

2 cups milk

¼ cup unsalted butter, melted, plus extra for greasing the tins

2 cups all-purpose flour

1½ teaspoons kosher salt

¼ teaspoon pepper

3 ounces crumbled blue cheese*

¼ cup roughly chopped fresh thyme

*Blue, Maytag, or Danish blue cheese may be used

COURTESY DON STRENCH

Kids enjoying the New Albany Classic Invitational Grand Prix & Family Day

Gruyère Cheese Puffs (Gougères)

THIS HOT CHEESE PASTRY MAKES A SPECTACULARLY EASY COCKTAIL SNACK SERVED WITH A GLASS OF RED WINE OR PORT.

1   Preheat the oven to 375°F. Lightly butter a baking sheet.

2   Combine the milk, butter, and salt in a medium, heavy saucepan and bring to a boil. Remove the pan from the heat and add the flour all at once. Whisk vigorously for a few moments, then return the pan to medium heat and cook, stirring constantly, until the batter has thickened and is pulling away from the sides and bottom of the pan—often less than a minute but sometimes as much as 5 minutes.

3   Again remove the pan from the heat. Stir in 6 of the eggs, one at a time and beating until incorporated before adding the next. When the batter is smooth and uniform, stir in the Gruyère cheese and 1 cup of the Parmesan cheese.

4   Drop the batter by scant tablespoons onto the baking sheet, spacing them about 1 inch apart. Beat the remaining egg in a small bowl. Brush the tops of the puffs with the beaten egg and sprinkle with the remaining 1 cup Parmesan cheese. (You can make the *gougères* to this point a few hours beforehand and refrigerate them, covered, until ready to bake.)

5   Set the baking sheet on the center rack of the oven, reduce heat to 350°F and bake for 15 to 20 minutes, or until the *gougères* are puffed and well browned. Serve immediately.

YIELD: 30 puffs

CHEF TIP: You can top the *gougères* with minced herbs, such as thyme or rosemary, in addition to the Parmesan if you desire.

1½ cups milk

12 tablespoons unsalted butter (1½ sticks)

1½ teaspoons salt

1½ cups sifted all-purpose flour

7 large eggs

1¼ cups shredded Gruyère cheese

2 cups grated Parmesan cheese

Jalapeño-spiked Deviled Eggs

THIS IS A SPICY TWIST ON THE TRADITIONAL DEVILED EGGS.

1 Cut the eggs in half lengthwise and carefully remove the yolks. Mash the yolks in a small bowl. Stir in the mayonnaise, jalapeños, mustard, cayenne, cumin, and salt; blend well. Spoon or pipe the yolk mixture evenly into the egg-white halves. Lightly sprinkle with chili powder and garnish with fresh parsley sprigs, if desired.

YIELD: 24 pieces

12 hard-boiled eggs

½ cup mayonnaise (chipotle-flavored is even more authentic)

3 tablespoons pickled jalapeño slices, drained and minced

2 tablespoons prepared mustard

½ teaspoon cayenne

½ teaspoon ground cumin

¼ teaspoon kosher salt

Chili powder and fresh parsley sprigs for garnish

Baked Brie with Caramel Sauce

RONDA HOBART'S APPETIZER IS SO EASY TO DO. IT IS ALWAYS A HIT AT COCKTAIL PARTIES, PARTICULARLY DURING THE COOL HOLIDAY SEASON.

1 Preheat the oven to 350°F.

2 Place the Brie in an ovenproof lidded serving dish (a ceramic pie plate would be ideal). Pour the caramel sauce over it. Warm it in the oven for 6 to 10 minutes, until the center feels soft when you push down with a spoon.

3 Sprinkle the top with the almonds, cherries, and apricots. Serve warm with sliced French bread or cocktail crackers.

SERVES: 6

CHEF TIP: An alternative to the caramel sauce would be ¼ cup of Kahlua mixed with 3 tablespoons of dark brown sugar, heated over medium heat in a saucepan until the brown sugar has completely dissolved and the sauce has thickened a little. Do not bake the Brie too long, as the hot Kahlua sauce will already have warmed it slightly.

1 (8-ounce) wheel or wedge of Brie

1 (9 to 12-ounce) jar caramel sundae topping

2 tablespoons toasted sliced almonds or chopped pecans

2 tablespoons finely chopped dried cherries

2 tablespoons finely chopped dried apricots

Sliced French bread or cocktail crackers

Blue Crab Stuffed Mushrooms

THESE SCRUMPTIOUS STUFFED MUSHROOMS CAN GO TWO WAYS: AS HORS D'OEUVRES OR A FIRST COURSE FOR A FORMAL DINNER—SIMPLY ARRANGE THREE TO FIVE PIECES ON A PLATE AND GARNISH WITH GREENS.

1 Preheat the oven to 350°F.

2 Place the mushroom caps in a colander and quickly rinse under running water. Drain mushrooms caps stem side down on paper towels. Gently pat dry with paper towels and set aside.

3 Carefully pick over crabmeat, without breaking up lumps. Discard any pieces of shell or cartilage. Place crabmeat in a large bowl. Add cheese, bread crumbs, parsley, green onions, salt, and cayenne.

4 Melt ¾ cup of the butter. Pour over crabmeat mixture. Toss gently to combine. Do not break up lumps of crabmeat.

5 In the oven, melt the remaining ¼ cup butter in a shallow baking pan large enough to hold the mushrooms in a single layer. Tilt pan to coat with melted butter. Fill each mushroom cap with stuffing, mounding the stuffing about ½ inch above the cap. Place stuffed mushrooms in the pan. Bake until the mushrooms are dark and juicy and the stuffing is slightly browned, about 10 minutes.

6 To serve as appetizers, arrange on platters. To serve as first course, arrange 3 to 5 mushrooms on each small plate and drizzle drippings from the baking pan over each serving.

YIELD: 40 pieces

40 medium or large mushroom caps

1 pound backfin lump blue crab meat or other crabmeat

1½ cups shredded Monterey Jack cheese (about 6 ounces)

¾ cup dry bread crumbs

¼ cup minced flat-leaf parsley

6 green onions, thinly sliced

1 teaspoon salt

1 teaspoon cayenne

1 cup unsalted butter

Oven-roasted Tomatoes with Goat Cheese

ROASTING SHRINKS THE TOMATOES, BUT WHAT'S LOST IN SIZE IS MADE UP FOR IN FLAVOR.

1 Preheat the oven to 200°F. (If your oven does not have this temperature setting, set it on low.)

2 In a large bowl, whisk 1 tablespoon of the oil with the vinegar. Add the halved tomatoes and toss very gently. Make sure each tomato is lightly coated with the dressing. Season with salt and pepper.

3 Arrange the tomatoes cut side up on a wire rack set on a baking sheet. Dry the tomatoes in the oven for 4 to 6 hours (or longer if the tomatoes are still juicy), turning the baking sheet frequently to promote even drying. The tomatoes will shrink considerably but will stay somewhat soft and syrupy. Do not let them dry completely (they should not resemble commercially produced chewy sun-dried tomatoes). Remove the tomatoes from the oven and let them cool on the rack. (The tomatoes can be dried a day ahead. Store in an airtight container in the refrigerator. Let them come to room temperature before continuing.)

4 Center a piece of cheese on each tomato. Fold the tomato slightly to cradle the cheese. Insert a rosemary sprig into one end of the tomato, through the cheese, and out the other end of the tomato to hold the tomato and cheese together. Repeat with the remaining tomatoes. Drizzle lightly with the remaining 1 tablespoon oil. Let stand for 30 minutes before serving.

SERVES: 6

CHEF TIP: You may substitute fresh mozzarella cheese for the goat cheese. Additionally, you may serve the roasted tomatoes on slices of French bread.

2 tablespoons extra virgin olive oil

1 tablespoon aged balsamic vinegar

6 Roma tomatoes, halved lengthwise and seeded

Salt and freshly ground pepper to taste

12 teaspoon-sized pieces fresh white goat cheese

12 sprigs rosemary

Spanish Potato Omelet (Tortilla Española)

*P*OTATO OMELET IS AN ALL-TIME TAPAS CLASSIC. IT IS A GOOD RECIPE TO MASTER, AS IT TASTES EQUALLY GOOD HOT, COLD, OR AT ROOM TEMPERATURE AND CAN THEREFORE BE DONE WELL AHEAD.

ANNUAL NEW ALBANY COMMUNITY FOUNDATION EVENT

*E*ach autumn the New Albany Community Foundation, in partnership with the New Albany Classic Signature Series and event hosts Abigail and Leslie Wexner, presents "A Remarkable Evening," an event benefiting innovative and forward-thinking community projects. The New Albany Library, the Community Performing Arts Center, and many other initiatives that enhance life in the community have benefited from the proceeds of this event. The evening has showcased world-renowned lecturers and performers, including Pulitzer Prize–winner David McCullough, Tony and Pulitzer Prize–winner the late Wendy Wasserstein, and acclaimed Irish tenor and champion disabled athlete, Dr. Ronan Tynan.

A sold-out event every year, "A Remarkable Evening" has been the venue for some outstanding community announcements, including a $1-million gift by the MI Homes Foundation to support the New Albany Community Performing Arts Center and the establishment of the Jeanne and John B. McCoy Community Award, which was first awarded in 2005 to New Albany Women's Network founder Janet Atwater.

— New Albany Community Foundation and New Albany Classic Signature Series

1 Heat the oil in a 12- or 14-inch skillet over medium heat. Add the potato slices one at a time so they don't stick together. Alternate layers of potato with the onion slices and lightly salt each layer. Cook slowly (the potatoes will boil in the oil rather than fry), lifting and turning the potatoes occasionally, until they are tender but not brown. The potatoes should not stick together. Drain the potatoes and onions in a colander, reserving about 3 tablespoons of the oil. (The onion and potato give the oil a wonderful flavor, so save the rest for another use.)

1¼ cups olive oil

3 large potatoes, peeled and cut into ⅛-inch slices

1 large onion, thinly sliced

Kosher salt to taste

5 large eggs

Tony and Pulitzer Prize-winner, the late Wendy Wasserstein at 2003 NACF Fundraiser

NEW ALBANY CLASSIC SIGNATURE SERIES PHOTOS
COURTESY DANIEL W. FLOSS & ASSOCIATES PHOTOGRAPHY

2 In a large bowl, beat the eggs with a fork until they are slightly foamy. Salt to taste. Add the potatoes to the beaten egg, pressing the potatoes down with a spatula so they are completely covered by the egg. Let sit for 15 minutes.

3 Heat 2 tablespoons of the reserved oil in a 10-inch omelet pan over high heat until it just begins to smoke. It must be very hot or the eggs will stick. Add the potato and egg mixture, spreading it out rapidly in the skillet with the aid of a spatula. Lower the heat to medium-high and shake the pan often to prevent sticking. When the eggs begin to brown underneath, invert a large plate over the skillet and flip the omelet onto the plate. Add the remaining 1 tablespoon reserved oil to the pan, then slide the omelet back into the skillet and cook until browned on the other side.

4 Lower the heat to medium and flip the omelet two or three more times, cooking briefly on each side. It should be firm but still moist inside. Transfer to a platter and let cool, then cut into thin wedges or into 1-inch squares that can be picked up with toothpicks. Serve with saffron sauce, if desired (see below).

SERVES: 8 to 10

CHEF TIP: Use a mandolin to slice the potatoes and onions to a uniform thickness.

SAFFRON SAUCE

1 Heat the olive oil in a medium skillet over low heat and cook the onion and garlic, stirring occasionally, until the onion is wilted, about 5 minutes. Add the tomato, turn up the heat to medium and cook for 2 minutes. Stir in the chicken stock and saffron. Cover and simmer for 15 minutes, then strain, pressing on the vegetables with the back of a wooden spoon to extract as much liquid as possible. Stir in the pimientos. Place omelet wedges or squares in the sauce, cover and simmer for 2 to 3 minutes. Cool to room temperature.

2 Transfer omelet pieces and sauce to a platter and serve.

1 tablespoon olive oil

1 small onion, finely chopped

1 clove garlic, minced

1 small tomato, chopped

¾ cup chicken stock

A few strands of saffron

1 (2-ounce) jar diced pimientos, drained

Shrimp Rémoulade

THIS COLD APPETIZER HAS A ZIP THAT AWAKENS YOUR TASTE BUDS AND GETS YOU READY FOR THE FOLLOWING COURSES.

1 Fill a large pot with water. Add the shrimp boil mix. Bring water to a roiling boil. Add the shrimp and boil, stirring occasionally, just until pink but still tender, no more than 3 minutes. Drain shrimp and rinse in cold water to stop the cooking; drain again.

2 To make the sauce, in a blender combine the lemon juice, vinegar, mustard, horseradish, garlic, paprika, salt, pepper, ginger, and cayenne. Blend until smooth. With the motor running, slowly add the oil to emulsify. Blend well. Pour into a bowl and stir in the celery and green onions. Add the cooked shrimp and stir well. Chill, covered, for at least 4 hours before serving.

3 To serve, mound shredded iceberg lettuce on a large platter. Spoon the shrimp rémoulade over the lettuce. Serve with toothpicks.

SERVES: 6 to 8

1 (3-ounce) bag shrimp and crab boil mix

2 pounds medium to large shrimp, peeled, tails removed and deveined

Shredded iceberg lettuce

Sauce:

¼ cup lemon juice

¼ cup tarragon vinegar

¼ cup Creole mustard

¼ cup prepared horseradish

2 cloves garlic, minced

2 teaspoons paprika

2 teaspoons salt

½ teaspoon black pepper

Dash of ground ginger

Dash of cayenne

1 cup olive oil

½ cup minced celery

½ cup minced green onions

Piquant Portuguese Shrimp

THESE HOT AND SPICY SHRIMP ARE WONDERFUL SERVED ON A BED OF SALAD GREENS AND EQUALLY GOOD AS COCKTAIL FINGER FOOD.

1 Rinse the shrimp and blot dry with paper towels. Place the shrimp in a shallow tray and set aside.

2 To make the spice paste, stir together the garlic, ginger, cayenne, brown sugar, black pepper, cumin, cinnamon, cloves, turmeric, and gin. Using your fingers, rub the paste evenly over the shrimp. Set aside for 30 minutes at room temperature.

3 In a 12-inch skillet over high heat, heat the oil. When it starts to smoke, add the shrimp and cook, tossing, until they turn pink and curl, no more than 5 minutes. Remove from the heat and sprinkle with the lemon juice. Serve immediately over a bed of salad greens.

SERVES: 8

1 pound jumbo or large (31 to 40 count) shrimp, peeled, with tails left on, and deveined

2 tablespoons olive oil

1 tablespoon fresh lemon juice

Salad greens

Spice Paste:

1 tablespoon minced garlic

1 tablespoon grated fresh ginger

2 teaspoons cayenne

1 teaspoon dark brown sugar

1 teaspoon black pepper

1 teaspoon ground cumin

½ teaspoon ground cinnamon

¼ teaspoon ground cloves

¼ teaspoon turmeric

2 tablespoons gin

Spicy Fried Calamari

WITH READY-TO-COOK CALAMARI NOW WIDELY AVAILABLE IN SUPERMARKETS, HOME COOKS CAN SERVE THIS ITALIAN RESTAURANT STAPLE IN NO TIME AT ALL.

1 Combine the flour and the Cajun Spice Mix. Place the calamari on a tray and dust with the flour mixture. Shake off excess mixture.

2 In a large, heavy pot or deep fryer over medium heat, heat the oil to 375°F, or until almost smoking. Working in 4 batches, fry the calamari for 1 minute, or until light golden brown. Using a slotted spoon, transfer to paper towels to drain. Serve immediately with lemon or lime wedges and Lemon Aïoli.

SERVES: 6

5 tablespoons all-purpose flour

5 tablespoons Cajun Spice Mix (recipe follows)

4 pounds calamari rings, washed and dried with paper towels

3 to 4 cups canola oil

Lemon or lime wedges

1 cup Lemon Aioli (recipe follows)

CAJUN SPICE MIX

1 Combine all the ingredients and mix well. Store in an airtight container in a cool, dry place.

YIELD: Makes about 1¼ cups

½ cup sweet paprika

2½ tablespoons cayenne

2½ tablespoons garlic powder

2½ tablespoons onion powder

1½ tablespoons black pepper

1½ tablespoons white pepper

1 tablespoon dried thyme

1 tablespoon dried oregano

1 tablespoon salt

LEMON AÏOLI

1 In a blender or food processor, combine the bread, egg yolks, lemon zest and juice, garlic, mustard, pepper, and salt; purée to a smooth paste. With the machine running, drizzle in the oil. If the aïoli appears too thick, add 2 tablespoons of water at a time to adjust the consistency. The aioli keeps, refrigerated in an airtight container, for up to 2 weeks.

CHEF TIP: The aïoli makes a wonderful dressing for poached salmon or grilled chicken breasts.

1½ slices white bread, crusts removed and bread torn into pieces

2 egg yolks

Grated zest and juice of 3 lemons

2 tablespoons minced garlic

1½ tablespoons Dijon mustard

1½ teaspoons white pepper

½ teaspoon salt

2 cups olive or canola oil

½ cup iced water (if needed)

Mini Crab Cakes with Lemon Dill Sauce

A SHOWSTOPPER THAT GETS MORE RAVES THAN BROADWAY. THE LEMON DILL SAUCE IS DIVINE.

1 In a medium bowl, lightly beat the egg. Add the mayonnaise, prepared mustard, Worcestershire sauce, lemon juice, parsley flakes, seafood seasoning, and dry mustard; beat well. Gently fold in the bread and crabmeat. Shape into 16 balls, flatten slightly into cakes and transfer to a baking sheet. Chill for 30 minutes.

2 Preheat the oven to 350°F.

3 Bake the crab cakes for 10 minutes. Then broil for another 2 minutes until golden brown. Serve immediately with Lemon Dill Sauce.

YIELD: 16 crab cakes

1 egg

1 heaping tablespoon mayonnaise

1 heaping teaspoon prepared mustard (your choice)

1 teaspoon Worcestershire sauce

1 teaspoon lemon juice

1 teaspoon parsley flakes

½ teaspoon Phillips Seafood Seasoning

¼ teaspoon dry mustard

2 slices white bread, torn into small pieces

1 pound lump (or backfin) crabmeat, picked over

LEMON DILL SAUCE

1 Mix all the ingredients together well. Keep refrigerated until serving time.

¾ cup mayonnaise

½ cup buttermilk

2 tablespoons minced fresh dill

1 tablespoon minced fresh parsley

1 tablespoon finely grated lemon zest

2 teaspoons fresh lemon juice

1 clove garlic, minced (optional)

Vietnamese Fresh Summer Rolls (Goi Cuon)

THESE DELICATE SUMMER ROLLS HAVE BECOME ENORMOUSLY POPULAR FOR THEIR REFRESHINGLY COOL, CLEAN TASTE. THEY ARE ESSENTIALLY LITTLE SELF-CONTAINED SALADS-TO-GO AND ARE TYPICALLY EATEN WITH YOUR HANDS. PERFECT FOR A LIGHT SUMMER MEAL, OR A DINNER-PARTY HORS D'OEUVRE.

1 Prepare the dipping sauce and set aside.

2 In a bowl, combine the shredded carrots and the sugar; let stand for 10 minutes to soften. In another bowl, soak the rice vermicelli in hot water for 10 minutes to soften; drain.

3 Bring a pot of water to a boil and cook the shrimp until pink and opaque, 2 to 3 minutes. Fish out the shrimp but keep the water boiling. Add the rice noodles and cook for 2 minutes. Drain and rinse in cold water; drain again. Peel the shrimp and slice in half lengthwise.

4 To assemble the summer rolls, have a basin of warm water ready to moisten the rice paper rounds. Work with only 2 rice paper rounds at a time. Dip each sheet into the warm water, then lay them flat on a dry towel (do not let the sheets touch one another or they will stick together). Lay one piece of lettuce over the bottom third of the rice paper round. On top of the lettuce, place 2 tablespoons of noodles, 2 tablespoons of the shredded carrot, and several mint leaves. Roll up the paper just enough to cover the filling. Fold both sides of the paper over the filling. Lay 2 shrimp halves, cut side down, along the crease. Tuck 2 chives under the shrimp at one end, leaving about 1 inch of the chives extending past the edge of the roll. Place several cilantro leaves next to the shrimp. Finish rolling the paper into a complete cylinder. Place the rolls on a plate and cover with a damp towel so they will stay moist. Continue filling the remaining rice paper rounds.

5 The rolls don't keep well, so serve them straight away with plenty of dipping sauce. If you're serving them as an appetizer, cut the rolls in half diagonally using a sharp knife.

SERVES: 4 as a light main dish, 12 as an appetizer

CHEF TIP: If you absolutely must make the rolls ahead of time, place them in an airtight container lined with a damp kitchen towel and store at cool room temperature, not in the refrigerator. They will keep for an hour or two.

Hoisin-Chili Dipping Sauce (recipe opposite)

2 carrots, shredded

1 teaspoon sugar

3 ounces rice vermicelli
24 medium shrimp, unpeeled
12 (8½-inch) rice paper rounds *(banh trang mong)**

½ small head green leaf, red leaf or romaine lettuce (10 to 12 leaves), thick stem ends removed and each leaf cut in quarters

½ cup fresh mint leaves

16 Chinese chives, trimmed to 5-inch lengths (optional)

½ cup fresh cilantro leaves

*available at most Asian groceries

Hoisin-Chili Dipping Sauce

1 Heat the oil in a saucepan over medium-high heat. Stir-fry the shallot for a minute or two, until softened. Stir in the hoisin sauce, water, and rice vinegar and bring to a boil. Add chili paste to taste. Remove from heat and let cool to room temperature. Pour into small individual dipping bowls, and garnish with chopped peanuts.

1 teaspoon vegetable oil

1 small shallot (or 2 cloves garlic), minced

½ cup hoisin sauce

¼ cup water

1 tablespoon rice vinegar

2 teaspoons Asian red chili paste

2 tablespoons chopped peanuts for garnish

The New Albany Classic Invitational Grand Prix & Family Day

Fried Spring Rolls (Lumpia Shanghai)

PERFECT FINGER FOOD! SERVED WITH THAI SWEET CHILI SAUCE OR TRADITIONAL CHINESE DUCK SAUCE, THESE NEVER FAIL TO ELICIT OOHS AND AHHS AT COCKTAIL PARTIES.

1 In a large bowl, combine the pork, shrimp, egg, water chestnuts, mushrooms, green onions, soy sauce, salt, and pepper. Mix well. Fry a tablespoon of the filling in hot oil to test for seasoning and adjust with salt and pepper.

2 Lay a spring roll wrapper on the counter. At one end of the wrapper, spoon 2 tablespoons of the filling across the width of the square. Roll tightly into a cylinder. Brush the end of the wrapper with egg white to seal. Repeat rolling until the filling is used up. (Spring rolls may be prepared ahead to this point and frozen in one layer in 1-gallon resealable plastic bags.)

3 In an electric frying pan or deep saucepan over medium heat, heat an inch of vegetable oil to 350°F. Working in batches and without crowding the pan, fry spring rolls for about 5 minutes on one side or until golden brown; turn over and fry for another 3 minutes or until golden brown. Drain on paper towels.

4 Serve with Thai sweet chili sauce or duck sauce.

SERVES: 20 or more

CHEF TIP: The spring rolls can be stored several months in the freezer, ready to fry at a moment's notice. Do not thaw before frying frozen rolls. Fry for about 7 minutes on one side, then turn and fry for 5 minutes or until golden brown.

2 pounds ground pork

1 pound medium shelled fresh shrimp, finely chopped

1 egg, lightly beaten

1 (5-ounce) can sliced water chestnuts

8 pieces dried shiitake mushrooms, soaked in hot water for 20 minutes, then minced

1 cup minced green onions

2 tablespoons soy sauce

2 teaspoons salt

1 teaspoon black pepper

4 packages spring roll wrappers (25 sheets, 8 inches square)

1 egg white

Vegetable oil for frying

Thai sweet chili sauce or duck sauce*

*both are available in jars in Asian groceries or the ethnic aisle of large supermarkets

Cashew Chicken Bites
with Apricot Dipping Sauce

A DELECTABLE PARTY NIBBLE. SERVE ON TOOTHPICKS, WITH THE TANGY DIPPING SAUCE ON THE SIDE.

1 Whisk together the egg white, cornstarch, sherry, Worcestershire sauce, salt, and pepper. Add the chicken and stir to coat. Marinate, covered and refrigerated, for at least 45 minutes.

2 Preheat the oven to 350°F. Lightly coat a baking sheet with butter-flavored cooking spray.

3 Spread the cashew nuts on a sheet of wax paper. Scoop up spoonfuls of the chicken pieces and dredge them in the nuts to coat, pressing on the nuts so they adhere. Place the chicken in one layer on the baking sheet. Lightly spray the chicken with butter-flavored spray. Bake for 20 to 30 minutes or until lightly browned.

4 Meanwhile, make the sauce. Slowly warm the apricot jam in a small saucepan, then stir in the vinegar.

YIELD: about 20 pieces

CHEF TIPS: Pecans may be substituted for cashews.

Do not microwave leftovers; reheat in the oven to keep the crunch.

1 egg white, lightly beaten

2 tablespoons cornstarch

2 tablespoons dry sherry or white wine

1 tablespoon Worcestershire sauce

1 teaspoon salt

¾ teaspoon pepper

1 pound boneless skinless chicken breast, cut into bite-sized chunks

Butter-flavored cooking spray

2 cups finely chopped cashew nuts

Apricot Dipping Sauce:

¾ cup apricot jam

2 tablespoons cider vinegar

Pork and Vegetable Potstickers with Soy Dipping Sauce

THIS IS ONE OF STELLA WOO'S FAMILY FAVORITES. SHE AND HER FRIENDS GET TOGETHER FOR AN INFORMAL DINNER WHERE EVERYONE WRAPS AND GABS, A FUN WAY TO VISIT. PILES OF POTSTICKERS ARE MADE AND THEN SERVED WITH A LIGHT SOUP.

HOMELESS FAMILIES FOUNDATION EVENT

The Homeless Families Foundation (HFF) began as a small volunteer-based family shelter in 1986 and evolved into the largest 90-day Emergency Family Shelter in Franklin County, Ohio. HFF focuses on supporting families in crisis, helping hundreds to stay together despite the traumatic events that lead to homelessness, helping them take the steps necessary to empower their independence, and assisting them in securing permanent housing.

Over the past several years, various homeowners in the New Albany Country Club community have been honored to host what has become the largest single fundraiser supporting HFF. Each year a different family, in partnership with the New Albany Classic Signature Series, opens their home to more than 200 guests in support of Central Ohio's homeless. The fundraising event consistently raises more than $200,000 thanks to the support of local companies and individuals who believe in the mission of the Homeless Families Foundation.

The event is also supported by many New Albany residents who volunteer at HFF and contribute their time and talent to see that the event raises the critical funds needed to continue HFF's good work.

— New Albany Classic Signature Series

1 To make the dipping sauce, in a bowl stir together the soy sauce, vinegar, and sugar until the sugar is dissolved. Stir in the ginger. Cover and set aside at room temperature.

2 If using dried shiitake mushrooms, soak in warm water until softened, about 20 minutes. Drain and squeeze dry. Remove and discard the stems. Finely chop the mushroom caps.

3 In a large bowl, toss the cabbage with the salt. Let sit for 20 minutes. Rinse well with water and squeeze out as much water as possible. There will be about 2 cups of squeezed-dry cabbage.

Soy Vinegar Dipping Sauce:

½ cup light soy sauce

¼ cup rice vinegar

1 teaspoon sugar

2 tablespoons finely julienned fresh ginger

6 dried shiitake mushrooms (optional)

½ pound Napa cabbage, shredded (approximately 3 cups)

1 tablespoon salt

½ pound lean ground pork

2 green onions, chopped

1 tablespoon minced fresh ginger

1 tablespoon soy sauce

1 tablespoon cornstarch

Homeless Families Foundation event

NEW ALBANY CLASSIC SIGNATURE SERIES PHOTOS
COURTESY DANIEL W. FLOSS & ASSOCIATES PHOTOGRAPHY

4 Return the cabbage to the bowl and add the ground pork, green onions, ginger, soy sauce, cornstarch, rice wine, sesame oil, sugar, and pepper. Mix well until thoroughly blended. Cover and refrigerate for 30 minutes to 2 hours.

5 Preheat the oven to 200°F. Line a baking sheet with lightly greased foil.

6 Working with one potsticker wrapper at a time, and keeping remaining wrappers covered with a damp kitchen towel, place a heaping teaspoon of filling in the center of a wrapper. Lightly brush the edge with water. Fold in half to form an open half-moon shape but do not press the edges together. Using your thumb and index finger, make 4 small pleats in the top piece of wrapper. Fold up the far edge and press the edges to seal. The potstickers will have a crescent shape, with the seam along the top. Place on a tray and cover with a damp kitchen towel. Repeat with the remaining wrappers and filling.

7 Heat a large skillet over medium-high heat until hot. Add 2 tablespoons of the peanut oil and swirl to coat the bottom of the pan. Arrange half of the potstickers, seam side up and without touching, in the pan. Cook for 3 to 4 minutes, until the bottoms are golden brown, being careful not to burn them. Reduce heat if necessary. Add ½ cup of the chicken stock. Cover and reduce heat to low. Cook until the liquid is absorbed, 5 to 7 minutes.

8 Transfer the cooked potstickers with a spatula to the prepared baking sheet, browned side up. Keep warm in the oven while cooking the second batch of potstickers.

9 Serve hot with Soy Vinegar Dipping Sauce.

YIELD: 24 potstickers

CHEF TIP: Potstickers taste best freshly cooked and served immediately. However, they may be made ahead on the same day and refrigerated until needed. Heat in a single layer on an oiled baking sheet in a preheated 350°F oven until heated through, about 15 minutes.

1 teaspoon rice wine or sherry wine

1 teaspoon toasted sesame oil

½ teaspoon sugar

½ teaspoon white pepper

24 potsticker wrappers*

¼ cup peanut or vegetable oil

1 cup chicken stock

*available in the refrigerator section of Asian groceries

Spicy Chicken Drummettes

THIS EXOTIC RECIPE CAME FROM AUSTRALIA. THE SOUTH ASIAN AND CHINESE INFLUENCE CAME BY WAY OF THE BRITISH COLONIES. GREAT PARTY FARE.

1 To make drummettes, cut the chicken wings in half at the main joint. Save the wing-tip segment for another use, such as chicken stock (see Chef Tip). Trim around the bone with a sharp knife. Cut, scrape and push the meat down to the large end of the piece of chicken. Pull the skin and meat down over the bottom joint so the wing resembles a baby drumstick. (Drummettes can be prepared up to 2 days ahead. Cover and refrigerate.)

2 Into a bowl, sift the self-rising flour, chickpea flour, chili powder, garam masala, cumin, and coriander; gradually stir in the water until the batter is smooth. (Batter can be prepared 3 hours ahead.)

3 To make the sauce, combine the barbecue sauce, water, and chiles in a small pan and bring to a boil. Set aside.

4 Heat an electric deep-fryer, or half-fill a deep 4-quart saucepan with oil and heat until very hot. Dip drummettes into the batter and deep-fry in hot oil until lightly browned and cooked through. Do not crowd the pan or it will steam up and not fry efficiently. Drain drummettes on paper towels. Serve hot with the sauce.

YIELD: 24 drummettes

CHEF TIP: At some grocery stores and meat markets you can buy chicken wing segments, sometimes referred to as buffalo wings; ask for the meaty segment of the wings only.

24 chicken wings

½ cup self-rising flour

¼ cup chickpea flour*

1 teaspoon chili powder

1 teaspoon garam masala**

½ teaspoon ground cumin

½ teaspoon ground coriander

1 cup water

Vegetable oil for deep frying

*also known as gram flour or besan flour; available at South Asian markets or the gourmet section of some supermarkets

**blend of dry-roasted, ground spices from India

Sauce:

1 (7-ounce) jar Chinese barbecue sauce

⅓ cup water

1 teaspoon chopped fresh chiles

Grilled Beef, Chicken, or Pork on Skewers (Satays)

VARIATIONS OF SATAYS ARE MADE ALL OVER SOUTHEAST ASIA. THIS THAI VERSION IS SERVED WITH A SWEET AND SPICY PEANUT SAUCE AND A CUCUMBER RELISH TO BALANCE THE FLAVORS.

1   In a shallow baking dish, whisk together the coconut milk, turmeric, and curry powder. Thread 3 or 4 meat strips onto each skewer. (The meat can be threaded onto skewers 1 day ahead.) Marinate the skewered meat in the coconut milk mixture for about 1 hour.

2   Grill or broil the satays, turning once and basting occasionally with the marinade, until the meat is cooked through, about 4 minutes total. Serve warm or at room temperature with Spicy Peanut Sauce and Thai Cucumber Relish. If the satay is a main course, serve with rice as well.

SERVES: 6 to 8

CHEF TIPS: Canned coconut milk separates naturally. The top layer can be spooned off for recipes calling for cream; the rest is thin coconut milk. Shake up the can to get the most commonly called for thick coconut milk.

If you are using chicken, choose thighs, as they remain moist during grilling.

SPICY PEANUT SAUCE FOR SATAY *(Naam Jim Satay)*

1   Stir together the tamarind paste and water until dissolved; set aside.

2   In a saucepan, cook the thick coconut milk over low heat until it thickens and becomes oily around the edges. Increase the heat to medium. Stir in the curry paste and cook for 3 to 5 minutes, being careful not to burn it. The mixture will turn a deep red and the curry odor will intensify as it cooks. Gradually stir in the thin coconut milk. Season with sugar, fish sauce, and the reserved tamarind water. Remove from the heat and stir in the ground peanuts.

YIELD: 2 cups

CHEF TIP: The peanut sauce may be prepared several days in advance. Keep refrigerated but serve at room temperature. The sauce will become spicier and thicker as it stands. If it is too thick when serving, dilute it with thin coconut milk or water.

Continued on next page

1¾ cups thin coconut milk (see Chef Tips)

1¼ teaspoons turmeric

¾ teaspoon curry powder

1 pound beef, chicken or pork, or an assortment, cut across the grain into thin slices ¼-inch thick and 3 inches wide

About 20 (6-inch) bamboo skewers, soaked in water for 1 hour to prevent burning

Spicy Peanut Sauce (recipe below)

Thai Cucumber Relish (recipe on page 82)

1 teaspoon tamarind paste*

1 tablespoon hot water

1 cup thick coconut milk (see Chef Tips above)

2½ tablespoons red curry paste*

¾ cup thin coconut milk (see Chef Tips above)

2 tablespoons light brown sugar

1 tablespoon fish sauce*

¼ cup ground unsalted roasted peanuts (or 3 tablespoons creamy peanut butter)

*available at Asian groceries or gourmet stores; tamarind paste may also be found in Hispanic groceries

Thai Cucumber Relish *(Arjard)*

1 Put the cucumbers in a bowl. In a small saucepan, bring the water to a boil; add the sugar and stir to dissolve. Stir in the vinegar and salt. Let cool. Pour over the cucumbers. Add the red onion and chiles. Toss well. Chill before serving.

YIELD: 1½ cups

1 cucumber, seeds removed, thinly sliced

1 cup water

5 tablespoons sugar

½ cup distilled white vinegar

1 teaspoon salt

2 tablespoons minced red onion

3 to 5 Thai or serrano chiles, seeded and thinly sliced

New Albany residence

Moorish Pork Kabobs (Pinchos Morunos)

THESE SUBSTANTIAL AND FLAVORFUL APPETIZERS CAN EASILY STAR AS THE MAIN COURSE AT A GRILL-OUT DINNER. SERVE WITH COUSCOUS AND A BOWL OF GAZPACHO AND YOU'RE ALL SET.

1 In a small skillet, combine the olive oil, cumin, coriander, paprika, cayenne, turmeric, oregano, salt and black pepper. Stir over low heat until warmed through and fragrant, about 3 minutes. Let cool to room temperature.

2 Place the pork pieces in a bowl and rub with the spice mixture. Add the parsley, lemon juice, and garlic and toss well. Cover and refrigerate overnight.

3 Preheat the grill to medium-high. Thread the meat onto 10 metal skewers and sprinkle with salt. Grill the pork, turning once, until just cooked through, about 4 minutes on each side. Serve with lemon wedges.

SERVES: 10

CHEF TIP: Use pork shoulder or a cut with a little fat in it. A very lean cut of pork will dry up when grilled as a kabob. You can also use boneless skinless chicken.

⅔ cup olive oil

3 tablespoons ground cumin

2 tablespoons ground coriander

1 tablespoon sweet paprika

1½ teaspoons cayenne

1 teaspoon ground turmeric

1 teaspoon dried oregano

1 teaspoon salt

½ teaspoon freshly ground black pepper

3 pounds pork, cut into 1-inch cubes (see Chef Tip)

¼ cup chopped flat-leaf parsley

¼ cup fresh lemon juice

3 tablespoons minced garlic

Lemon wedges

Pork and Red Pepper Mini Skewers with Mango Salsa

*K*ATE THOMAS MADE THESE SKEWERED APPETIZERS ALL THE RAGE. THEY'RE BEST WHEN CHARCOAL-GRILLED BUT THEY CAN ALSO BE PREPARED INDOORS UNDER A BROILER. SERVE WITH PLENTY OF ICE-COLD BEER.

1 To make the mango salsa, combine the mango, pineapple juice, lime juice, and salt in a blender or food processor and process until well blended but still chunky. Pour into a bowl and stir in the onion, cilantro, and jalapeño. Refrigerate until chilled. (The salsa can be made a day ahead. It will thicken; stir in pineapple juice until it reaches the desired consistency.)

2 Soak the skewers in water for 1 hour. Preheat the oven to 450°F or a gas grill to medium-high.

3 Place the pork and bell peppers in 2 separate bowls; drizzle with the olive oil and toss. In a small bowl, stir together the paprika, onion powder, cinnamon, allspice, and salt; add to the pork. Toss to coat.

4 Slide a piece of red pepper, skin side first, onto a skewer followed by a piece of pork. Repeat until all ingredients have been used. If broiling, place skewers on a foil-lined baking sheet and broil, turning once, until the meat is barely cooked in the center, 10 to 15 minutes. If grilling, arrange skewers in a grill basket and cook until meat is barely cooked in the center, 4 to 6 minutes per side.

5 To serve, slice off the top of the orange pepper and remove the seeds and membranes. Trim a thin slice from the bottom of the pepper so it stands up straight. Fill with the mango salsa. Put in the center of a platter and surround with the skewers.

SERVES: 8

Mango Salsa:

1 cup coarsely chopped mango (about 2 mangoes)

2 tablespoons pineapple juice

2 teaspoons fresh lime juice

¼ teaspoon kosher salt

2 tablespoons chopped red onion

1 tablespoon chopped fresh cilantro

1 teaspoon minced jalapeño, unseeded

1 orange bell pepper, to hold the dip

1 pound boneless pork loin, trimmed of fat and cut into ¾-inch cubes

1 to 2 red bell peppers, cut into ¾-inch cubes

2 tablespoons olive oil

2 teaspoons paprika

2 teaspoons onion powder

2 teaspoons cinnamon

1 teaspoon ground allspice

1 teaspoon kosher salt

32 (5-inch) bamboo skewers

Soups

New Albany High School Commons

Pursuit of Lifelong Learning

THE path to greater knowledge begins for many at the New Albany branch of the Columbus Metropolitan Library in Market Square. Striving to make New Albany a center for lifelong learning and intellectual stimulation, New Albany residents immediately embraced the new library and what it represents. "A whole world of free ideas and learning, free to the people," were the words of Pulitzer Prize–winner David McCullough at the May 2002 library fundraiser. Residents have flocked to public programs, including book clubs, which are a "best seller" with New Albany's children, teens, and adults.

Residents know that strong schools build strong communities. In 1874 a school bell was hung at the original New Albany School of Plain Township. In 1996 this bell was included in the dedication of the New Albany Learning Community Campus, linking the community's history to its future. The centrally located Learning Campus features eight school buildings connected by tree-lined walkways and surrounded by an 80-acre nature preserve that includes 34 acres of wetlands, woods, ponds, a creek, and pathways. Expanding educational settings beyond the four walls of the classroom, teachers and students use the preserve for hands-on environmental studies. Residents and local employees also enjoy the trails and wildlife in the center of the village.

New Albany High School was recognized as one of the top high schools in the country and was designated a Lighthouse School after winning the nationally prestigious 21st Century Schools of Distinction Award from the Intel Foundation. The award acknowledged the partnerships and collaborations between the school district and local businesses, government agencies, non-profits, and parents that further academic improvement. Through one such partnership, the Learning Campus has two Kinko's for Kids Technology Centers, where students learn the advantages of adopting professional media options. Through another, Mount Carmel Health Systems provides community and school programs in the New Albany Center for Wellness located on the school campus. Physicians see patients there, and programs ranging from nutrition to CPR certification to babysitting workshops are offered to residents and students alike.

The New Albany Children's Ballet Theatre and Broadway Bound Dance Centre offer classes for both children and adults. Self-defense classes are provided by the New Albany Police Department to local groups and businesses, and the New Albany Safety Town program teaches lifelong safety lessons to the youngest and most vulnerable members of our community.

As the community continues to grow, residents will find new and exciting programs that will ensure lifelong learning for everyone. — *Diane Forrest LaHowchic*

Chilled Cucumber Soup 89

Summer Tropical Fruit Soup 90

White Gazpacho 91

Dilled Summer Soup 92

Creamy Asparagus Tarragon Soup 93

Five-Onion Bisque 94

Tomato and Eggplant Gratin Soup 95

Minted Sweet Pea and Spinach Soup 96

Sweet Potato Vichyssoise 97

Elegant Cauliflower Soup 98

Lentil Soup *(Masoor Dal)* 99

Roasted Mushroom Soup
(Potage aux Champignons Rôtis) 100

Hearty Minestrone Soup 101

South-of-the-Border Corn Chowder 102

Corn and Crab Soup, Thai Style
(Kaeng Poo Kab Kao Phod) 103

Pork and Cucumber Noodle Soup 104

Chilled Cucumber Soup

IN SUMMER WHEN CUCUMBERS ARE ABUNDANT, SERVE THIS EASY, REFRESHING SOUP.

1 Cut 6 to 8 thin slices from one unpeeled cucumber and set aside for garnish.

2 Peel, seed and chop the cucumbers. Place half the chopped cucumber in a blender, add 1 cup of the buttermilk, half the parsley, and half the green onions; blend until smooth. Transfer to a large bowl. Repeat with the remaining cucumber, another 1 cup buttermilk, parsley, and green onions.

3 Whisk in the remaining buttermilk, sour cream, lemon juice, and salt. Stir in the chopped dill. Taste and adjust seasonings. Chill for at least 4 hours.

4 Serve cold, garnished with cucumber slices and sprigs of dill.

SERVES: 6 to 8

3 cucumbers (about 2½ pounds)

6 cups buttermilk

½ cup chopped fresh parsley

3 green onions (white part only), chopped

3 cups sour cream

3 tablespoons fresh lemon juice

2 teaspoons salt

3 tablespoons chopped fresh dill or to taste

Sprigs of fresh dill for garnish

COURTESY LORN SPOLTER

New Albany Learning Community Campus

Summer Tropical Fruit Soup

THIS IS A REFRESHING DESSERT SOUP. IT ALSO WORKS WELL AS AN INTERMEZZO BETWEEN COURSES.

1 Peel and core the pineapples. Cut into ¼-inch-thick wedges. Reserve 2 cups of the wedges for the broth. Chill the remaining pineapple for the salad.

2 To make the broth, combine 2 cups of the pineapple, the coconut milk, and nutmeg in a blender and purée for about 1 minute. Transfer to a bowl and chill for at least 3 hours.

3 Just before serving, slice the bananas. Ladle the broth into each bowl and arrange the remaining pineapple, the bananas, kiwi fruits, and mango on top. Decorate each bowl with a mint leaf.

SERVES: 8

CHEF TIP: If using canned coconut milk, vigorously shake the can before opening. Purchase coconut milk from the Asian section of the supermarket. Thai brands are the best.

Broth:

2 cups fresh pineapple wedges (from salad ingredients below)

3½ cups coconut milk

¼ teaspoon grated nutmeg

Salad:

2 pineapples

4 large bananas

4 kiwi fruits, peeled and sliced

2 mangoes, peeled, seeded, and cut into chunks

Mint leaves for garnish

Children enjoying music at Lambton Park

NEW ALBANY CLASSIC SIGNATURE SERIES PHOTOS
COURTESY DANIEL W. FLOSS & ASSOCIATES PHOTOGRAPHY

White Gazpacho

A COMMON MISCONCEPTION IS THAT GAZPACHO IS ALWAYS RED BECAUSE IT IS TOMATO-BASED. CARLINE WEDDINGTON'S INNOVATIVE WHITE VERSION IS CREAMY AND TANGY AT THE SAME TIME. IT ALWAYS PUTS A SMILE ON THE DINER, WHO IS PLEASANTLY SURPRISED THAT A WHITE VERSION OF THE FAMOUS SUMMER SOUP CAN TASTE EQUALLY GOOD.

1 Peel and dice the cucumbers. Place in a blender with the garlic and 1 cup of the chicken stock. Purée the mixture. Add the remaining stock and thoroughly blend.

2 Mix the sour cream and yogurt in a medium bowl and thin with about one-third of the cucumber mixture. Stir in the remaining cucumber mixture. Season with the vinegar, salt, and pepper. Chill for 6 to 8 hours.

3 Serve in large chilled bowls. Put the tomatoes, green onions, parsley, and almonds in smaller bowls so each guest can garnish their gazpacho as desired.

SERVES: 8

3 medium cucumbers

1 clove garlic

3 cups chicken stock

2 cups sour cream

1 cup plain yogurt

3 tablespoons white vinegar

2 teaspoons salt

2 teaspoons white pepper

Garnish:

4 medium tomatoes, peeled, seeded, and chopped

½ cup chopped green onions (including the green tops)

½ cup chopped fresh parsley or cilantro

¾ cup toasted slivered almonds or sunflower seeds

Dilled Summer Soup

SIMPLE AND QUICK FOR WHEN IT GETS TOO HOT TO COOK. THE DEFINING FLAVOR IS THE DILL, SO ADJUST THE QUANTITY TO SUIT YOUR TASTE.

1 Heat the oil in a large saucepan over medium heat. Add the leeks and cook, stirring occasionally, until tender, about 5 minutes. Add the zucchini and stock; simmer for 8 to 10 minutes or until zucchini is tender. Let cool slightly.

2 Purée the mixture in batches in a blender or food processor. Transfer to a bowl and stir in the half-and-half, sour cream, chopped dill, and salt. Cover and chill for at least 3 hours. Serve chilled, garnished with dill sprigs.

SERVES: 8

CHEF TIP: Use homemade chicken stock for a heartier, more flavorful soup. If you don't have time to make stock from scratch, use these supermarket brands that have consistently won high ratings in surveys: Swanson Certified Organic broth, Better Than Bouillon base, or Swanson Natural Goodness broth.

2 tablespoons vegetable oil

2 small leeks (white part only), washed, trimmed, and cut into 1-inch pieces

1½ pounds zucchini or yellow squash, sliced

3 cups chicken stock

1 cup half-and-half

1 cup sour cream

⅓ cup chopped fresh dill

½ teaspoon salt

Fresh dill sprigs for garnish

COURTESY ROD BERRY / EXPERIENCE COLUMBUS

Jack Nicklaus at The Memorial Tournament

Creamy Asparagus Tarragon Soup

A SPRINGTIME AND SUMMER SOUP, WITH THE DELICATE YET ASSERTIVE FLAVOR OF TARRAGON.

1 Cut off the dark green top of the leek, leaving about 2 inches of the paler green part, and trim off the root end. Beginning about ½ inch up from the root end, slice the leek in half lengthwise. Fan out the leaves in a bowl of cold water and swish them gently to loosen dirt. If necessary, repeat with a fresh bowl of water until the leek is completely rid of dirt. Slice into ½-inch pieces.

2 Heat the oil and butter in a saucepan over low heat. Add the leek, onion, and parsnip; cook, stirring occasionally, until softened, about 15 minutes. Add the stock and tarragon; bring to a boil. Add the asparagus, cover and simmer for 30 minutes or until vegetables are very tender. Uncover and let cool.

3 Purée the soup in a blender or food processor. Pour through a fine strainer, pressing on the solids. Stir in the cream.

4 The soup may be served chilled or reheated over low heat; do not let it boil. Serve 1½ cups of soup per bowl, placing 3 cantaloupe balls in the center of each serving, surrounded by 4 mint leaves. Add a dollop of sour cream on one side of each bowl.

SERVES: 5

1 large leek

2 tablespoons olive oil

2 tablespoons unsalted butter

1 onion, chopped

1 parsnip, peeled and chopped

6 cups chicken stock

3 tablespoons chopped fresh tarragon

2 pounds medium asparagus, ends trimmed, cut into 2-inch pieces

½ cup whipping cream or half-and-half

15 small cantaloupe balls for garnish

20 small fresh mint leaves for garnish

⅓ cup sour cream for garnish

Five-Onion Bisque

THIS IS A RICHER ONION SOUP THAN THE USUAL KIND. USING FIVE ONION VARIETIES LENDS A COMPLEX ONION FLAVOR.

1   Preheat the oven to 350°F. Lightly spray a small baking sheet with vegetable oil. Spread the garlic cloves on the baking sheet pan and bake until very soft, about 10 minutes. Set aside.

2   Cut off the dark green top and trim off the root end of each leek. Beginning about ½ inch up from the root end, slice the leeks in half lengthwise. Fan out the leaves in a bowl of cold water and swish them gently to loosen dirt. If necessary, repeat with a fresh bowl of water until the leek is completely rid of dirt. Slice into 1-inch pieces.

3   Melt the butter in a 5 or 6-quart stockpot over low heat. Cook the Vidalia and Maui onions, stirring occasionally, until caramelized, 30 to 40 minutes. Add the leeks and green onions. Cook an additional 10 to 15 minutes. Peel the roasted garlic and add to the pot. Add the champagne and cook, stirring, until almost evaporated. Add the stock and simmer for 30 minutes.

4   Remove from the heat and stir in the chives. Let cool slightly. Working in batches if necessary, purée the soup in a blender while adding sour cream, salt, and pepper. Wipe clean the saucepan and reheat the soup until hot, but do not let it boil.

5   Serve garnished with the basil and sourdough croutons.

SERVES: 8

CHEF TIPS: Non-alcoholic champagne may be replaced with equal parts ginger ale and apple cider (or white grape juice).

The Maui and Vidalia onions may be substituted with onions of the sweet, succulent variety such as Texas onion and Walla-Walla.

10 cloves garlic, unpeeled

2 leeks

1 tablespoon butter

3 cups sliced Vidalia onions

1½ cups sliced Maui onions

1¼ cups chopped green onions

¼ cup non-alcoholic champagne

5 cups chicken stock

1 cup chopped fresh chives

⅔ cup sour cream

2 teaspoon kosher salt

½ teaspoon freshly ground black pepper

Shredded fresh basil and sourdough croutons for garnish

Tomato and Eggplant Gratin Soup

THE SOUP TO SERVE WHEN THE HEART NEEDS WARMING AND THE STOMACH NEEDS FILLING. IT MAKES ONE THINK OF COMING HOME TO MAMMA.

1 Peel the eggplant and cut crosswise into ⅓-inch-thick slices. Salt lightly on both sides. Place on paper towels in a single layer. Let stand for 30 minutes.

2 Preheat the oven to 400°F.

3 Rinse the eggplant slices and pat dry with paper towels. Brush heavily with olive oil and place on a baking sheet. Bake, turning occasionally, until golden on each side, 15 to 20 minutes. Cut each slice into quarters. (Do not turn off the oven.)

4 Blanch the tomatoes in boiling water for 30 seconds. Transfer to a bowl of ice water, then core, peel, and slice tomatoes ⅜-inch thick.

5 Stir together the minced garlic and the parsley.

6 Rub a 2-quart gratin dish with the whole garlic clove and lightly oil the dish. Starting at one end of the dish, arrange a row of tomatoes, followed by a row of eggplant, slightly overlapping. Continue to alternate rows until the dish is filled. Sprinkle with salt and pepper and all but 1 tablespoon of the parsley mixture. Ladle 1 cup of the hot chicken stock into the gratin dish. Sprinkle with ¾ cup of the cheese. Bake until the liquid is almost absorbed, about 45 minutes.

7 Season the remaining hot chicken stock with salt and pepper. Spoon a large scoop of the gratin into each soup bowl. Ladle the stock into the bowls. Garnish with the remaining tablespoon of parsley mixture and the remaining ¼ cup cheese. Serve immediately.

SERVES: 6

CHEF TIP: Use homemade chicken stock for a heartier, more flavorful soup. If you don't have time to make stock from scratch, use these supermarket brands that have consistently won high ratings in surveys: Swanson Certified Organic broth, Better Than Bouillon base, or Swanson Natural Goodness broth.

1 (1-pound) eggplant

Salt

1 tablespoon olive oil

8 plum tomatoes (1½ pounds)

3 cloves garlic, 2 minced, 1 whole

¼ cup chopped fresh parsley

Freshly ground black pepper

5 cups chicken stock, heated

1 cup finely grated Parmigiano-Reggiano cheese

Minted Sweet Pea and Spinach Soup

A SOUP FOR ALL SEASONS. THIS CREAMY GREEN SOUP MAKES AN ELEGANT APPETIZER FOR A FORMAL DINNER.

1   Melt the butter in a saucepan over low heat. Add the onions, cover and cook, stirring occasionally, until tender and lightly colored, about 25 minutes. Meanwhile, drain the spinach and squeeze out excess liquid. Add the spinach, peas, and stock to the onions and bring to a boil. Reduce heat and simmer, partially covered, until peas are tender, about 20 minutes.

2   Add the mint. Cover and simmer for another 5 minutes.

3   In two or three batches, transfer the soup to a blender and purée until smooth. Strain the puréed soup through a chinois or fine-mesh strainer into a clean saucepan, pressing on the solids. Stir in the cream. Season to taste with salt and pepper. Just before serving, simmer briefly to heat through.

SERVES: 8

CHEF TIP: A chinois is a conical strainer usually made of stainless steel that prevents lumps, seeds, and skins from passing through. The chinois rests over a pot. A wooden pestle helps push ingredients through.

6 tablespoons unsalted butter

4 cups finely chopped yellow onions

2 (10-ounce) packages frozen chopped spinach, thawed

2 (10-ounce) packages frozen peas, thawed

6 cups chicken stock

4 cups fresh mint leaves

2 cups whipping cream or half-and-half

Salt and freshly ground black pepper

COURTESY DOON STRENCH

The New Albany Learning Community Campus

Sweet Potato Vichyssoise

AN UNUSUAL VARIATION OF VICHYSSOISE. DON'T OVERLOOK THE CHIVES FOR GARNISH—THEY ADD ANOTHER LEVEL OF FLAVOR.

1   Preheat the oven to 400°F.

2   Prick the sweet potatoes several times with a fork and bake for about 1 hour, until soft. Let cool, then scoop out the potato pulp from the skins.

3   Meanwhile, in a medium saucepan, combine the green onions with 1 cup of the chicken stock. Simmer over medium heat, stirring occasionally, until the onions are tender, about 10 minutes. Pour the stock mixture into a food processor. Add the sweet potato pulp and ½ cup more of the chicken stock. Purée until smooth, about 30 seconds.

4   Return to the saucepan and stir in the remaining 1 cup stock. Bring to a boil over medium heat, reduce the heat to low and simmer for 5 minutes to allow the flavors to blend. Season to taste with salt and white pepper. Let the soup cool to room temperature, then cover and refrigerate until chilled, about 4 hours.

5   Just before serving, beat the cream until slightly thickened. Pour the soup into chilled bowls and swirl into each 1 tablespoon of the thickened cream. Garnish with the chives.

SERVES: 4

CHEF TIP: For an unusual presentation at parties where guests mill around rather than sit down at the table, serve in small cups so guests can sip rather than spoon the soup.

1¼ pounds sweet potatoes (2 large)

1 cup sliced green onions (including 2 inches of the green part)

2½ cups chicken stock

Salt and white pepper

¼ cup whipping cream

2 teaspoons snipped fresh chives

Elegant Cauliflower Soup

THE CREATIVE PRESENTATION MAKES THIS AN ATTRACTIVE FIRST COURSE.

1 Blanch asparagus tips until tender-crisp. Refresh under cold water to stop the cooking, then drain well. Set aside.

2 In a large saucepan, heat the oil over medium heat. Add the onion, shallots, and garlic and cook, stirring frequently, until tender, about 5 minutes. Stir in the stock and bring to a boil. Add the cauliflower; cook, stirring occasionally, until tender, about 15 minutes.

3 Process the soup in batches in a blender until smooth; return to the pot. Stir in the cream, salt, and white pepper; cook over low heat, stirring often, until thoroughly heated. Ladle into bowls. Fan out asparagus tips (3 per bowl) over soup and sprinkle cracked pepper at the base of the fan.

SERVES: 4

CHEF TIPS: Using an immersion blender saves a lot of time and effort and does the puréeing just as well as a blender.

In place of the asparagus tips, for a colorful presentation use a sprinkling of cut chives or minced red or orange pepper.

12 asparagus tips (cut 3 inches from the tip)

1 tablespoon olive oil

1 large onion, sliced

2 shallots, sliced

½ clove garlic, sliced

2 (14-ounce) cans chicken stock or homemade stock

1 large cauliflower, cut into florets

1½ cups whipping cream

1 teaspoon salt

⅛ teaspoon white pepper

Cracked black pepper for garnish

Lentil Soup (Masoor Dal)

A HEALTHFUL AND HEARTY SOUP BEST SERVED WITH RICE—PREFERABLY INDIAN BASMATI.

1 Rinse the lentils, drain and put in a large saucepan. Add 7 cups of water, the turmeric, and chili powder. Cover loosely and bring to a boil, then reduce heat and simmer, stirring every so often, until the lentils are soft and mashed, about 25 minutes. Add water to desired consistency and bring to a boil again, stirring until the mixture is well blended. Add salt to taste.

2 Melt the ghee in a small skillet over medium-high heat. Add the nigella seeds and the onion and fry until the onion is golden brown. Add the onion to the hot lentils and serve immediately, garnished with chopped cilantro or chiles.

SERVES: 6

CHEF TIP: Do not add salt during the cooking or the lentils will not soften completely.

2 cups red lentils *(masoor dal)**

7 cups water (approx.)

⅛ teaspoon turmeric

⅛ teaspoon Indian chili powder*

Salt to taste

1 tablespoon ghee (clarified butter)*

½ teaspoon nigella seeds *(kalonji)**

1 small onion, sliced

Chopped cilantro or chopped green chiles for garnish

*available at South Asian groceries

New Albany student Rachel Welty and two-time Pulitzer Prize-winner David McCullough at the 2003 dedication of the New Albany Library

NEW ALBANY LIBRARY

"*W*e must not think of learning as only what happens in schools. It is an extended part of life. The most readily available resource for all of life is our public library system."
—David McCullough, speaking at the dedication of the New Albany Library, October 2003

On a vibrant autumn day in 2003, community members and students gathered at Market Square to celebrate the culmination of a community dream, the opening of a public library in the heart of the village of New Albany. Inspirational thoughts were shared by two-time Pulitzer Prize–winning author David McCullough, who had previously visited during the library fundraising campaign. As promised, McCullough returned to celebrate this major milestone in our community. New Albany High School senior and aspiring writer Rachel Welty also spoke, serving to remind the audience that the library will be an ongoing and vital resource for students of all ages.

The library was made possible through collaboration between the Columbus Metropolitan Library, New Albany Company, and members of our community. Private donors from New Albany contributed more than $1 million to purchase a book collection of more than 120,000 volumes and enable the purchase of state-of-the-art library operations technology.

The library, a cornerstone of the community, has become one of the busiest branches in the Columbus Metropolitan Library system. It will continue to serve as a valued community resource and enrich lives for generations to come.
— *New Albany Classic Signature Series*

Roasted Mushroom Soup
(Potage aux Champignons Rôtis)

THIS DELIGHTFUL SOUP WILL WORK WONDERS ON A CHILLY EVENING. TRY OUT VARIOUS MUSHROOMS IN SEASON AND DISCOVER WHICH COMBINATION YOU LIKE BEST.

1 Preheat the oven to 450°F. Line a baking sheet with parchment paper.

2 In a large bowl, toss the mushrooms and shallots together and spread out on the baking sheet. Drizzle with olive oil, then sprinkle with thyme, salt, and pepper. Roast the mushrooms for 15 to 20 minutes. They should be roasted but not dry and crunchy; return to oven if some liquid still remains.

3 In a large saucepan, melt the butter over medium heat until it is slightly brown and smells nutty. Add the flour and cook for several minutes, stirring the entire time. Stir in the roasted mushrooms. Add the stock, cream, and sherry. Whisk until blended. Simmer for 5 minutes.

4 Adjust seasonings and serve hot sprinkled with chopped chives.

SERVES: 8

2 pounds assorted mushrooms (button, shiitake, and portobello), wiped clean and finely chopped

½ cup minced shallots

1 tablespoon olive oil

1 teaspoon chopped fresh thyme

Pinch each of salt and pepper

4 tablespoons unsalted butter

2 tablespoons all-purpose flour

2 cups chicken stock

2 cups light cream

¼ cup dry sherry

¼ cup snipped fresh chives for garnish

This historic school bell was hung in 1874 at the New Albany School of Plain Township located on North High Street.

In 1996 the bell was included in the dedication of the Learning Community Campus and is on loan from the New Albany-Plain Township Historical Society.

New Albany school bell plaque

Hearty Minestrone Soup

This is Susan Corley's family favorite for the holidays, especially when served with cracked crab. Being from the Bay City, she recommends serving San Francisco sourdough bread with it.

1 Heat the butter and oil in a large saucepan over medium heat. Add the onions and cook, stirring frequently, until translucent, about 10 minutes. Add the potatoes, cabbage, carrots, zucchini, green beans, white beans, celery, basil, and oregano. Cook for 6 minutes, then add the stock, tomatoes, and rice. Wrap the cheese rind in a piece of cheesecloth to prevent it from sticking to the bottom of the pan and add to the soup. Simmer, stirring occasionally, for 2 hours on low heat. Remove cheese rind before serving.

2 Serve hot with a sprinkling of the Parmesan cheese on top of each bowlful.

SERVES: 8

CHEF TIP: Make soup the day before, as it tastes great the second day. This soup also freezes well.

3 tablespoons unsalted butter

½ cup olive oil

2 medium onions, thinly sliced

3 red potatoes, diced

6 to 8 cups shredded cabbage

2 cups chopped carrots

2 cups chopped zucchini

1½ cups chopped green beans

1½ cups white beans (canned may be used)

1 cup chopped celery

2 tablespoons dried basil

1½ teaspoons dried oregano

2 (32-ounce) cans chicken stock

1 (14.5-ounce) can stewed tomatoes

½ cup risotto rice such as Arborio

1 (4-ounce) wedge Parmesan cheese, rind reserved and the rest grated for topping

South-of-the-Border Corn Chowder

SALSA, CHILI POWDER, AND CUMIN ADD A SOUTH-OF-THE-BORDER ACCENT TO THIS NATIVE AMERICAN DISH.

1 In a large saucepan over medium-high heat, melt the butter. Sauté the onions until translucent, about 8 minutes. Stir in the flour, chili powder, and cumin. Add the corn, salsa, pimientos, and stock. Bring to a boil, then remove from heat.

2 In a small bowl, gradually stir ¼ cup of the hot corn mixture into the cream cheese, stirring until well blended. Return the cream cheese mixture to the saucepan, add the milk and cook over medium-low heat, stirring, until well blended and heated through. Do not let boil.

3 Top each serving with a sprig of cilantro and serve immediately.

SERVES: 6

CHEF TIP: Stretch any leftovers by adding chopped chicken or ham and serve with cornbread or tortillas.

2 tablespoons unsalted butter or margarine

1 cup chopped onion

1 tablespoon all-purpose flour

1 tablespoon chili powder

1 teaspoon ground cumin

2 cups fresh corn kernels (from 3 to 4 ears), boiled (or frozen corn)

2 cups salsa

1 (4-ounce) jar diced pimientos, drained

1 (14-ounce) can chicken stock

8 ounces cream cheese, softened

1 cup whole milk

Cilantro sprigs for garnish

COURTESY DIANE FORREST LaHOWCHIC

Geroux Herb Garden, Gahanna, Ohio

Corn and Crab Soup, Thai Style
(Kaeng Poo Kab Kao Phod)

THIS IS A SOUP OF CHINESE ORIGIN THAT THE THAIS HAVE ADAPTED BY USING FISH SAUCE AS THE MAIN SEASONING. IT'S A SNAP TO PREPARE.

1 Heat a 5-quart saucepan over high heat. Add the oil and heat until almost smoking. Fry the garlic and shallots until fragrant. Add the chicken stock, fish sauce, crabmeat, and corn. Stir until the soup comes to a boil. Reduce heat to low and simmer 1 minute. The soup can be prepared a day ahead up to this point.

2 Just before serving, reheat to a simmer. Pour the beaten eggs in a wide circle over the soup and stir gently a few times with a wooden spoon to form ribbons. Remove from the heat and stir in the pepper and cilantro. Adjust seasonings by adding more salt or fish sauce, if desired.

SERVES: 8

CHEF TIP: Shrimp may be substituted for crabmeat.

3 tablespoons vegetable or peanut oil

5 cloves garlic, minced

4 shallots, minced

8 cups chicken stock

2½ tablespoons fish sauce (nam pla)*

1 pound crabmeat, picked over

2 (15-ounce) cans cream-style corn

2 large eggs, beaten with ½ teaspoon salt

Pinch of white pepper

5 tablespoons chopped fresh cilantro leaves

*available in Asian groceries or in the ethnic aisles of supermarkets

Pork and Cucumber Noodle Soup

FIONA GAUNTLETT SHARED HER GRANDMOTHER'S RECIPE FROM HONG KONG. THIS SOOTHING SOUP COMFORTS WHENEVER A FAMILY MEMBER IS FEELING UNDER THE WEATHER.

1 Soak the noodles in 1 cup of hot water for about 20 minutes. Do not drain the noodles.

2 Meanwhile, cut the cucumber in half lengthwise, then cut into ¼-inch slices.

3 In a medium bowl, stir together the soy sauce, sugar, and white pepper until the sugar is dissolved; add the ground pork and mix well.

4 Heat the oil in a wok over high heat until just beginning to smoke. Stir-fry the onion until wilted. Add the ground pork and stir-fry until half-done. Add the cucumber. Continue to fry until the pork is cooked through. Immediately stir in the chicken stock and remaining 5 cups of hot water. Bring to a boil. Add the noodles with the water in which they soaked. Return to a boil, then remove from the heat. Salt to taste and serve hot.

SERVES: 8

1 (2-ounce) package vermicelli or bean thread noodles*

6 cups hot water

1 cucumber

2 tablespoons soy sauce

2 teaspoons sugar

⅛ teaspoon white pepper

1 pound ground pork

2 tablespoons vegetable or peanut oil

1 small onion, minced

2 (14-ounce) cans chicken stock

Salt

*available at Asian groceries

Salads

2006 New Albany 10K Walking Classic

Pursuit of Health and Wellness

THE pursuit of a healthy lifestyle was a key consideration when scenic walking trails lined with white fences were designed to connect New Albany's neighborhoods. The white fences provide a stark backdrop to the green wavy grass of summer, autumn's brilliant red sugar maples, or the snow-frosted landscapes of winter days. It is not unusual to see residents enjoying a vigorous stroll over the paths while others train for marathons at a rabbit-fast pace. Roller-bladers whoosh by on occasion with a few even practicing pro speed-skating techniques, bent from the waist, one arm tucked firmly behind and the other swinging for added speed.

Children and adults of all ages and skill levels are encouraged to pursue their sports interests in New Albany. If golf is their game, there are plenty of courses in and around New Albany to test their abilities, including the award-winning Jack Nicklaus–designed New Albany Country Club course with 27 challenging holes that meander through New Albany neighborhoods. Tennis players have year-round options, from sharpening their skills with lessons from the tennis pro to discovering rigorous competition in league tennis. Hockey and skating enthusiasts enjoy the Chiller at Easton, where valuable ice time is available for both youth leagues and adult skaters. And Broadway Bound Dance Centre and the New Albany Children's Ballet Theatre turn out talented dancers, many of whom participate in the Columbus production of *The Nutcracker* at holiday time.

Nothing could be more fun than putting all those athletic skills to the test in New Albany's own backyard. One of the most popular races is the Abercrombie & Fitch Challenge, a well-attended event held at the company's New Albany headquarters each September. Pick your sport—a 5K run, a 20-mile bike, or a 5K roller-blading competition. And competitors enjoy a huge post-race picnic courtesy of Abercrombie, complete with a full meal, drinks, and a live band. Another superb event, the New Albany 10K Walking Classic, debuted in September 2005. Walking is gaining popularity as a sport, and whether strolling or striding, many residents, including former runners, find it a gentler way to stay in shape.

Several gyms are located in the New Albany area, including a state-of-the-art fitness facility at the New Albany Country Club. Whether Pilates, kick-boxing, or yoga is your passion, you can find it at the New Albany Country Club's Bath & Tennis facility. Lifetime Fitness at Easton Town Center offers indoor climbing walls, racket sports, children's sport programs, and much more.

Staying fit takes time, commitment, and willpower at any age. With the numerous resources at New Albany's fingertips, healthy living is made easy. No matter the sport, there's likely an avenue to making fitness goals a reality—and a friend to accompany you along the way.

— *Rhonda Koulermos*

Asparagus and Red Pepper Salad
(Insalata di Asparagi e Peperoni Rossi) 109

Cranberry Cashew Salad 110

Beet, Pear, and Bitter Leaf Salad 111

Mixed Greens with Oriental Vinaigrette 112

Spinach Salad with Cranberry Vinaigrette, Walnuts,
and Goat Cheese 112

Warm Spinach Salad with
Creamy Mustard Dressing 113

Arugula and Figs with Warm Shallot Vinaigrette 114

Summer Peach Salad 115

Creamy Beet and Apple Salad *(Rödbetssallad)* 116

Oriental Cole Slaw 117

Caraway Cabbage Salad 118

Quinoa Salad 119

Carrot and Green Bean Salad with
Sesame-flavored Noodles 120

Chopped Salad with Russian Dressing 121

Tex-Mex Salad 122

Couscous and Shrimp Salad 123

Charlie's Grilled Chicken Caesar Salad 124

Bon Bon Chicken Salad 125

Beef and Avocado Deluxe 126

Asparagus and Red Pepper Salad (Insalata di Asparagi e Peperoni Rossi)

A COLORFUL DO-AHEAD SALAD THAT CAN BE SERVED WARM OR COLD.

1 Preheat the broiler. Place the peppers on a broiler pan and broil, turning four times, until all sides are blackened, about 15 minutes. Be sure to roast the ends of the peppers as well. Put the peppers in a brown paper bag or a plastic bag and let cool. Peel, core, and seed the peppers, and cut into ¼-inch-wide strips. Set aside.

2 Preheat the oven to 350°F. Brush a baking sheet with 1½ tablespoons of the olive oil. Place the asparagus on the sheet and turn to coat with the oil. Roast for 20 to 30 minutes, until a knife is easily inserted in the stalk.

3 Line a platter with Bibb lettuce. Arrange the asparagus on top of the lettuce and top with the pepper strips.

4 Whisk together the remaining olive oil and the balsamic vinegar. Add salt to taste. Drizzle the dressing over the salad. Cover and let marinate at room temperature for several hours before serving.

SERVES: 8

CHEF TIP: Make this salad early in the day to allow the flavors to mingle. This salad can be served as a side dish or as part of an antipasto selection.

4 red bell peppers (about 2 pounds)

¼ cup plus 3 tablespoons extra virgin olive oil

2 pounds thin asparagus, stalks trimmed

Bibb lettuce leaves

¼ cup balsamic vinegar

Fine sea salt

Cranberry Cashew Salad

CRISP APPLES, DRIED CRANBERRIES, AND CASHEW NUTS TOP THIS SALAD, GIVING IT A CRUNCHY AND CHEWY TEXTURE. THE MANGO CHUTNEY AND CURRY GIVE THE DRESSING AN EXOTIC NOTE.

1 Whisk together the dressing ingredients (or shake in a jar). Let stand for at least 2 hours. You can make the dressing 1 or 2 days ahead; store in the refrigerator. Before using, bring to room temperature.

2 Just before serving, whisk (or shake) the dressing again. Toss with the salad ingredients and serve immediately.

SERVES: 6 to 8

CHEF TIPS: If you cannot find dried cranberries, substitute white raisins. Other greens such as baby greens may be added to the spinach.

Two recommended good-quality mango chutneys are Major Grey and Stonewall Kitchen brands.

Dressing:

½ cup white wine vinegar

¼ cup mango chutney

1½ teaspoons sugar

1 teaspoon curry powder

1 teaspoon salt

¼ teaspoon Tabasco sauce

⅔ cup salad, safflower, or olive oil

Salad:

6 cups baby spinach

1 large unpeeled Granny Smith or Red Delicious apple, thinly sliced

⅓ cup dried cranberries

¾ cup roasted cashew halves

GOLF NEW ALBANY!

Golfers will feel welcome and excited to play at one of the many beautiful courses in New Albany. Jack Nicklaus, the Golden Bear, was born only a few miles away, in Columbus, where you can visit the Jack Nicklaus Museum and walk through a celebration of golf's history and Jack's legendary career. The championship 27-hole golf course at the New Albany Country Club was designed by Jack. His imprint is visible in the varying terrain of the course, with some areas having the lush feel of the Carolinas and others suggesting the ruggedness of the Scottish links. The Golf Academy at New Albany Country Club is the most extensive in Central Ohio, with state-of-the-art video and digital scoring analyses that provide the ultimate instructional experience year-round.

If you are a beginner or a scratch golfer, you will find a course to your liking in or around New Albany. In addition to the New Albany Country Club, there are three private courses in New Albany—The Golf Club, New Albany Links, and Winding Hollow Country Club—and about 20 courses nearby. They include five of the country's top 100 golf courses (rated by *Golf Digest* in May 2006)—Muirfield Village Golf Club in Dublin (No. 18), the Golf Club in New Albany (No. 51), Scioto Country Club in Columbus (No. 59), Double Eagle Club in Galena (No. 68), and Longaberger Golf Club (No. 65 among public courses). Muirfield Village Golf Club, Jack Nicklaus's dream, hosts the annual Memorial Tournament, often called the Fifth Major. — *Diane Forrest LaHowchic*

New Albany Country Club golf course

COURTESY NEW ALBANY COUNTRY CLUB

Beet, Pear, and Bitter Leaf Salad

SLIGHTLY BITTER RADICCHIO AND FRISÉE LEAVES ARE SET OFF BY SWEET BEETS AND PEARS FOR A WONDERFUL BLEND OF FALL FLAVORS.

1 In a food processor or with an immersion blender, blend the dressing ingredients until smooth.

2 Preheat the broiler.

3 Place the walnut pieces on a baking sheet and broil for 2 to 3 minutes, turning often, until golden.

4 Arrange the salad leaves, sliced beets, and pear slices on serving plates. Sprinkle with the walnut pieces, then top with thin slivers of Parmesan cheese made using a vegetable peeler. Spoon the dressing over the salad and garnish with whole chives.

SERVES: 4

CHEF TIPS: Fresh beets can be quickly cooked in a microwave. Place unpeeled beets in a microwaveable dish, add 1 inch of water, and cook on high for 10 to 15 minutes, until tender.

If preparing the salad ahead of time, toss the pears in lemon juice to prevent browning. Granny Smith apples may be substituted for pears.

Dressing:

¼ cup walnut oil

2 tablespoons chopped fresh herbs, including basil, chives, mint, and parsley

2 tablespoons extra virgin olive oil

1 tablespoon honey

2 teaspoons red wine vinegar

1 clove garlic, crushed

Salt and black pepper to taste

Salad:

½ cup walnut pieces

½ pound mixed salad leaves, including radicchio and frisée

½ pound cooked beets in natural juices, sliced (see Chef Tips)

2 pears, quartered, cored, and sliced

1½-ounce piece Parmesan cheese

Fresh chives for garnish

Mixed Greens with Oriental Vinaigrette

THIS VERSATILE SALAD DRESSING CAN BE SERVED WITH ANY SELECTION OF SALAD GREENS OR STEAMED VEGETABLES.

1 Whisk together the vinegar, tamari, mustard, garlic, and pepper in a bowl. Slowly whisk in the olive oil. If you want a creamy dressing, add a small amount of cream.

2 Toss the dressing with the mixed greens.

SERVES: 8

16 cups mixed greens (1½ pounds)

Dressing:

½ cup apple cider vinegar

2½ tablespoons tamari or soy sauce

1 tablespoon Dijon mustard

2 cloves garlic, minced

Freshly ground black pepper

1¼ cups olive oil

1 to 2 tablespoons whipping cream (optional)

Spinach Salad with Cranberry Vinaigrette, Walnuts, and Goat Cheese

THIS SALAD IS ESPECIALLY WONDERFUL FOR THE HOLIDAYS. FOR A FORMAL DINNER, USE RED PLATES FOR AN EXTRA-SPECIAL TOUCH.

1 Preheat the oven to 350°F.

2 Toast the walnuts on a baking sheet, shaking the pan occasionally, until golden brown, 5 to 10 minutes. If using whole walnuts, put the nuts in a plastic bag and lightly smash with a rolling pin to break into smaller pieces.

3 To make the dressing, in a blender, combine the vinegar, cranberries, shallots, mustard, and sugar. Blend until smooth. With the machine running, slowly drizzle in the oil. Season with salt and pepper.

4 Toss the walnuts and spinach with half of the dressing. If the salad seems too dry, add some more of the dressing. Gently crumble the goat cheese on top.

SERVES: 8

Salad:

1 cup walnuts

3 (6-ounce) bags baby spinach (about 9 cups)

8 ounces goat cheese

½ cup red wine vinegar

⅓ cup dried cranberries

1 tablespoon chopped shallots

1 teaspoon Dijon mustard

½ teaspoon sugar

⅔ cup olive oil

Salt and pepper to taste

Warm Spinach Salad
with Creamy Mustard Dressing

THIS SALAD SHARES DRESSING WITH THE GRILLED CHICKEN PAILLARDS ON PAGE 173. PAIR THESE TWO DISHES FOR A MEAL AND YOU ONLY MAKE THE SAUCE ONCE.

1 To make the dressing, in a medium saucepan, combine all the dressing ingredients. Place over medium heat and simmer, stirring occasionally, for 20 minutes. Remove from the heat and whisk for 1 to 2 minutes, until the sauce begins to thicken. Taste and adjust the seasoning if necessary. Set aside and keep warm.

2 Put the spinach in a serving bowl.

3 In a large, heavy skillet over medium heat, brown the bacon until crisp. Using a slotted spoon, transfer the bacon to paper towels to drain. Pour off all but 2 tablespoons of the bacon fat.

4 Cook the green onions and mushrooms in the bacon fat over medium heat for 2 minutes or until lightly browned. Add the sherry and stir to scrape the browned bits from the bottom of the pan. Cook until the liquid is reduced by half. Add the dressing, parsley, cilantro, salt, and pepper. Pour the mixture over the spinach, add the Parmesan cheese and gently toss. Sprinkle with the bacon bits. Serve immediately.

SERVES: 6

Creamy Mustard Dressing:

1 cup whipping cream

2 tablespoons minced fresh basil

1 tablespoon plus 2 teaspoons Dijon mustard

1½ teaspoons Worcestershire sauce

⅛ teaspoon salt

⅛ teaspoon black pepper

Salad:

3 (6-ounce) bags baby spinach (about 9 cups)

6 slices bacon, diced

1 bunch green onions, including some green tops, cut into ¼-inch pieces

10 white mushrooms, thinly sliced

¼ cup dry sherry

2 tablespoons chopped fresh parsley

2 tablespoons chopped fresh cilantro

Salt and freshly ground pepper to taste

1 cup grated Parmesan cheese

Arugula and Figs with Warm Shallot Vinaigrette

THE SUBTLE SWEETNESS OF THE FIGS ENHANCES THE PEPPERY, PUNGENT TASTE OF THE ARUGULA. THIS IS SOPHISTICATED FARE THAT INTRODUCES FIGS TO MANY WHO ONLY KNOW THAT TASTE FROM THOSE UBIQUITOUS NEWTONS.

1 Place the arugula and figs in a serving bowl.

2 Thinly slice 2 shallots and separate into rings. In a resealable plastic bag, toss the shallots with the flour, salt, and pepper until well coated. Shake the shallots in a sieve to remove any excess flour.

3 In a 10-inch skillet, heat the olive oil over medium heat. Add the sliced shallots in batches and cook, stirring, until golden brown and crisp, 2 to 3 minutes. Remove shallots with a slotted spoon; drain on paper towels.

4 To make the dressing, in a small saucepan over low heat, heat the olive oil, minced shallot, lemon juice, thyme, salt, and pepper until just warm, about 1 minute.

5 Pour the dressing over the arugula and figs and toss well. Sprinkle with the crisp shallots and serve warm.

SERVES: 4

Salad:

6 cups baby arugula

6 ripe figs, trimmed and quartered lengthwise

2 shallots

¼ cup all-purpose flour

¾ teaspoon salt

⅛ teaspoon freshly ground pepper

⅓ cup olive oil

Dressing:

2 tablespoons extra virgin olive oil

1 shallot, minced

1 tablespoon fresh lemon juice

1 teaspoon chopped fresh thyme

¼ teaspoon salt

⅛ teaspoon pepper

Summer Peach Salad

PERFECT FOR A SUMMER PICNIC.

1 Whisk together (or shake in a jar) all the dressing ingredients until emulsified. Taste and adjust seasonings.

2 Toss the mesclun with the peaches and just enough dressing to coat. Serve immediately, garnished with the cheese.

SERVES: 4

Dressing:

1 small shallot, finely diced

3 tablespoons champagne vinegar

1½ teaspoons honey (optional)

½ cup extra virgin olive oil

Salt and freshly ground pepper to taste

Salad:

½ pound mesclun*

2 ripe but firm peaches, peeled, pitted, and cut into bite-sized wedges

½ cup shaved Romano or Parmesan cheese (use a vegetable peeler)

*a potpourri of small young salad greens, available at specialty produce markets and many supermarkets

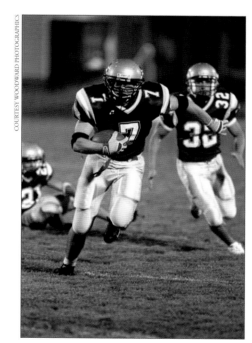

New Albany High School Eagles football team

NEW ALBANY ATHLETICS

Do you remember your first touchdown, personal best time, or even your first game? All of the hours spent practicing, the meetings, doing homework on the bus, the Friday-night games, and the championships? Those precious moments helped shape who we are today, and many of us would go back in a second to relive the thrill of winning and even the agony of defeat.

New Albany students are creating similar memories daily. It is an important piece of their educational framework. With over 80 percent of our student body participating in athletics, coaches are mentors helping students formulate and achieve their goals. In order to support and sustain academic success, personal fulfillment, and athletic achievement, the schools emphasize educating the whole person to develop the intellectual, social, and leadership qualities needed in a changing world.

Students at New Albany have the opportunity to participate in 22 varsity sports including soccer, cross-country, football, tennis, golf, cheerleading, volleyball, basketball, swimming, wrestling, track, lacrosse, baseball, and softball. Our facilities include four gyms, a 25-yard Olympic swimming pool, a weight room, a full-size wrestling room, eight tennis courts, a stadium/track complex that seats more than 5,000 spectators, three 100-yard practice fields, a middle-school competition field, and a baseball/softball complex.

We are all truly fortunate to have a learning community that has a vision to create so many opportunities for our students.

— *Rex Reeder on behalf of New Albany High School Athletic Department*

Creamy Beet and Apple Salad (Rödbetssallad)

THIS IS MIA JOHANSSON-STRENCH'S VERSION OF A SCANDINAVIAN STAPLE. IT IS DELICIOUS SERVED WITH SLICED SMOKED HAM, ROAST BEEF, OR SWEDISH MEATBALLS. IT IS OFTEN USED ON OPEN-FACED SANDWICHES AND GARNISHED WITH A SPRIG OF PARSLEY.

1 Chop the beets into small pieces and put in a salad bowl. Grate the apple over the beets. Add the lemon juice, pepper, salt, and sugar; toss.

2 Mix together the mayonnaise and cream, and pour over the salad. Toss well. Chill for at least 4 hours. Serve chilled.

SERVES: 4

CHEF TIP: For an attractive presentation, serve in individual bowls lined with a whole leaf of Boston lettuce.

1 (16-ounce) jar pickled beets

1 unpeeled apple

1 teaspoon fresh lemon juice

Pinch each of white pepper, salt, and sugar

⅓ cup mayonnaise

⅓ cup whipping cream

COURTESY DON STRENCH

New Albany Learning Community Campus track & field

Oriental Coleslaw

A CINCH TO PREPARE. ORIENTAL VINAIGRETTE AND CRUNCHY TEXTURE GIVE A MODERN BOOST TO AN OLD STANDBY.

1 Using your hands or a rolling pin, coarsely crush the noodles in their packages; do not pulverize. Toss all the salad ingredients in a serving bowl.

2 To make the dressing, whisk together (or shake in a jar) all the dressing ingredients. Pour over the noodles and cabbage just before serving and toss well.

SERVES: 10

Salad:

2 (3-ounce) packages ramen noodles (Oriental flavor preferred)

1 cup slivered almonds, toasted

2 tablespoons toasted sesame seeds*

1 medium Napa or other green cabbage (about 2 pounds), shredded

4 green onions, thinly sliced

*toasted sesame seeds are available at Asian groceries

Dressing:

½ cup salad oil

3 tablespoons white vinegar

¼ cup sugar

¼ teaspoon salt

Seasoning packs from the ramen noodle packages

Bicycles outside New Albany Library

Caraway Cabbage Salad

THIS EASTERN EUROPEAN SALAD GOES WELL WITH PORK, CHICKEN, OR TURKEY. BACON BITS AND THE ANISE-LIKE FLAVOR OF CARAWAY MAKE THE SALAD APPEALING EVEN TO PEOPLE WHO OTHERWISE TEND TO SHUN CABBAGE.

PARKS AND RECREATION IN NEW ALBANY

New Albany is a wonderful place where adults and children of all skills levels are encouraged to get involved in sports and enjoy the beautiful green spaces sprinkled throughout the community. Each year New Albany Parks programs promote wellness, development of skills, team unity, and sport competitions and offer vehicles for all members of the family to get to know their neighbors. One great example is New Albany baseball, which earned its Little League Baseball International charter in 2006, allowing local players to enter the international Little League tournament that ends with the nationally televised World Series in August.

The number of parks and acres of green space continue to grow to keep up with the increased number of residents signing up for the sports programs each season. Bevelhymer Park and Thompson Park offer acres of green space filled with softball and baseball diamonds, tennis courts, soccer fields, playgrounds, walking trails, picnic areas, and restroom facilities. The Wexner Community Park is a leisurely playground park with a great pavilion for community gatherings and the site of the future Recreation Center. The New Albany Plain Township Aquatic Center is a tremendous asset both for families who just want to enjoy the pool and for athletes who want to compete with other swimmers.

— *Dave Wharton on behalf of New Albany Parks*

1 Finely shred the cabbage, transfer it to a bowl and sprinkle with 2 teaspoons of the salt. Let sit for 15 minutes. Squeeze the cabbage to remove excess water. Transfer to a serving bowl.

2 Fry the bacon until crisp and drain on paper towels. Add the vinegar and sugar to the bacon fat and cook, stirring, until the sugar has dissolved. Pour the hot dressing over the cabbage and let sit for 1 minute. Add the vegetable oil, caraway seeds, pepper, and remaining 1 teaspoon salt; toss well.

3 Serve at room temperature, sprinkled with the bacon.

SERVES: 6

1 small red cabbage (or ½ large head), 1 to 1½ pounds

3 teaspoons salt

½ cup chopped bacon (about 5 slices)

¼ cup white vinegar

1 teaspoon sugar

2 tablespoons vegetable oil

1 tablespoon caraway seeds

¼ teaspoon pepper

COURTESY DON STRENCH

Wexner Community Park

Quinoa Salad

$\mathcal{Q}$UINOA HAS BEEN HAILED AS THE "SUPERGRAIN OF THE FUTURE" BECAUSE IT CONTAINS MORE PROTEIN THAN ANY OTHER GRAIN AND LOWER CARBOHYDRATES THAN MOST GRAINS; IT ALSO PROVIDES A RICH AND BALANCED SOURCE OF VITAL NUTRIENTS. THIS SPA STAPLE GETS AN ORIENTAL TWIST IN THIS RECIPE CONTRIBUTED BY ELEANOR SEDLUK, WHO BROUGHT IT FROM SEATTLE.

1 Whisk together (or shake in a jar) the dressing ingredients. Set aside.

2 Rinse the quinoa with warm water and drain it in a fine strainer. Place the quinoa in a 3-quart saucepan with the water and salt; bring to a boil. Turn heat to low, loosely cover and simmer for 15 minutes. Uncover the quinoa and let it sit on the lowest heat setting for another 5 minutes so it dries out. This makes the grain fluffier for salads. Remove from the heat, toss the quinoa with a fork and let cool.

3 Transfer the quinoa to a salad bowl; stir in the carrots, parsley, sunflower seeds, and garlic. Whisk (or shake) the dressing again, pour it over the quinoa and toss well. Serve garnished with tomato wedges.

SERVES: 6

CHEF TIP: Tamari is a premium soy sauce with a richer, less salty flavor than regular soy sauce. Tamari is wheat free and popular with those who have wheat allergies.

Dressing:

⅓ cup fresh lemon juice

3 tablespoons extra virgin olive oil

3 tablespoons tamari (see Chef Tip)

Salad:

1⅔ cups dry quinoa*

3 cups water

Pinch of sea salt

1 cup chopped carrots

¾ cup minced fresh parsley

⅓ cup sunflower seeds, toasted

4 cloves garlic, minced

Tomato wedges for garnish

*available in the rice, pasta, and grain section of the supermarket and in most health food or gourmet stores

Carrot and Green Bean Salad
with Sesame-Flavored Noodles

*T*HE SESAME OIL LENDS THIS HEFTY SALAD AN ORIENTAL FLAVOR.

1 Whisk together (or shake in a jar) all the dressing ingredients. Set aside for at least 30 minutes to blend the flavors. Taste and correct seasoning with salt. Whisk (or shake) again before using.

2 Meanwhile, cook the green beans in a large pot of boiling water until tender-crisp, about 5 minutes. Using a slotted spoon, transfer beans to a bowl of ice water to cool. (Do not drain the water.) Drain the beans well and pat dry.

3 Return the water to a boil. Add the pasta and cook, stirring often, until just tender but still firm to the bite, about 12 minutes. Drain. Rinse pasta under cold water.

4 Combine green beans, pasta, carrots, green onions, and the dressing in large bowl. Toss to coat. Season with red pepper flakes.

SERVES: 6

CHEF TIP: For extra texture, add toasted sliced almonds.

Dressing:

¼ cup fresh lime juice (from about 3 limes)

3 tablespoons canola oil

3 tablespoons soy sauce

2 tablespoons dark brown sugar

1 tablespoon sesame oil

1 tablespoon minced garlic

Salt and pepper to taste

Salad:

½ pound green beans, cut into ½-inch pieces

½ pound linguine

2 cups shredded carrots

1 cup thinly sliced green onions

Red pepper flakes to taste

Chopped Salad with Russian Dressing

Don't be put off by the litany of ingredients. Serve this at a gathering and we guarantee someone will request the recipe.

1   To make the dressing, heat the oil in a small saucepan over medium-high heat. Add the shallots; sauté until they begin to caramelize, about 3 minutes. Add the vodka; simmer, stirring, until nearly evaporated. Add the V8, Worcestershire sauce, vinegar, sugar, mustard, horseradish, celery seeds, and lemon juice. Boil, stirring occasionally, for 5 minutes. Remove from the heat and season with salt and pepper. Refrigerate until cold.

2   Toss the salad ingredients together. Toss again with just enough dressing to coat the salad. Serve immediately.

SERVES: 4

Dressing:

1 teaspoon olive oil

2 teaspoons minced shallots

¼ cup vodka or chicken stock

1 (5.5-ounce) can spicy V8 juice

2 teaspoons Worcestershire sauce

2 teaspoons red wine vinegar

1 teaspoon sugar

1 teaspoon Dijon mustard

1 teaspoon prepared horseradish

½ teaspoon celery seeds

Juice of ½ lemon

Salt and pepper to taste

Salad:

8 ounces cooked medium shrimp

2 cups chopped Roma tomatoes

1 cup sliced celery

½ cup diced cucumber

⅓ cup sliced pimiento-stuffed green olives

1 tablespoon chopped fresh parsley

1 teaspoon olive oil

Salt and pepper to taste

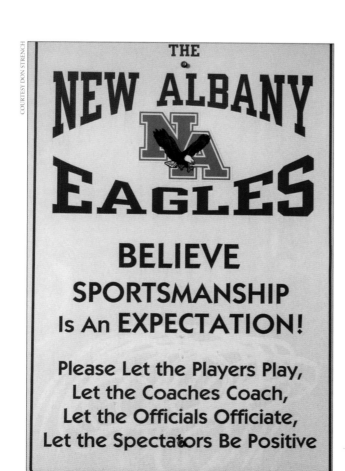

Eagles' Code of Conduct

Tex-Mex Salad

THIS "BIG" SALAD IS ALL YOU NEED FOR A ONE-DISH LUNCHEON.

1 In a nonreactive dish large enough to hold the steak, stir together the garlic, half the lime juice, 3 tablespoons of the olive oil, salt, and pepper. Add the steak, turning to coat all sides, and let marinate at room temperature for 1 hour (or longer, covered and refrigerated).

2 To make the dressing, combine the remaining lime juice and olive oil with the vinegar, chili powder, cumin, paprika, and sugar. Taste and add more sugar if needed. Set aside.

3 Panfry the steak on medium-high, or cook under a preheated broiler, until browned on the outside and cooked to your liking. Cut into strips and set aside.

4 Toss the green onions with the lettuce and arrange on a serving platter or in a salad bowl. Pour about half the dressing over the leaves, and then arrange the beans, avocado, and tomatoes over the top. Sprinkle with the chile pepper, cilantro, and corn kernels. Arrange the strips of steak and the tortilla chips on top, then pour over the rest of the dressing. Serve immediately.

SERVES: 10

6 garlic cloves, chopped

Juice of 1 lime

7 tablespoons olive oil

Salt and pepper to taste

12 ounces tender steak, such as sirloin

1 tablespoon red wine vinegar

½ teaspoon chili powder

½ teaspoon ground cumin

½ teaspoon paprika

½ teaspoon sugar

5 green onions, thinly sliced

8 ounces crisp lettuce leaves such as romaine

1 (14-ounce) can pinto, black, or red kidney beans, drained and rinsed

1 avocado, sliced and tossed with a little lime juice

2 ripe tomatoes, diced

A 2-inch piece jalapeño or 1-inch piece serrano pepper, chopped (or ½ teaspoon red pepper flakes)

3 tablespoons chopped fresh cilantro

1 (8-ounce) can corn kernels, drained

Generous handful of crisp tortilla chips, broken into pieces

Couscous and Shrimp Salad

THIS CITRUS-FLAVORED AND MINTY SALAD GOES WELL WITH A MEDITERRANEAN BUFFET.

1 Whisk together (or shake in a jar) all the dressing ingredients. Set aside.

2 In a large saucepan, bring the water to a boil. Stir in the couscous, cover, remove from the heat and let sit until the couscous has absorbed the water, about 10 minutes. Fluff the couscous with a fork and transfer it to a salad bowl. Add the shrimp, tomatoes, celery, green onions, mint, and capers; toss well.

3 Whisk (or shake) the dressing again and add to the couscous mixture. Toss. Chill couscous salad until cold, about 30 minutes and up to 2 hours. Serve cold.

SERVES: 6

Dressing:

½ cup olive oil

¼ cup fresh lime juice

1 clove garlic, minced

1 teaspoon celery seeds

½ teaspoon salt

¼ teaspoon freshly ground pepper

Salad:

2¼ cups water

2 cups couscous

1 pound cooked, peeled medium shrimp

2 medium ripe tomatoes, seeded and chopped (about 2 cups)

2 stalks celery, cut into ¼-inch dice

½ cup chopped green onions

⅓ cup chopped fresh mint

2 tablespoons capers, drained and rinsed

COURTESY NEW ALBANY COUNTRY CLUB

Tennis match on Stadium Court, New Albany Country Club

Charlie's Grilled Chicken Caesar Salad

*T*HIS VERSION OF THE FAMOUS SALAD REPLACES THE TRADITIONAL RAW EGG WITH PASTEURIZED EGG. UNTRADITIONAL INGREDIENTS—PECANS, CRANBERRIES, AND APPLE—EMBELLISH THIS OLD STANDBY.

1 In a large salad bowl, layer the lettuce, chicken, pecans, cranberries, green onions, and feta cheese. Keep cool until ready to serve. Just before serving, chop the apple and add it to the salad with the croutons and dressing; toss to combine.

SERVES: 8

CHEF TIP: Use packaged grilled chicken available in your grocer's deli or freezer section for a quick fix. Bring to room temperature before using.

4 cups bite-sized pieces romaine lettuce (about 2 heads)

½ pound chicken tenderloin, grilled, cooled, and cut into bite-sized pieces

½ cup pecans, toasted and chopped

¼ cup dried cranberries

¼ cup sliced green onions

4 ounces feta cheese

1 apple (Braeburn or Fuji preferred), unpeeled

1 cup croutons

½ cup Classic Caesar Salad Dressing (recipe below)

CLASSIC CAESAR SALAD DRESSING

1 In a small bowl, mash the anchovies with a fork to make a paste. Whisk in the egg. Add the oil, lemon juice, dry mustard, garlic, salt, and pepper; mix well.

1 (2-ounce) can anchovies (regular or with capers)

1 pasteurized egg

¼ cup olive oil

Juice of ½ lemon

½ teaspoon dry mustard

Pressed garlic to taste

Salt and pepper to taste

Bon Bon Chicken Salad

THIS PORTABLE SALAD OF CHINESE PROVENANCE IS SAVORY AND SWEET; EVEN KIDS LOVE IT.

1 Whisk together (or shake in a jar) all the dressing ingredients. Set aside.

2 Put the chicken in a saucepan, cover with water and bring to a boil. Boil the chicken until it is cooked through (the juices run clear when you pierce the thickest part of the breast with a knife), about 20 minutes. Drain the chicken and let cool.

3 Finely shred the chicken and put it in a bowl. Toss the chicken with the green onions, the dressing, and the sesame seeds, if desired. Refrigerate for at least 3 hours. Serve cold, wrapped in lettuce leaves.

SERVES: 8

Dressing:

¼ cup brown sugar

¼ cup sesame seed paste

¼ cup soy sauce

2 tablespoons sesame oil

1½ teaspoons Chinese chili oil

1½ tablespoons cane or rice vinegar

1 tablespoon minced fresh ginger

1 tablespoon minced garlic

1½ teaspoons salt

Salad:

2 pounds boneless skinless chicken breasts

5 green onions, chopped

½ cup toasted sesame seeds (optional)

Lettuce leaves for wraps

Beef and Avocado Deluxe

SHOW OFF THE LAYERS OF THIS COLORFUL SALAD BY STACKING THEM IN A TRIFLE BOWL OR OTHER LARGE GLASS BOWL. PAIR IT WITH A RICE SALAD FOR A MAIN COURSE.

1   Whisk together (or shake in a jar) all the dressing ingredients.

2   In a deep glass bowl, layer the avocado, beef, and onion; repeat layers until all these ingredients are used. Pour the dressing over the salad and let marinate, loosely covered at room temperature, for several hours. Garnish with parsley sprigs before serving.

SERVES: 4 to 6

CHEF TIP: Purchase good-quality beef from the deli.

Dressing:

½ cup chopped fresh parsley

½ cup wine vinegar

½ cup vegetable oil

¼ cup olive oil

2 teaspoons Dijon mustard

2 teaspoons salt

¼ teaspoon pepper

Salad:

3 avocados, peeled and thinly sliced

2 pounds thinly sliced rare roast beef

1 sweet red onion, thinly sliced

Parsley sprigs for garnish

Walking path in New Albany

G.W.Acock 06

New Albany Ballet Company recital

Fostering of the Arts and Cultural Life

As the community of New Albany grows, cultural opportunities become tradition for area residents. Under a crystal blue July sky in Lambton Park, picnickers savor cool salads and enjoy the melodies of the Columbus Symphony Orchestra. In August, a concert by the Columbus Jazz Orchestra in Market Square finds families and friends relaxing on the green, nodding in time to the classic jazz notes of familiar standards. A crisp autumn afternoon brings out parents with young children to the Harvest the Arts Festival. And many a young girl begins her classical ballet training at the New Albany Ballet Company: her long hours at the barre and in class translate into elegant recitals and a *Babes in Toyland* production during the holidays.

New Albany's residents planned for the future with great hope and pride when they joined together to launch the New Albany Community Performing Arts Center. Truly the most visible symbol of our dedication to the arts, the center features a 750-seat concert hall/auditorium and houses much-needed classroom space where our district's children can learn about all facets of the arts. From fly-loft to set-building, the backstage and technical aspects of a performance will draw talented, curious students to an area of performing arts they otherwise may not have explored. The vision behind the center provided for programming to meet the needs of all community members, with guest speakers, adult workshops, and master classes a strong part of the dream. Collaborative efforts with existing arts groups in Columbus, such as BalletMet, the Columbus Museum of Art, Columbus Association for the Performing Arts, and the Columbus Symphony Orchestra, to name a few, will continue to further enhance the programming schedule.

As New Albany develops and expands throughout the next decade, not only will residents continue to take advantage of the many cultural happenings throughout the greater Columbus area, they will strive to put their mark on the local cultural landscape as well. The concept of "right in your own backyard" has never been more exciting!

— *Rhonda Koulermos*

Roasted Asparagus with Goat Cheese and Bacon 131

Mia's Berry Glazed Asparagus 132

Roasted Beets with Thyme and Orange 133

Broccoli with Ginger 133

Sautéed Collard Greens 134

Never-Fail Corn Pudding 135

French Beans with Mushrooms 135

French Green Bean "Kindling"
(*Fagotins des Haricots Verts*) 136

Green Beans Poriyal 137

Braised Leeks and Tomatoes, Greek Style *(Prasa)* 137

Sautéed Mushrooms 138

Chinese Roasted Peppers 139

Roasted Pepper Pasta 140

Roasted Peppers and Potatoes with Rosemary 141

Roasted Potatoes with
Herbs and Parmesan Cheese 142

Sweet Potato Purée with Bourbon
and Buttered Pecans 143

Potato Parmesan au Gratin 144

Summer Squash and Zucchini 144

Stir-fried Snow Peas with Shrimp 145

Spinach with Chickpeas *(Espinacas con Garbanzos)* 146

Pearl Couscous with Olives and Roasted Tomatoes 147

Lemon Rice 148

Saffron Rice Pilaf with Almonds and Raisins 149

Wild and Brown Rice Casserole 150

Lemon and Roasted Garlic Risotto 151

Mélange of Roasted Root Vegetables
with Herb Vinaigrette 152

Vegetable Kabobs with Balsamic Vinegar Toss 153

Macaroni with Five Cheeses 154

Caramelized Onion and Tomato Galette 155

Goat Cheese and Potato Pie *(Tarte au Fromage
de Chèvre et aux Pommes de Terre)* 156

Elsa's Smoked Ham and Vegetable Quiche 158

Roasted Asparagus with Goat Cheese and Bacon

As SOON AS THE ASPARAGUS SEASON ARRIVES, SERVE THIS DISH WITH YOUR CHOICE OF EGGS FOR BRUNCH, HAVE A GLASS OF MIMOSA, AND YOU'LL FEEL THE JOY THAT SPRING HAS INDEED SPRUNG.

1 Preheat the oven to 500°F.

2 Fry the bacon until crisp. Drain on paper towels. Crumble bacon; set aside.

3 Position racks in upper and lower thirds of oven. Arrange asparagus on 2 large, heavy baking sheets. Drizzle each sheet with 1 tablespoon of oil and turn asparagus to coat well. Sprinkle generously with salt and pepper. Roast the asparagus, switching racks after 4 minutes, until tender-crisp when pierced with a knife, about 8 minutes.

4 Arrange asparagus in a single layer on a serving platter. Sprinkle with the goat cheese, then with the bacon. Drizzle with lemon juice and the remaining 2 teaspoons oil. Sprinkle with lemon zest. Serve immediately or let stand, covered with plastic wrap, for no more than 1 hour and serve at room temperature.

SERVES: 6

CHEF TIP: Thirty minutes before the goat cheese will be crumbled, put it in the freezer. The hardened consistency makes crumbling much less messy.

6 slices bacon

2 pounds medium asparagus, tough ends trimmed

2 tablespoons plus 2 teaspoons olive oil

Salt and pepper to taste

1 (4-ounce) log soft fresh goat cheese, crumbled

2 teaspoons fresh lemon juice

Grated zest of 1 lemon

Mia's Berry Glazed Asparagus

A SWEET AND TANGY BERRY GLAZE TURNS SIMPLE ASPARAGUS SPEARS INTO A COLORFUL AND ENTICING SIDE DISH.

CSO CONCERT IN LAMBTON PARK

A much-loved tradition in our community established by the New Albany Classic Signature Series, the annual July concert features one of Central Ohio's premier arts organizations, the Columbus Symphony Orchestra. Free and open to the public, this concert draws hundreds of people of all ages to enjoy an evening of rousing symphonic music. Past program themes have included patriotic selections, Broadway favorites, and movie themes.

Picnic baskets, lawn chairs, and casual clothing are the order of the day as families and friends gather to get the best spot on the lawn in Lambton Park before the concert begins.

Many New Albany residents have made this concert an opportunity to entertain families and friends who might not live in the community. And of course the symphony loves coming to New Albany, especially conductor Albert George Schramm, whose talent for getting toddlers through teenagers up to dance the hokey pokey and other classics is legendary. The concert in the park offers summer entertainment that everyone looks forward to year after year.

— *New Albany Classic Signature Series*

1 Stir together the jam, wine, honey, and lemon juice in a microwavable cup. Set aside.

2 In a 12-inch skillet over medium heat, warm the olive oil and butter. Add the asparagus and cook, shaking occasionally, until tender yet firm, about 8 minutes. Add salt and pepper to taste. Move asparagus to the side of the pan, then add the almonds and cook, stirring, until browned. Remove from the heat.

3 Microwave the jam mixture until warm and melted, about 30 seconds on high. Arrange asparagus with almonds on a platter. Drizzle with the berry glaze and serve.

SERVES: 8

Glaze:

¼ cup mixed berry jam

2 tablespoons dry red wine

1 teaspoon honey

Juice of 1 lemon

2 teaspoons olive oil

1 tablespoon unsalted butter

3 pounds asparagus, tough ends trimmed

Salt and pepper

¼ cup sliced almonds

Children enjoying music played by CSO in Lambton Park

Roasted Beets with Thyme and Orange

NUTRITIOUS AND DELICIOUS, BEETS ARE ONE OF THE BEST DIETARY SOURCES OF FOLATE. SPRINKLE WITH THE ZEST FROM AN ORANGE FOR AN ATTRACTIVE PRESENTATION.

1 Preheat the oven to 400°F.

2 Remove the tops and the roots of the beets and peel each one. Cut the beets into quarters. Make sure that the chunks of beets are of a uniform size. Put the beets in a bowl and toss with the olive oil, thyme, salt, and pepper.

3 Place the beets on a baking sheet and roast for 40 to 50 minutes, turning once or twice with a metal spatula, until the beets are tender. Remove from the oven and immediately toss with the vinegar and orange juice. Adjust salt and pepper, if desired.

SERVES: 6

12 medium beets

3 tablespoons olive oil

1½ teaspoons minced fresh thyme

2 teaspoons kosher salt

1 teaspoon freshly ground black pepper

2 tablespoons raspberry vinegar

Juice of 1 large orange (about ¼ cup)

Broccoli with Ginger

THE GINGER FLAVOR INFUSES THE BROCCOLI IN NO TIME AT ALL. THIS IS A VERY QUICK DISH TO PREPARE.

1 Cut the broccoli stalk off where it branches. Cut the florets from the stem; cut individual florets into bite-sized pieces, if necessary. Cut the stem into ½-inch pieces.

2 Heat the oil in a wok over medium heat. Stir-fry the ginger until golden. Add the broccoli stems and stir-fry until just tender; sprinkle with a little water if needed to prevent burning. Add florets and oyster sauce. Reduce heat to low and simmer for about 3 minutes, until the florets are tender-crisp and still bright green.

3 Serve with steamed white rice.

SERVES: 6

CHEF TIP: Use Loriva roasted peanut oil for the best flavor.

1 large head broccoli (2 pounds)

2 tablespoons peanut oil

3-inch piece fresh ginger, peeled and julienned (about 3 tablespoons)

3 tablespoons oyster sauce,* or more to taste

*available in most Asian groceries or the ethnic aisles of a large supermarket

Sautéed Collard Greens

A TASTY ALTERNATIVE TO STEAMED SPINACH.

1 Bring chicken stock and water to a boil in a stockpot.

2 Meanwhile, clean the collard greens thoroughly, rinsing 3 or 4 times in a sink full of water, until the water is clear. Cut away the large stems, roll several leaves together and cut with kitchen shears or tear into bite-sized pieces. Add the greens to the boiling stock. Cover and boil for 30 minutes, stirring once about midway to ensure thorough cooking. If greens are still a bit tough, add a pinch or two of baking soda and continue to boil for 5 minutes. Drain in a colander.

3 Fry the bacon in large skillet until crisp. Remove bacon, drain on paper towels, crumble and set aside. Sauté the onions in the bacon fat until transparent. Add the garlic and sauté for another minute. Add the collard greens and sauté for about 5 minutes, or until thoroughly heated. Add crumbled bacon. Serve immediately.

SERVES: 6

8 cups water

4 cups chicken stock

8 bunches collard greens
(2½ to 3 pounds)

Pinch of baking soda (if needed)

6 slices of bacon

1 medium onion, finely chopped

3 cloves garlic, minced

Salt and pepper to taste

Columbus Symphony Orchestra concert in Lambton Park

Never-Fail Corn Pudding

IN AUGUST WHEN THE CORN IS TENDER AND SWEET YOU CAN MAKE THIS DISH EVERY DAY AND NOT TIRE OF IT. IT IS A WONDERFUL ACCOMPANIMENT TO A SUMMER BARBECUE.

1 Preheat the oven to 375°F. Grease a 1-quart baking dish.

2 Stir all the ingredients together and pour into the baking dish. Bake for 30 to 40 minutes, or until the center is set. Serve immediately.

SERVES: 4

2 cups fresh or frozen corn (from about 4 ears)

2 eggs, lightly beaten

2 tablespoons sugar

1 tablespoon all-purpose flour

1 cup whole milk

2 tablespoons unsalted butter, melted

Pinch of salt

French Beans with Mushrooms

THE GARLIC DEFINES THE FLAVOR OF THIS SIMPLE DISH, BUT THE MUSHROOMS ADD A DEPTH OF FLAVOR.

1 Snip off both ends of the beans, then blanch them in boiling water for 4 minutes, or until barely tender. Drain and rinse under cold running water to stop the cooking; drain again and pat dry with paper towels.

2 Heat the oil in a large skillet over high heat. Add the garlic and mushrooms; cook, stirring, for 3 to 4 minutes. Add the green beans. Cook, stirring, for 1 minute. Add the chicken stock, soy sauce, and salt. Cook, stirring, until the vegetables are well coated with the sauce. Taste and correct the seasoning and serve.

SERVES: 4

CHEF TIP: Put ice cubes on top of the beans after blanching to enhance the green color.

1 pound haricots verts*

3 tablespoons corn or olive oil

3 cloves garlic, minced

1 medium portobello mushroom, stemmed and cap sliced into ½-inch wedges

¼ cup chicken stock

1 teaspoon soy sauce

½ teaspoon coarse or kosher salt

*a small and slender type of green string bean

French Green Bean "Kindling" (Fagotins des Haricots Verts)

*"K*INDLING" REFERS TO THE BUNDLING OF THE BEANS LIKE FIREWOOD. A PRETTY PRESENTATION ESPECIALLY FOR PLATED DINNERS.

1 Trim the beans and blanch in boiling salted water until tender-crisp, about 7 minutes. Drain and plunge into ice water; drain again when cooled and pat dry with paper towels. Gather in bunches of about 6 to 8 beans and tie each bundle with a strip of stretched bacon.

2 In a large skillet over medium-high heat, melt the butter in the oil. Sauté the bundles of beans, turning frequently, until the bacon fat starts to melt and the bacon is brown on all sides, 4 to 5 minutes. Season with salt and pepper.

SERVES: 6

CHEF TIP: Blanched green onions or strips of carrots may be used to tie the bundles. You may also garnish with pieces of roasted red pepper or pimiento.

2 pounds haricots verts* or green beans

12 slices bacon (approx.; 1 slice per bundle)

1 tablespoon unsalted butter

1 tablespoon vegetable oil

Salt and freshly ground pepper to taste

*a small and slender type of green string bean

New Albany walking path scene

Green Beans Poriyal

A PORIYAL IS A SAUCELESS VEGETABLE DISH, ALSO KNOWN AS A DRY CURRY. THIS SIMPLE SIDE DISH GOES WELL WITH CURRIED MEAT DISHES.

1 Trim the beans if necessary and thinly slice them on the diagonal. Put the beans in a heavy saucepan with just enough cold water to cover, add the turmeric and salt, and bring to a boil. Cook the beans until tender-crisp, about 5 minutes; drain and set aside.

2 In the same saucepan, heat the oil over medium-high heat. Add the mustard seeds, dal and dried red chiles and cook, stirring. When the mustard seeds begin to crackle, add the onion and green chiles. Stir-fry for 4 minutes. Add the beans and stir-fry until the beans are tender, about 2 minutes. Add salt to taste and the coconut; stir and remove from heat. Serve hot.

SERVES: 4 to 6

1 pound green beans

1 teaspoon turmeric

Salt to taste

1 tablespoon vegetable oil

1 teaspoon black mustard seeds*

1 teaspoon black gram dal or urad dal (optional)*

2 whole dried red chiles

1 small onion, chopped

2 fresh green chiles, chopped

1 teaspoon unsweetened desiccated coconut

*available at South Asian groceries

Braised Leeks and Tomatoes, Greek Style (Prasa)

M EDITERRANEAN-FLAVORED SEPHARDIC FARE. YOU CAN WALK AWAY FROM THE COOKING AFTER THE INITIAL SAUTÉING AND COME BACK TO THE ALLURING DELICATE AROMA OF LEEKS AND TOMATOES AFTER A LONG SIMMER. SIMPLY DELECTABLE.

1 In a large saucepan, heat the olive oil and tomatoes (without their juices) over medium heat. When the tomatoes start to get tender, add the garlic. Continue cooking for about 5 minutes. Add the leeks and about half of the tomato juice. Cover and simmer over low heat for about an hour, stirring every 15 minutes and adding some of the tomato juices (or water) if it is getting dry.

2 Add the lemon juice, sugar, salt, and pepper; simmer, uncovered, another 15 minutes or until the leeks are tender.

3 Serve hot, cold, or at room temperature. This dish keeps in the refrigerator for a few days and tastes best if prepared the day before.

SERVES: 8

¼ cup olive oil

20 Roma tomatoes, seeded and chopped in large pieces, any juices reserved

4 cloves garlic, minced

10 large leeks, washed and chopped into 1-inch pieces (about 5 pounds)

Juice of 2 lemons or to taste

2 tablespoons brown sugar or to taste

Salt and pepper to taste

Sautéed Mushrooms

THESE MUSHROOMS MAKE A GREAT SIDE DISH FOR MEAT OR POULTRY MAIN COURSES BUT CAN ALSO STAND ALONE AS AN APPETIZER WHEN SERVED WITH PIECES OF FRESH SOURDOUGH BREAD OR WARM FRENCH BREAD TO SOP UP THE DELICIOUS SAUCE.

1 Remove the stems from the mushrooms and reserve for another use. In a large, heavy skillet, heat 2 tablespoons of the olive oil over medium-high heat until it begins to smoke. Add the mushroom caps and sauté for 2 minutes, stirring constantly.

2 Add the remaining 2 tablespoons olive oil, the garlic, basil, oregano, thyme, green onions, and pepper flakes; sauté for 2 minutes. Stir in the sherry and cook to reduce it by half, about 8 minutes. Swirl in the butter a tablespoon at a time to glaze the mushrooms. Season with salt and pepper. Serve immediately.

SERVES: 4

1½ pounds whole white mushrooms

4 tablespoons olive oil

2 tablespoons minced garlic

½ teaspoon crumbled dried basil

½ teaspoon crumbled dried oregano

½ teaspoon dried thyme

3 green onions (white part only), finely chopped

Pinch of red pepper flakes

⅔ cup dry sherry

4 tablespoons unsalted butter, cut into 4 parts

Salt and freshly ground pepper to taste

Byron Stripling, Columbus Jazz Orchestra Artistic Director

JAZZ ARTS GROUP PHOTOS COURTESY CHRISTIN McCABE

Chinese Roasted Peppers

THIS MAKES A GREAT PASTA, SALAD, OR SANDWICH ACCOMPANIMENT.

1 Trim off the bottom and top of the peppers. Slice each pepper in half lengthwise. Lightly press each half so it lies flat. While pressing down on the pepper, slide a knife along the underside of the pepper and cut away the white pith, the seeds, and the top layer of the translucent flesh. Cut into strips 1 inch wide and then cut the strips into triangles. Put peppers in a bowl. Toss with the salt. Let them stand at least 1 hour. Rinse, drain and dry the peppers with paper towels.

2 Make the seasoning sauce by mixing all the ingredients in a small bowl until the sugar has dissolved.

3 Place a wok over high heat for about 2 minutes until it smokes. Add the peanut oil; heat until hot but not smoking. Add the peppers; stir-fry for 5 to 7 minutes, pressing down on them with a spatula to aid the scorching. If they are scorching too quickly and unevenly, reduce the heat. You want the peppers to be charred; the scorched skin gives the peppers the desired char-broiled flavor.

4 Add the seasoning sauce. Stir-fry until all the liquid is absorbed. Transfer peppers to a bowl and serve at room temperature.

YIELD: 3 cups

CHEF TIPS: Do not include green bell peppers in the mix. They do not taste good in combination with the other peppers mentioned above.

Use Loriva roasted peanut oil for the best flavor.

3½ pounds red, yellow, and orange bell and poblano peppers* (about 7 peppers)

1 tablespoon salt

3 tablespoons peanut oil

*a dark green, almost black or purplish Mexican pepper with a sweet flavor

Seasoning Sauce:

2 tablespoons light soy sauce

4 teaspoons red wine vinegar

1 tablespoon Chinese chili sauce or to taste

2 teaspoons sugar

Roasted Pepper Pasta

A WONDERFULLY AROMATIC AND DELICIOUS FUSION OF EAST/WEST FLAVORS.

1   Heat a 12-inch skillet or large wok over high heat for 1 minute. Add the peanut oil; reduce the heat to low. Add the shallots, garlic, and salt; sauté until the garlic is golden, about 2 minutes. Add the green onions; sauté 1 minute. Add the roasted peppers, cilantro, sesame oil, and hot sauce. When the mixture begins to simmer, turn off the heat.

2   In a large pot of boiling salted water, cook the farfalle until just tender but still firm to the bite, about 12 minutes. Drain the pasta, reserving ¼ cup of the cooking water.

3   Add the pasta to the pepper mixture. Stir in the Parmesan cheese and 3 or 4 tablespoons of the pasta water. Toss well. Serve hot or at room temperature.

SERVES: 6

2 tablespoons peanut oil

½ cup chopped shallots

2 tablespoons chopped garlic

½ teaspoon salt

½ cup thinly sliced green onions (white and green parts)

2 cups Chinese Roasted Peppers with their juice (see page 139)

¼ cup chopped fresh cilantro

2 tablespoons dark sesame oil

2 teaspoons Chinese hot sauce (or 1 teaspoon chili oil)

1 tablespoon salt

1 pound farfalle*

⅔ cup freshly grated Parmesan cheese

*bow-tie or butterfly-shaped pasta

New Albany flowers in spring

Roasted Peppers and Potatoes with Rosemary

WITH NEW POTATOES AND PEPPERS ROASTED WITH ROSEMARY, YOU HAVE A TASTY, SOMEWHAT GOURMET DISH THAT YOU CAN TAKE TO A PICNIC OR A COOK-OUT.

1   Preheat the oven to 450°F.

2   Cut the potatoes in halves or quarters depending on their size so that all the pieces are approximately the same size. In a 13 by 9-inch roasting pan, toss the potatoes with the oil, vinegar, rosemary, salt, and pepper. Roast for 20 minutes.

3   While the potatoes are roasting, remove the seeds and ribs from the peppers; cut the peppers into quarters. After the potatoes have roasted for 20 minutes, add the peppers and toss them with the potatoes to coat them with the oil, vinegar, and rosemary. If the pan is dry, add 1 tablespoon of olive oil. Continue roasting the potatoes and peppers for at least 20 minutes more or until the potatoes are easy to pierce with a fork and the peppers have begun to brown and blister. Serve hot or at room temperature.

SERVES: 8 to 10

CHEF TIP: The vegetables may also be grilled in a grill basket.

1½ pounds new potatoes, unpeeled

2 tablespoons olive oil

1 tablespoon balsamic vinegar

2 tablespoons minced fresh rosemary

Salt and pepper to taste

3 large yellow or orange bell peppers

3 large red bell peppers

Roasted Potatoes with Herbs and Parmesan Cheese

THESE GARLICKY ROASTED POTATOES ARE ENRICHED WITH THE ADDITION OF GRATED PARMESAN CHEESE.

NEW ALBANY ARTS COUNCIL

Since 1993, the New Albany Arts Council has provided quality arts programs for area residents, including Summer Art Camp for children 5 to 13, a summer musical for children 9 to 15, and a year-round mixed chorus. The council also presents Concert on the Commons each June and the Harvest the Arts Festival in October, a festival for all ages that celebrates the area's cultural heritage.

The council works closely with school arts groups, providing additional funding for special needs, and has contributed thousands in scholarship funds for high-school seniors and mini-grants for special projects. Residents interested in learning more about this non-profit group's promotion of the arts may visit their website at **www.naarts.org.**

— *Kathy Mayhorn on behalf of New Albany Arts Council*

1 Preheat the oven to 425°F.

2 In a 13 by 9-inch casserole dish, toss the potatoes with the olive oil, herbes de Provence, salt, and pepper. Bake for 1 hour, stirring about midway to ensure even cooking, or until the potatoes are tender. About 15 minutes before the potatoes are done, sprinkle with Parmesan cheese and add a sprig of rosemary. Serve hot.

SERVES: 8

CHEF TIP: Consorzio garlic-flavored olive oil is highly recommended for this recipe.

3 pounds baby red-skinned potatoes, halved or quartered

2 tablespoons garlic-flavored olive oil

1 teaspoon herbes de Provence

Salt and pepper to taste

1 cup freshly grated Parmesan cheese

Sprig of fresh rosemary

New Albany Harvest the Arts Festival

Sweet Potato Purée
with Bourbon and Buttered Pecans

A GOOD ITEM FOR THE THANKSGIVING DINNER MENU. THE SWEET POTATO PURÉE CAN BE MADE UP TO TWO DAYS AHEAD. WARM THE PURÉE OVER LOW HEAT, THEN TRANSFER TO A LARGE BOWL AND SERVE.

1 Preheat the oven to 425°F.

2 Prick sweet potatoes with a fork, put them in a foil-lined baking pan, and bake until tender, about 1 hour. Remove sweet potatoes from the oven and reduce the temperature to 325°F.

3 When the sweet potatoes are just cool enough to handle, peel them. Transfer half of them to a food processor. Add the orange juice, bourbon, and 6 tablespoons of the butter; process for 30 seconds. Transfer the purée to a large bowl. Purée the remaining potatoes until completely smooth and transfer to the bowl. Stir until well combined and season with salt and pepper to taste. Transfer the purée to a 2-quart gratin dish or other shallow baking dish. (The purée may be made 2 days ahead and chilled, covered. Bring purée to room temperature before proceeding.)

4 In a shallow baking pan, spread the pecans in one layer and bake, shaking the pan occasionally, until fragrant, about 10 minutes. Toss the hot pecans with the remaining 2 tablespoons butter and 1 teaspoon kosher salt. (Pecans may be made 2 days ahead and kept in an airtight container at room temperature.)

5 Arrange the pecans on top of the purée and sprinkle with brown sugar. Bake in the upper third of the oven until heated through and pecans are slightly browned, about 30 minutes.

SERVES: 12

6 pounds sweet potatoes (about 8 large)

⅓ cup fresh orange juice

3 tablespoons bourbon

½ cup (1 stick) unsalted butter, softened

Salt and pepper to taste

2 cups pecan halves

1 teaspoon kosher salt

2 tablespoons packed dark brown sugar

Potato Parmesan au Gratin

THIS IS A DELICIOUSLY CREAMY POTATO CASSEROLE. WITH THE PARMESAN CHEESE AND WHIPPING CREAM, IT IS ROBUST ENOUGH TO SERVE AS A MAIN COURSE WITH A SIMPLE GREEN SALAD. FOR VARIATION ADD SLICED SMOKED HAM OR CHOPPED ANCHOVIES TO END UP WITH THE CLASSIC SWEDISH DISH JANSSON'S TEMPTATION.

1 Preheat the oven to 375°F.

2 Coat the sides and base of 13 by 9-inch casserole dish with the butter. Arrange a layer of potatoes in the dish. Add a thin layer of onion rings. Sprinkle with Parmesan, salt, and pepper. Repeat layering the potatoes, onions, Parmesan, salt, and pepper until it reaches ½ inch from the top of the dish. Pour the cream over the potatoes (it should cover them; add more if it doesn't). Sprinkle the remaining Parmesan and the bread crumbs on top. Cover and bake for 50 minutes. Uncover and bake for 20 minutes more or until the potatoes are tender. Serve hot.

SERVES: 8

CHEF TIP: Use a mandoline or V-slicer to slice the potatoes and onions into an even thickness.

1½ teaspoons unsalted butter

3½ pounds potatoes (approximately 10 large ones), peeled and cut into ¼-inch slices

1 large yellow onion, thinly sliced into rings

1 cup freshly grated Parmesan cheese

Salt and pepper to taste

3 cups whipping cream (approx.)

½ cup dry bread crumbs

Summer Squash and Zucchini

THE MINT GIVES THIS SIDE DISH A VERY CLEAN TASTE, MAKING IT A REFRESHING ACCOMPANIMENT TO ANY MEAT DISH.

1 Slice the squash and zucchini into ¼-inch-thick rounds. Melt the butter in a 12-inch skillet over medium-high heat. When the foam subsides, add the squash and zucchini; sprinkle with salt and pepper.

2 Raise the heat to high and cook, stirring occasionally, until the vegetables become tender and the edges begin to brown, about 20 minutes. Stir in the honey and mint, adjust the seasoning, and serve.

SERVES: 4

1 pound summer squash (about 2 to 3 medium)

1 pound zucchini (about 3 small)

¼ cup unsalted butter

Salt and freshly ground black pepper to taste

1 tablespoon honey

¼ cup minced fresh mint

Stir-fried Snow Peas with Shrimp

An EASILY PREPARED, COLORFUL STIR-FRY THAT COMBINES CRISPY GREEN SNOW PEAS WITH DELICATE SHRIMP.

1 Stir together 1 teaspoon of the cornstarch and 1 tablespoon of the water. Set aside.

2 Rinse shrimp in cold water and pat dry with paper towels. In a large bowl beat the egg white; stir in the remaining 1 teaspoon cornstarch, the sherry, salt, and pepper. Add the shrimp and stir to coat the shrimp well.

3 Heat 2 tablespoons of the oil in a wok over medium-high heat until very hot. Add the shrimp. Stir-fry for 1 minute. Add the garlic and ginger; stir-fry for 30 seconds. Add the green onions. Stir-fry until the shrimp turns opaque. Immediately transfer the shrimp to a bowl.

4 Heat the remaining 2 tablespoons oil in the wok. Add the snow peas and stir-fry until peas are evenly coated with the oil. Add the remaining 3 tablespoons water. Cover and cook for about a minute; the snow peas should still be green and crispy. Return the shrimp to the wok and toss with the snow peas. Stir the cornstarch mixture and swirl it into the wok. Heat through. Serve immediately.

SERVES: 4

CHEF TIP: Have all the ingredients prepared ahead of time but do the stir-frying as close to serving time as possible.

2 teaspoons cornstarch

4 tablespoons water

1 pound small (36 to 45 count) shrimp, peeled and deveined

1 egg white

2 teaspoons dry sherry

1 teaspoon salt

Freshly ground black pepper to taste

4 tablespoons vegetable oil

1 clove garlic, chopped and smashed

2 tablespoons chopped fresh ginger

2 green onions (white and green parts), chopped

1 pound snow peas, strings removed

3 tablespoons water

Spinach with Chickpeas (Espinacas con Garbanzos)

THIS NUTRITIOUS SPANISH SIDE DISH GOES WELL WITH CRUSTY BREAD.

1 Rinse the spinach, drain well, remove tough stems and tear the leaves into pieces. Place in a microwavable dish, cover and cook on high for 4 minutes (or simmer about 10 minutes in a pot of water on the stove). Drain well and chop finely.

2 Heat 1 tablespoon of the oil in a skillet over medium-high heat. Sauté the bread and garlic until they are golden on all sides. Transfer the bread and garlic to a mortar or mini processor. Add the vinegar and salt and mash to a paste.

3 Add the remaining 1 tablespoon oil to the skillet and heat over medium-high heat. Quickly sauté the spinach, then add the chickpeas, bread mixture, thyme, oregano, rosemary, paprika, cumin, and red pepper flakes. Cook 1 minute, adding a little water if the mixture seems too dry. Remove from the heat and let sit 10 minutes to blend flavors. Serve hot or at room temperature.

SERVES: 4

CHEF TIP: If using canned chickpeas, rinse and drain thoroughly before using. Fresh chickpeas that are ready for use are typically found in Middle Eastern groceries.

½ pound spinach leaves

2 tablespoons olive oil

2 thin slices white bread

2 cloves garlic

½ teaspoon wine vinegar

⅛ teaspoon salt

¾ cup cooked or drained canned chickpeas

1 teaspoon fresh thyme (or ⅛ teaspoon dried)

1 teaspoon minced fresh oregano (or ⅛ teaspoon crumbled dried)

1 teaspoon minced fresh rosemary (or ⅛ teaspoon crumbled dried)

¼ teaspoon sweet paprika

¼ teaspoon ground cumin (preferably freshly ground)

Red pepper flakes to taste

Pearl Couscous with Olives and Roasted Tomatoes

PEARL COUSCOUS HAS BEEN TURNING UP IN SOPHISTICATED SALAD MENUS IN THE LAST DECADE BECAUSE ITS PASTA-LIKE QUALITY GOES WELL WITH A WIDE RANGE OF DRESSINGS.

1 Preheat the oven to 250°F.

2 Using a serrated knife, halve the tomatoes lengthwise and arrange cut sides up in 1 layer on a baking sheet. Add the garlic cloves. Roast until the tomatoes are slightly shriveled around the edges, about 1 hour. Cool in the pan on a rack for 30 minutes.

3 Peel the garlic and put it in a blender. Add the oil, water, lemon juice, salt, pepper, and ½ cup of the roasted tomatoes; blend until the dressing is very smooth. (Set aside the rest of the roasted tomatoes for the couscous.)

4 To make the couscous, bring the stock to a boil in a large, heavy saucepan. Stir in couscous and simmer, uncovered, 6 minutes. Cover and remove from the heat. Let stand 10 minutes. Spread couscous in an even layer on a baking sheet and let cool 15 minutes.

5 Transfer couscous to a salad bowl and stir in the oil, olives, parsley, mint, thyme, dressing, reserved roasted tomatoes, and salt and pepper to taste.

SERVES: 6

CHEF TIP: Roasted tomatoes, dressing, and couscous can be made 1 day ahead and kept separately, covered and chilled. Bring to room temperature before proceeding.

Roasted Tomatoes and Dressing:

1½ pounds red grape or cherry tomatoes

4 cloves garlic, unpeeled

¼ cup extra virgin olive oil

¼ cup warm water

1 teaspoon fresh lemon juice

1 teaspoon salt

¼ teaspoon black pepper

Couscous:

2¾ cups chicken stock

2¼ cups pearl (Israeli) couscous*

1 tablespoon olive oil

½ cup Kalamata or other brine-cured black olives, pitted and chopped

⅓ cup chopped fresh flat-leaf parsley

¼ cup chopped fresh mint

1 teaspoon chopped fresh thyme

*also known as Middle Eastern or toasted couscous, it is the size of peppercorns and is very different from the commonly available coarse-ground couscous associated with Moroccan cuisine. Usually found in the kosher section of the supermarket.

Lemon Rice

A RICH, FULL-FLAVORED RICE PREPARATION. THE PINE NUTS GIVE IT A DECIDEDLY ITALIAN UNDERTONE.

1 In a 3-quart heavy saucepan, bring the water to a boil. Stir in 1 tablespoon of the butter and the salt. Stir in the rice. Reduce heat to very low. Cover tightly and cook 20 minutes. Turn off the heat and let rice sit for 10 minutes before lifting the lid. If excess moisture remains, cook an additional 5 minutes, uncovered, until all the water is absorbed into the rice.

2 In small saucepan, melt the remaining 2 tablespoons butter over low heat. Add the pine nuts, lemon juice and zest. Stir until heated through. Pour over the rice and toss with a fork. Adjust salt to taste. Serve immediately.

SERVES: 4

2½ cups water

3 tablespoons unsalted butter

1¼ teaspoons salt

1 cup white rice

¼ cup pine nuts

¼ cup fresh lemon juice

1 tablespoon grated lemon zest

Groundbreaking for the New Albany Community Performing Arts Center

NEW ALBANY CLASSIC SIGNATURE SERIES PHOTOS
COURTESY DANIEL W. FLOSS & ASSOCIATES PHOTOGRAPHY

Saffron Rice Pilaf with Almonds and Raisins

THE GLORIOUS SAFFRON SPICE TAKES THIS PILAF FROM PLAIN TO EXQUISITE. IT IS A TERRIFIC ACCOMPANIMENT TO LAMB, BEEF, OR SHRIMP.

1 Preheat the oven to 350°F.

2 Melt 2 tablespoons of the butter in a skillet over medium heat. Cook the almonds until browned, about 3 minutes. Watch carefully, as they burn easily. Drain on paper towels.

3 In a 5-quart casserole, melt the remaining butter over medium-high heat. Sauté the celery and onions until lightly coated with butter, 4 to 5 minutes. Add the rice and stir to coat the grains with butter. Stir in the almonds, raisins, stock, salt, pepper, and saffron. Cover and bake until all the liquid is absorbed, 50 minutes to 1 hour.

4 Fluff the rice with a fork before serving. Serve warm.

SERVES: 8

CHEF TIP: The pilaf can be baked in advance and held in a warm oven for up to 40 minutes.

1 cup unsalted butter (2 sticks)

¾ cup slivered blanched almonds

1¼ cups chopped celery

1¼ cups chopped onions

2 cups long-grain white rice

⅓ cup golden raisins

2¼ cups chicken stock

2½ teaspoons salt

¼ teaspoon pepper

⅛ teaspoon crumbled saffron

COURTESY DON STRENCH

New Albany winter scene

Wild and Brown Rice Casserole

THIS MAKES A DELICIOUS WINTERTIME ACCOMPANIMENT TO ANY GAME OR ROASTED DUCK DISH.

1 Preheat the oven to 350°F.

2 Bring 3 cups water to a boil in a medium, heavy saucepan. Add the wild rice, stir, and reduce the heat to low. Cover and simmer until the rice is just tender, about 35 minutes. (Wild rice can vary considerably in its cooking time.) Drain the rice, if necessary, and transfer it to a large bowl.

3 Meanwhile, bring 2 cups water to a boil in a heavy saucepan. Add the brown rice, stir, and reduce the heat to low. Cover tightly and simmer until the water is absorbed and the rice is just tender, about 20 minutes. Add the brown rice to the wild rice.

4 Add the currants, pine nuts, parsley, orange zest, orange juice, olive oil, salt, and pepper; toss to combine. Transfer to a large casserole dish.

5 Cover the casserole tightly with the lid or foil. Bake until the rice is soft but not mushy and the casserole is heated through, 20 to 30 minutes. Serve hot.

SERVES: 6 to 8

CHEF TIP: Toast the pine nuts in a small skillet over medium-low heat until just browned.

1 cup wild rice

1 cup brown rice

1 cup currants (or dried cranberries)

½ cup pine nuts, toasted

¼ cup chopped flat-leaf parsley

2 tablespoons grated orange zest

2 tablespoons fresh orange juice

¼ cup olive oil

Salt and freshly ground black pepper to taste

Lemon and Roasted Garlic Risotto

THE COMBINATION OF MUSHROOMS AND RISOTTO FLAVORED WITH LEMON AND ROASTED GARLIC IS HARD TO BEAT.

1 Bring the chicken stock to a simmer in a saucepan. Reduce heat to low.

2 In a separate large saucepan over medium heat, heat the olive oil and 2 tablespoons of the butter. Add the mushrooms and shallots and sauté for 3 to 4 minutes, stirring frequently. Add the rice and cook for 4 to 5 minutes, stirring continuously to coat the rice with the oil-butter mixture.

3 Carefully add the wine and lemon juice (it may steam up when poured into the hot pan) and simmer until it is nearly evaporated. Slowly add the heated stock ½ cup at a time, stirring until each addition of stock is absorbed into the rice before adding more. After 2 cups of stock have been added, taste the rice to see if it is cooked al dente (cooked completely through but slightly firm). If not, continue adding small amounts of stock until the rice is al dente. (You may not need all the stock.)

4 Add the goat cheese, roasted garlic, green onions, lemon zest, and the remaining 2 tablespoons butter; stir thoroughly. Season with pepper and remove from the heat.

5 To serve, place risotto in a large serving bowl. Spread halved cherry tomatoes on top.

SERVES: 6

CHEF TIP: To roast garlic, preheat the oven to 325°F. Cut ½ inch from the top of 1 or more heads of garlic, trimming just enough to expose the tips of the cloves. Remove any loose papery skin. Place the garlic on a sheet of foil, drizzle generously with olive oil and wrap tightly in the foil. Roast on a small baking sheet until tender when pierced, about 1 hour.

3½ cups hot chicken stock

¼ cup olive oil

4 tablespoons unsalted butter

1 cup chopped shiitake mushrooms

¼ cup chopped shallots

1 cup Arborio rice

¾ cup dry white wine

¼ cup fresh lemon juice

⅔ cup crumbled goat cheese

¼ cup roasted garlic (see Chef Tip)

¼ cup chopped green onions

1 tablespoon finely grated lemon zest

Freshly ground pepper

12 cherry tomatoes, halved, for garnish

Mélange of Roasted Root Vegetables with Herb Vinaigrette

THE VEGETABLES, ONCE PREPARED AND CUT TO THE PRESCRIBED SIZES, ALL ROAST IN THE SAME PAN FOR THE SAME LENGTH OF TIME. ONCE IN THE OVEN, THE DISH REQUIRES NO TENDING UNTIL THE VEGETABLES ARE DONE, SOME FORK TENDER, SOME SLIGHTLY CARAMELIZED.

1 Whisk together (or shake in a jar) the vinaigrette ingredients. Set aside.

2 Position racks in the upper and lower thirds of the oven and preheat the oven to 425°F. Spray 2 large baking sheets with vegetable oil.

3 In a large bowl whisk together the olive oil, thyme, and marjoram. Add the sweet potatoes, carrots, parsnips, rutabaga, and onions; toss to coat. Sprinkle vegetables generously with salt and pepper and divide between the baking sheets. Roast vegetables, turning occasionally, until tender and brown in spots, about 50 minutes. (Vegetables can be roasted 4 hours ahead. Let stand at room temperature. If desired, reheat in a 350°F oven for about 15 minutes, or microwave on high until heated through, about 6 minutes, before continuing.)

4 Drizzle the vinaigrette over the roasted vegetables. Sprinkle with chopped parsley and lemon zest. Season with more salt and pepper, if desired. Transfer to a platter and garnish with parsley sprigs. Serve hot or at room temperature.

SERVES: 10

Vinaigrette:

3 tablespoons balsamic vinegar

3 tablespoons extra virgin olive oil

1½ teaspoons chopped fresh thyme

1½ teaspoons chopped fresh marjoram

⅓ cup extra virgin olive oil

2 tablespoons chopped fresh thyme

2 tablespoons chopped fresh marjoram

2 pounds medium sweet potatoes, peeled, halved lengthwise, then cut crosswise into 1¼ to 1½-inch pieces

1½ pounds carrots, peeled, cut into ¾-inch rounds (about 4 cups)

1½ pounds parsnips, peeled, cut into ¾-inch rounds (about 4 cups)

1½ pounds rutabaga, peeled, cut into ½-inch pieces (about 4 cups)

2 medium red onions (about 1 pound), peeled, root ends left intact, cut into ½-inch wedges

Salt and pepper to taste

3 tablespoons chopped fresh parsley

2 teaspoons grated lemon zest

Fresh parsley sprigs for garnish

Vegetable Kabobs with Balsamic Vinegar Toss

THE FRESH TASTE OF THE HERBS IN THE VINAIGRETTE THAT COATS THE VEGETABLES REALLY COMES THROUGH. SIMPLY DELECTABLE.

1 Soak bamboo skewers in water for at least 1 hour to prevent burning on grill.

2 If using potatoes, parboil them for 10 minutes; drain. Slice or chop all the vegetables into bite-sized pieces and transfer to a bowl.

3 Whisk together (or shake in a jar) all the vinaigrette ingredients. Pour over the vegetables and toss. Thread the vegetables onto the skewers, leaving a few inches empty at each end. Grill (or broil) the kabobs, turning occasionally to prevent burning, until the peppers are slightly charred and the potatoes are easily pierced with a knife.

SERVES: 12

CHEF TIP: Instead of skewering the vegetables, you may grill them in a grill basket or roast them in a large shallow roasting pan at 450°F for about 20 minutes.

1 dozen (12-inch) bamboo skewers

3 pounds vegetables of choice such as red, yellow, and orange bell peppers, zucchini, halved red potatoes, mushrooms, shallots

Vinaigrette:

3 tablespoons balsamic vinegar

3 tablespoons olive oil

1 clove garlic, crushed

1 tablespoon chopped fresh rosemary

1 tablespoon chopped fresh thyme

1 tablespoon chopped fresh basil

Salt and pepper to taste

Macaroni with Five Cheeses

COMFORT FOOD AT ITS BEST. YOUR WHOLE FAMILY WILL LOVE THIS.

1 Preheat the oven to 350°F. Lightly butter a deep 2½-quart casserole dish.

2 Bring a large pot of salted water to a boil. Add the oil, then the elbow macaroni; cook until the macaroni is just tender, about 7 minutes. Do not overcook. Drain well and return to the pot. Melt ½ cup of the butter; stir into the macaroni.

3 Mix together the Muenster, mild and sharp cheddar, and Monterey Jack cheeses. To the macaroni add 1½ cups of the shredded cheeses, the processed cheese, half-and-half, eggs, parsley, salt, and pepper. Stir well and transfer to the casserole dish. Sprinkle with the remaining shredded cheeses. Sprinkle with the bread crumbs and dot with the remaining 2 tablespoons of butter.

4 Bake until bubbling around the edges, about 35 minutes. Serve hot.

SERVES: 6

CHEF TIP: For a festive look, add chopped red and green bell peppers, chopped ripe tomatoes, or finely chopped sun-dried tomatoes.

1 tablespoon vegetable oil

1 pound elbow macaroni

½ cup (1 stick) plus 2 tablespoons unsalted butter

½ cup shredded Muenster cheese

½ cup shredded mild cheddar cheese

½ cup shredded sharp cheddar cheese

½ cup shredded Monterey Jack cheese

8 ounces American processed cheese (preferably Velveeta), cut into small cubes

2 cups half-and-half

2 large eggs, lightly beaten

2 tablespoons finely chopped fresh parsley

¼ teaspoon salt

⅛ teaspoon pepper

⅓ cup dry bread crumbs

Caramelized Onion and Tomato Galette

THIS GALETTE COULD BE A MAIN COURSE AT LUNCH OR DINNER FOR VEGETARIANS. YOU CAN ALSO CUT IT INTO WEDGES AND SERVE IT ALONGSIDE ROASTED CHICKEN.

1 In a large, heavy, dry saucepan, cook the onions and thyme over medium heat, stirring once or twice, until the onions start to turn golden brown, about 15 minutes. Add 3 tablespoons of the oil, reduce the heat to low, cover and cook, scraping the pan every 10 minutes, until the onions are browned, about 1 hour. Season with salt, pepper, and 2 teaspoons of the fresh rosemary (or all of the dried rosemary). Remove from the heat and discard the thyme sprigs. Let cool for at least 20 minutes.

2 Preheat the oven to 400°F.

3 On a lightly floured cookie sheet, roll out the pie dough into a 14-inch round. Spread the onions over the dough, leaving a 2-inch border. Sprinkle with the Gorgonzola, then arrange the tomatoes in rings (overlap sliced tomatoes) over the cheese. Season with salt and pepper and drizzle with the remaining 1 tablespoon oil. Fold edge of pastry up and over to create a border. Pleat the border using your thumb and forefinger about every inch. Brush the pastry with the egg.

4 Bake the galette until the crust is golden brown, about 35 minutes. Sprinkle the remaining 1 teaspoon fresh rosemary over the top and serve hot or warm.

SERVES: 10

CHEF TIP: You may use a purchased puff pastry or ready-made dough in place of the homemade pie dough.

PIE DOUGH

1 In a bowl, toss the flour with the salt and sugar. With a pastry blender or using your fingers, cut in the butter until the mixture resembles coarse meal and some of the butter is the size of small peas. Using a fork, stir in the ice water by tablespoons, until the dough holds together when pressed. Sprinkle in more water by the teaspoon if needed. Flatten the dough into a disk, wrap well and refrigerate for 15 minutes before rolling out.

2½ pounds yellow onions, coarsely chopped

6 fresh thyme sprigs (or 2 pinches of dried thyme)

4 tablespoons olive oil

Salt and freshly ground pepper

3 teaspoons minced fresh rosemary (or 1 teaspoon crumbled dried)

Pie dough (recipe below)

3 ounces Gorgonzola cheese, crumbled

1 pound large cherry tomatoes or plum tomatoes sliced crosswise ⅓-inch thick

1 large egg, beaten

1½ cups all-purpose flour

½ teaspoon salt

½ teaspoon sugar

½ cup (1 stick) plus 1 tablespoon cold unsalted butter, cut into pieces

About ¼ cup ice water

Goat Cheese and Potato Pie
(Tarte au Fromage de Chèvre et aux Pommes de Terre)

THIS SAVORY TART OF THE FRENCH COUNTRYSIDE IS A SUITABLE FIRST COURSE FOR A MULTI-COURSE TRADITIONAL FRENCH DINNER.

NEW ALBANY CHILDREN'S BALLET THEATRE

Could any item be more symbolic of a little girl's childhood than a pink tutu? Perhaps not, and that could be why the New Albany Children's Ballet Theatre (NACBT) has been so successful in its mission to be a catalyst for the arts in New Albany. As the community has grown with young families, the number of children involved in athletic and artistic activities has literally grown by leaps and bounds.

The New Albany Children's Ballet Theatre was established as a non-profit organization in 2001. Its mission is to create an environment where children can learn the value of artistic expression and experience dancing in professional venues. At the same time, the theater strives to maintain the affordability of the experience.

Every December the group presents *Babes in Toyland*. Several hundred dancers of different ages participate in this wonderful production, which has become a cherished holiday tradition for many families. The dancers are excited to perform the classic piece in a professional environment after months of hard work and training. The fruition of their efforts draws a full house and serves as a spirited kickoff to the holiday season.

— *Hinson Ltd.*

1 Preheat the oven to 350°F.

2 On a floured surface, roll out the pastry to ¼ inch thickness. Using a bench scraper, lift the dough onto the rolling pin. Keep rolling the dough over the pin and unroll it evenly onto a 12-inch tart pan with removable bottom. Ease the dough into the corners of the pan and press the dough into the sides. Trim the overhang. Line the tart shell with wax paper and fill with pie weights. Bake for 12 minutes, or until golden brown. Remove the wax paper and pie weights and let the shell cool on a rack.

1 recipe *pâte brisée* (recipe below)

1 pound Yukon gold potatoes (3 to 4 medium)

Salt and pepper to taste

¾ to 1 cup whipping cream

1 (10-ounce) log mild aged goat cheese, chilled

½ cup diced shallots

1 tablespoon minced fresh parsley

COURTESY LORN SPOLTER

NACBT's Babes in Toyland *production*

3 Meanwhile, put the potatoes in a saucepan and add enough cold water to cover; bring to a boil and boil for 20 minutes or until a skewer slides through them but meets little resistance. Drain; peel potatoes when cool enough to handle. Coarsely chop the potatoes and spread them in a gratin dish; season with salt and pepper and add ¾ cup of the cream. Bake for 10 minutes. Let cool. (Potatoes can be made 2 hours ahead. Let stand at room temperature.)

4 Reheat the oven to 350°F.

5 Cut 9 slices, about ¼ inch thick, from the log of goat cheese and crumble the rest over the potatoes. Add the shallots and parsley. Mix everything with a fork to break up the bigger pieces. Thin with the remaining cream; the mixture should be moist.

6 Fill the pie crust with the potato mixture. Arrange the slices of goat cheese over the filling, evenly spacing them in a circle and placing one in the center for presentation.

7 Bake for 10 minutes, just enough to melt the cheese and brown the surface.

SERVES: 6 to 8

CHEF TIP: You may substitute a variety of soft cheeses for the goat cheese. Try Brie, Camembert, or Roquefort.

Pastry Dough with Egg (*Pâte Brisée à l'Oeuf*)

1 Put the flour, salt, butter, and egg in a food processor. Pulse until evenly mixed, about 30 seconds; do not over-process. With the machine running, drizzle in the water until the dough comes away from the side of the bowl.

2 Turn the dough out onto a clean surface. Roll into a flat disk. It should be smooth to the touch; if not, drizzle with 2 teaspoons cold water and knead until the dough is smooth. Wrap in plastic wrap, flattening it a little, and refrigerate for at least 1 hour before using.

CHEF TIP: Dough will keep 3 weeks in the refrigerator, 6 months in the freezer.

2¼ cups all-purpose flour, unsifted

Pinch of salt

1 tablespoon butter

1 egg, lightly beaten

2 tablespoons cold water

Elsa's Smoked Ham and Vegetable Quiche

THIS JOHANSSON FAMILY TREASURE IS A COMPLETE MEAL IN ITSELF. PAIR THIS WITH A SIMPLE SALAD AND TAKE TO A NEIGHBOR OR FRIEND IN NEED—A CONTEMPORARY ALTERNATIVE TO TRADITIONAL CASSEROLE DINNERS.

1 To make the pastry, in a bowl, combine the flour and the butter. With a pastry blender or using your fingers, cut in the butter until the mixture resembles coarse meal and some of the butter is the size of small peas. Using a fork, stir in the ice water by tablespoons, until the dough holds together when pressed. Sprinkle in more water by the teaspoon if needed. Flatten the dough into a disk, wrap well and refrigerate for at least 1 hour.

2 Preheat the oven to 400°F.

3 Boil the green onions and leeks for 5 minutes in lightly salted water; drain.

4 On a lightly floured surface, roll out the pastry to a 12-inch circle and fit it into a 10-inch quiche or pie dish. Trim the overhang. Line the shell with wax paper and fill with pie weights. Bake for 10 minutes. Remove the wax paper and weights. Sprinkle 3 tablespoons of the shredded cheese over the bottom of the crust. Evenly spread the green onions and leeks over the cheese. Top with the ham.

5 Whisk together the egg, cream, salt, and pepper. Pour over the filling. Bake for 35 minutes, covering loosely with foil after 15 minutes to prevent the crust from burning. Sprinkle the remaining cheese over the quiche and serve warm.

SERVES: 4

CHEF TIP: Smoked ham can be replaced with cooked chicken, diced mushrooms, or corn.

Pastry:

1½ cups all-purpose flour

1½ sticks butter (12 tablespoons), cut into pieces

3 tablespoons ice water plus more as needed

Filling:

¾ pound green onions (about 3 bunches), sliced into 1-inch pieces

¾ pound leeks (about 2 medium), rinsed well and sliced into 1-inch pieces

1 cup shredded Swiss cheese

1 cup smoked ham cut into ½-inch cubes (½ pound)

1 large egg

¾ cup whipping cream

Salt and pepper to taste

Main Courses

G.W. ACOCKOS

Market Square community event

Support of a Vibrant Community Center

NEW Albany's central location has contributed to the rapid growth of the community's commercial sector, which includes a good mix of large corporations, service companies, and locally owned boutique enterprises. New Albany is located in Franklin County, Ohio, just 15 minutes northeast of Columbus, the state capital, and it takes less than 20 minutes to commute to downtown Columbus, drive to Port Columbus International Airport, or get to Rickenbacker Air Freight Port.

New Albany Business Campuses were designed to promote economic development with easy access to highways, state-of-the art technology infrastructure, and surrounding wooded areas, meadows, and leisure trails. Office facilities are ready for additional tenants, and further expansion is planned to accommodate technical parks, medical providers, research institutes, offices, and distribution centers. Today, New Albany's Business Campuses house several large corporations, including Abercrombie & Fitch, Tween Brands, Discover Financial Services, State Farm, Aetna, U.S. Healthcare, and American Electric Power.

Residents of New Albany benefit from the community's proximity to Easton Town Center and Polaris Fashion Center, huge shopping, dining, and entertainment complexes just 10 minutes away. But the real New Albany shopping experience happens in Market Square, located in the village center, where a cluster of boutique shops, small offices, and restaurants serve residents, employees, and visitors. Leisure shoppers enjoy the quiet pace, personal attention from local shop owners, unique products, and convenient parking.

New Albany's village center is also a place where neighbors shop, socialize, and conduct business. There are a number of casual dining spots where the community can gather, such as Rusty Bucket, Chocolate Octopus, Gibby's New Albany Grill, Starbucks, and, a longtime favorite, Eagles Villa Pizza. Each summer the Chamber of Commerce encourages exploration of the area's food establishments. It sponsors "Taste of New Albany," during which residents can sample offerings from 30 restaurants while enjoying a performance by the New Albany Classic Signature Series' presentation of the Columbus Jazz Orchestra.

Local government agencies, businesses, non-profits, and residents have a shared vision for New Albany's future. Their vision includes a vibrant community with strong economic, cultural, and social services accessible to all its residents, employees, and visitors.

— *Diane Forrest LaHowchic*

Citrus Angel Hair Pasta with Mint 163

Baked Pasta Supreme 164

Baked Scallops with Garlic and Shallots 165

Greek Shrimp with Feta 166

Shrimp Étouffée 167

Thai Fried Noodles *(Pad Thai)* 168

Magdalena's Salmon with Capers 169

Poached Salmon with Cucumber Mayonnaise 170

Sole Meunière with Browned Butter Caper Sauce 171

Mediterranean Seafood Stew 172

Grilled Chicken Paillards with
Creamy Mustard Sauce 173

Grilled Chicken Provençal 174

Grilled Plum Chicken 175

Kung Pao Chicken 176

Chicken with Snow Peas 177

Chicken Clemenceau 178

Chicken Sautéed with Curried Pear Sauce 179

Chicken Paprikash 180

Chicken Adobo *(Adobong Manok)* 181

Chicken Mediterranean *(Pollo Mediterraneo)* 182

Deep-fried Turkey 183

Black Pepper and Herb-crusted Rack of Lamb 184

Beef Tenderloin with Mustard Peppercorn Sauce 185

Grilled Beef Tenderloin with Oriental Seasonings 186

Flank Steak with Papaya-Kiwi Marinade 187

Grilled Flank Steak with Far East Seasonings 188

Stuffed Flank Steak 189

Rolled Stuffed Beef, Calabrian Style
(Braciole di Manzo alla Calabrese) 190

Korean Barbecued Beef with
Asian Pear Dipping Sauce *(Bulgogi)* 191

Fragrant Beef Curry 193

Malaysian Beef Stew *(Rendang)* 194

Moroccan Meat-filled Phyllo Pastry
(Briouat Bil Kefta) 195

Veal Braciola 196

Osso Buco (Braised Veal Shanks) 197

Barbecued Ribs with Spicy Lime Sauce 198

Stir-fried Bean Curd and Pork *(Ma-Po Tofu)* 199

Cantonese Pork Tenderloin *(Char Siu)* 200

Pork Medallions in Crème Fraiche 201

Pork Tenderloin in Baguette *(Porc en Baguette)* 202

Pork Tenderloin with Shallot Sauce 203

Spicy Grilled Pork Tenderloin 204

Rum-glazed Smoked Easter Ham 204

Citrus Angel Hair Pasta with Mint

THIS RECIPE IS ADAPTED BY SHERYL ZANGARDI FROM TRATTORIA GARGA, HER FAVORITE TRATTORIA IN FLORENCE, ITALY. IT IS ESPECIALLY ELEGANT WHEN GARNISHED WITH A PEACH-COLORED ROSE.

1 In a heavy skillet over medium heat, combine the cream, lemon and orange zests, and salt. Cook, stirring frequently, until slightly thickened, about 2 minutes. Add the cognac and mint. Cook, stirring occasionally, another 3 minutes.

2 Bring a large pot of salted water to boil. Add pasta and cook until just tender but still firm to the bite, 2 to 4 minutes; drain. Add pasta to the cream mixture and cook for 3 to 4 minutes. Stir in the Parmesan cheese. Serve immediately.

SERVES: 4

CHEF TIP: Italian grocers almost always have fresh pasta in the freezer section of the grocery.

2 cups whipping cream

Grated zest of 1 lemon

Grated zest of 1 orange

Pinch of salt

2 tablespoons cognac or fresh orange juice

2 tablespoons minced fresh mint

1 pound fresh angel hair pasta

1 cup coarsely grated Parmesan cheese

New Albany residence

Baked Pasta Supreme

A HEARTY PASTA DISH. SERVE A GREEN SALAD AFTER THE PASTA AND YOU HAVE A COMPLETE MEAL.

1 Preheat the oven to 375°F. Butter a 4-quart baking dish.

2 In a large (at least 12-inch) skillet, heat the olive oil over medium heat. Sauté the onion, garlic, basil, oregano, and red pepper flakes until the onion is softened. Add the mushrooms; cook, stirring occasionally, until the mushrooms are tender, 10 to 12 minutes. Transfer the mushroom mixture to a large bowl.

3 In the same skillet, melt 3 tablespoons of the butter over medium-low heat. Whisk in the flour and cook, stirring, for 3 minutes. Slowly add the milk, whisking for 2 minutes or until sauce is thickened. Pour over the mushroom mixture; add the tomatoes, prosciutto, fontina, Gorgonzola, 1¼ cups of the Parmesan, and the parsley. Stir gently.

4 In a large pot of boiling salted water, cook the pasta for 5 minutes; drain well. (The pasta will not be tender.) Add the pasta to the mushroom mixture and combine well. Adjust seasonings. (The pasta can be made ahead to this point; cover and refrigerate overnight. Bring to room temperature before continuing.)

5 Sprinkle pasta mixture with the remaining ¼ cup Parmesan cheese and dot with the remaining 1 tablespoon butter. Bake, uncovered, 25 to 30 minutes or until the top is golden and the pasta is tender.

SERVES: 8 to 10

2 tablespoons olive oil

2 cups finely chopped onion

2 large cloves garlic, minced

1 teaspoon dried basil, crumbled

1 teaspoon dried oregano, crumbled

¼ teaspoon dried hot red pepper flakes, or to taste

1 pound shiitake mushrooms, stems discarded and caps sliced

4 tablespoons unsalted butter

3 tablespoons all-purpose flour

2 cups milk

2 (28-ounce) cans Italian tomatoes, drained well and chopped

¼ pound thinly sliced prosciutto, cut into thin strips

1 cup shredded fontina cheese

1 cup crumbled Gorgonzola cheese

1½ cups freshly grated Parmesan cheese

⅔ cup minced fresh parsley

1 pound farfalle*

*bow-tie or butterfly-shaped pasta

Baked Scallops with Garlic and Shallots

THESE DELICIOUS BAKED SCALLOPS LITERALLY TAKE MINUTES TO PREPARE.

1 Preheat the oven to 425°F.

2 In a large bowl toss the scallops with the melted butter, garlic, shallots, nutmeg, salt, and pepper. Transfer to a 2-quart baking dish and distribute the scallops evenly in the dish. Stir together the oil and bread crumbs and sprinkle the crumbs all over the scallops. Bake for 12 to 15 minutes or until the bread crumbs are deep golden and the scallops are opaque.

3 Serve with a green salad for a complete meal.

SERVES: 4 to 6

2 pounds sea scallops

4 tablespoons butter, melted

3 cloves garlic, minced

2 shallots, chopped

½ teaspoon freshly grated nutmeg

Salt and freshly ground pepper to taste

3 tablespoons extra virgin olive oil

1 cup seasoned dry Italian bread crumbs

½ cup minced fresh parsley

NEW ALBANY CLASSIC SIGNATURE SERIES PHOTOS
COURTESY DANIEL W. FLOSS & ASSOCIATES PHOTOGRAPHY

Market Day at Market Square

Greek Shrimp with Feta

This colorful and flavorful Mediterranean entrée has been part of Diane Forrest LaHowchic's dinner repertoire for years and it is always a crowd pleaser. Served with salad and bread, it makes a lovely meal. You have the option of spooning the shrimp onto a bed of rice or orzo, or just using crusty bread to soak up the juice.

1 In a medium skillet over low heat, heat 2 tablespoons of the olive oil. Cook the onion until it is soft but not browned. Add the tomatoes, parsley, wine, garlic, salt, and pepper; stir. Cook, uncovered and stirring occasionally, until the sauce is thickened, about 25 minutes.

2 Meanwhile, preheat the oven to 400°F.

3 In another skillet, heat the remaining 3 tablespoons oil over medium-high heat. Sauté the shrimp until they are almost pink, turning once, 2 to 3 minutes; do not overcook. Add the lemon juice and toss.

4 Spread the shrimp in a 12 by 9-inch baking pan. Top with the onion mixture. Crumble the feta cheese over the sauce. (The shrimp can be prepared to this point one day ahead. Let cool, cover and refrigerate overnight. Let stand at room temperature for about 10 minutes before baking.)

5 Bake until the cheese is bubbly, about 10 minutes. Serve over rice or pasta.

SERVES: 4 to 6

5 tablespoons olive oil

1 medium onion, chopped

1 (14½-ounce) can stewed tomatoes

⅓ cup chopped fresh parsley

⅓ cup white wine

1 clove garlic, minced

Salt and pepper to taste

2 pounds medium shrimp (31 to 35 per pound), peeled and deveined

2 tablespoons lemon juice

4 ounces feta cheese

Shrimp Étouffée

You NEED NOT GO TO NEW ORLEANS TO SAVOR THIS CAJUN SPECIALTY.

1 Thoroughly combine the seasoning mix ingredients in a small bowl and set aside. In a separate bowl, combine the onions, celery, and bell pepper.

2 In a large, heavy skillet (preferably cast iron), heat the oil over high heat until it begins to smoke, about 4 minutes. With a long-handled metal whisk, gradually stir in the flour, stirring until smooth. Continue cooking, whisking constantly, until the roux is dark red-brown, 3 to 5 minutes. (Be careful not to let it scorch in the pan.) Remove from the heat and, using a wooden spoon, immediately stir in the vegetables and 1 tablespoon of the seasoning mix. Continue stirring until cooled, about 5 minutes.

3 In a large saucepan bring 2 cups of the stock to a boil over high heat. Gradually add the roux mixture and whisk until the roux is thoroughly dissolved. Reduce heat to low and cook until the flour taste is gone, about 2 minutes, whisking almost constantly. (If any of the mixture scorches, don't continue to scrape that part of the pan bottom.) Remove from the heat.

4 Heat the serving plates in a 250°F oven.

5 In a 4-quart saucepan, melt 1 stick of the butter over medium heat. Stir in the shrimp and green onions and sauté about 1 minute, stirring constantly. Add the remaining stick of butter, the stock mixture, and the remaining 1 cup stock. Cook until the butter melts and is mixed into the sauce, 4 to 6 minutes, constantly shaking the pan in a back and forth motion (instead of stirring). Add the remaining seasoning mix, stir well and remove from the heat. If at any point the sauce starts separating, add 2 tablespoons more stock or water and shake the pan until it combines. Serve immediately over cooked rice.

SERVES: 8

Seasoning Mix:

2 teaspoons salt

2 teaspoons cayenne

1 teaspoon white pepper

1 teaspoon black pepper

1 teaspoon crumbled dried sweet basil

½ teaspoon dried thyme

¼ cup chopped onions

¼ cup chopped celery

¼ cup chopped green bell pepper

½ cup vegetable oil

¾ cup all-purpose flour

3 cups fish stock

½ pound (2 sticks) unsalted butter

2 pounds medium shrimp (31 to 35 per pound), peeled and deveined

1 cup very thinly sliced green onions

4 cups hot cooked rice

Thai Fried Noodles (Pad Thai)

ONE OF THE BEST-KNOWN THAI DISHES, THIS SHRIMP AND RICE-NOODLE DISH IS USUALLY SERVED FOR LUNCHEON, MIDDAY SNACK, OR AS A LATE SUPPER. IT IS A MEAL-IN-ONE AND NEEDS NO ACCOMPANIMENT.

1 Soak the noodles in lukewarm water for 40 minutes to 1 hour, or until the noodles are limp but still firm to the touch. Drain and set aside.

2 Meanwhile, in boiling water, blanch the bean sprouts for 30 seconds. Refresh under cold water. Drain and set aside.

3 Heat the oil in a large wok over high heat. Fry the garlic and shallots until golden. Stir in the shrimp powder, then add the shrimp; stir-fry until opaque, just a minute or two. Add the fish sauce, vinegar, sugar, ketchup, and chili powder. Stir until the sugar dissolves. Pour the beaten eggs over the other ingredients and let them set slightly, then stir to scramble. Add the noodles and stir well to evenly coat noodles. If the noodles are still too firm to your liking, sprinkle 1 to 2 tablespoons of water over them to help cook. Taste and adjust flavors as needed to your liking by adding more fish sauce and/or sugar.

4 Spoon the Pad Thai onto a platter. Sprinkle with the peanuts, chili flakes, green onions, and cilantro. Arrange lime wedges around the edge of the platter. Put the bean sprouts and cucumber slices in separate bowls and serve with the Pad Thai.

SERVES: 6

CHEF TIPS: You can prepare the sauce and cook the shrimp ahead of time. Combine with the drained noodles at serving time.

Use shredded pork or chicken or a combination of both in place of the shrimp.

1 pound dried flat rice noodles (also labeled Pad Thai noodles in Asian markets)

2 cups fresh bean sprouts, rinsed

⅔ cup vegetable or peanut oil

2 tablespoons minced garlic

½ cup minced shallots

1 tablespoon shrimp powder or shrimp paste (optional)

20 medium shrimp, peeled, deveined, and butterflied

5 tablespoons fish sauce (nam pla)*

2 tablespoons rice vinegar

¼ cup light brown sugar

5 tablespoons ketchup

½ to 1 teaspoon chili powder (optional)

5 eggs, lightly beaten

*available at Asian groceries or in the ethnic section of large supermarkets

Garnishes:

⅔ cup coarsely ground unsalted peanuts

½ teaspoon red pepper flakes (optional)

4 green onions, thinly sliced

2 tablespoons chopped fresh cilantro

3 limes, cut into wedges

1 large cucumber, sliced

Magdalena's Salmon with Capers

Kim Tarnapoll got hold of this recipe from a friend in Connecticut. Magdalena's family hailed from Venice, and a distant uncle was a Pope. They still have family properties in Rome and on the canals of Venice. Her grandfather opened international shipping offices for Cunard in the early 1900s and while in Chile met his soon-to-be wife. Magdalena came to Connecticut from Santiago speaking only Spanish and Italian. This is a recipe she concocted.

1   Preheat the oven to 350°F. Dot the bottom of a 13 by 9-inch baking pan with half of the butter. Place the salmon in the pan and dot with the remaining butter.

2   In a measuring cup mix the wine, vinegar, and lemon juice. Pour over the salmon. Arrange the onion slices over the salmon, then sprinkle with salt, pepper, and capers.

3   Bake, uncovered, for 30 to 40 minutes, or until the juice is boiling and the salmon is cooked through and browned.

4   Serve with rice or spicy lentils and garnish with lemon wedges.

SERVES: 6

CHEF TIP: It is better to err on having more liquid than less in the pan. Just add more of the liquid ingredients directly to the pan, if needed. For variety, serve the dish with a dill sauce.

3 tablespoons unsalted butter

6 (5-ounce) skinless salmon fillets

½ cup white wine

3 tablespoons white vinegar

Juice of 2 lemons

1 large yellow onion, thinly sliced

Salt and pepper to taste

1 (6-ounce) jar capers, drained

Lemon wedges for garnish

Poached Salmon with Cucumber Mayonnaise

THIS ELEGANT, PORTABLE ENTRÉE IS PERFECT FOR A PICNIC OR A SUMMER GARDEN LUNCH.

1   Pour about 2 quarts water into a roasting pan or fish poacher large enough to hold the salmon. Add the bay leaves, lemon, celery, onion, oil, salt, and pepper; bring to a boil.

2   Add the salmon, reduce heat to a simmer, and poach salmon, uncovered, about 20 minutes or until the fish flakes easily when pierced with a fork. Cool the salmon to room temperature in the poaching liquid.

3   Drain the salmon on paper towels, then chill for at least 4 hours. Garnish with watercress and serve with Cucumber Mayonnaise.

SERVES: 8

CHEF TIP: You may add ¼ cup white wine to the poaching liquid for a more robust flavor.

4 bay leaves

1 lemon, sliced

4 stalks celery, chopped

1 large onion, sliced

¼ teaspoon vegetable oil

1 teaspoon salt

¼ teaspoon pepper

8 (6-ounce) center-cut skinless salmon fillets

Watercress sprigs for garnish

Cucumber Mayonnaise (recipe follows)

CUCUMBER MAYONNAISE

1   Stir together the mayonnaise, lemon juice, Tabasco, and curry powder. Drain the cucumber and combine with mayonnaise mixture. Chill for several hours before serving.

1 cup mayonnaise (or ½ cup mayonnaise and ½ cup sour cream)

3 tablespoons fresh lemon juice

Dash of Tabasco sauce

¼ teaspoon curry powder

½ cup cucumber, diced and drained

Sole Meunière with Browned Butter Caper Sauce

"*Meunière*" means miller's wife and refers to the technique of dusting a food with flour before sautéing it. This is the classic version with a slight twist—we've added capers to the recipe. This dish is simple but elegant fare.

1 Put the flour on a plate. Season the fillets with salt and pepper, then dredge them in the flour.

2 Melt 2 tablespoons of the butter in each of 2 large sauté pans over medium-high heat. Sauté the fish until light golden brown on each side, 2 to 3 minutes per side. Transfer the fillets to a platter; sprinkle with parsley and cover loosely with foil.

3 Pour the butter from one of the skillets into the other; add the remaining 2 tablespoons butter. Heat over medium-high heat until the butter begins to foam and turn light brown. Remove from the heat and stir in the lemon juice and capers. Pour sauce over fish and serve immediately.

SERVES: 4

½ cup all-purpose flour

4 (8-ounce) sole fillets

Salt and freshly ground white pepper

6 tablespoons butter

¼ cup finely chopped parsley

Juice of 1 lemon

1½ tablespoons drained brined capers

New Albany winter scene

Mediterranean Seafood Stew

Patrice Douglas's robust stew gets a little kick from red pepper flakes, which you can adjust to your liking.

1 In a stockpot, heat the oil over medium-high heat. Add the garlic, onion, and red pepper flakes. Sauté until the onion is translucent, 5 minutes. Add the stock, wine, tomatoes, tomato paste, sugar, oregano, basil, bay leaf, and potato. Bring to a boil, reduce the heat, cover and simmer, stirring occasionally, until the soup is thick but still fairly liquid, about 30 minutes. Season with salt and pepper.

2 Discard any clams that are cracked or open. Add the clams to the pot along with the fish and shrimp. Raise the heat slightly, cover and cook until the fish flakes, the shrimp turn pink, and the clams open, 7 to 10 minutes. Discard any clams that do not open during cooking. Discard the bay leaf. Serve hot.

SERVES: 8

2 tablespoons olive oil

2 cloves garlic, finely chopped

1 yellow onion, finely chopped

1 teaspoon red pepper flakes

1 cup fish stock or clam juice

¼ cup dry red wine

2 (14.5-ounce) cans Italian-style chopped tomatoes

2 tablespoons tomato paste

1½ tablespoons sugar

1 teaspoon crumbled dried oregano

1 teaspoon crumbled dried basil

1 bay leaf

1 large baking potato (about ¾ pound), peeled and cut into ½-inch pieces

Salt and pepper to taste

12 small clams or mussels, well scrubbed, de-bearded if using mussels

½ pound tuna, salmon, or sea bass, cut into 1-inch cubes

½ pound shrimp, peeled and deveined

Grilled Chicken Paillards with Creamy Mustard Sauce

Serve this with the Warm Spinach Salad on page 113, which uses the same dressing, and save time on meal preparation.

1. In a medium saucepan, combine all the sauce ingredients. Place over medium heat and simmer, stirring occasionally, for 15 to 20 minutes. Remove from the heat and whisk for 1 to 2 minutes or until the sauce begins to thicken. Taste and adjust the seasoning if necessary. Set aside and keep warm.

2. Cut each chicken breast crosswise into 2 equal parts. Using the smooth side of a meat pounder, gently pound each piece to a ¼-inch thickness. Brush each paillard with olive oil and season with salt and pepper. (If not using immediately, cover and refrigerate. Remove the chicken from the refrigerator 30 minutes before grilling.)

3. Preheat the grill to medium. Grill the chicken for 2 to 3 minutes on each side. Pool 3 tablespoons of the mustard sauce on each plate and arrange paillard on top. Serve at once.

SERVES: 8

Creamy Mustard Sauce:

2 cups whipping cream

3 tablespoons minced fresh basil

3 tablespoons Dijon mustard

1 tablespoon Worcestershire sauce

¼ teaspoon salt

¼ teaspoon black pepper

Chicken:

4 boneless skinless chicken breasts (about 2 pounds)

2 to 3 tablespoons olive oil

Salt and pepper

Grilled Chicken Provençal

THIS GRILLING FAVORITE CAN EASILY BE DOUBLED OR TRIPLED TO SERVE A LARGE CROWD.

1 Combine the mustard, vinegar, lemon juice, garlic, and herbes de Provence; whisk in the olive oil until well blended. Put the chicken in a 1-gallon resealable plastic bag and add the marinade. Marinate in the refrigerator for about 4 hours, turning the chicken several times to coat all sides. Bring the chicken to room temperature before grilling.

2 Preheat the grill. Grill the chicken on both sides, about 15 minutes in all, until no longer pink inside but still moist and tender. Serve immediately or at room temperature—it is delicious either way—garnished with the rosemary and lemon.

SERVES: 6

2 to 3 pounds boneless skinless chicken breasts

Fresh rosemary sprigs and lemon slices for garnish

Marinade:

½ cup Dijon mustard

¼ cup balsamic vinegar

¼ cup freshly squeezed lemon juice

6 cloves garlic, minced or pressed

2 tablespoons herbes de Provence

½ cup olive oil

New Albany Fourth of July Celebration

Grilled Plum Chicken

A VERY EASY DISH TO PREPARE FOR THE WEEKNIGHT MEAL.

1 Place the chicken in a shallow nonreactive dish.

2 In small bowl, combine the vinegar, mustard, salt, and pepper. Gradually whisk in the oil. Pour over the chicken. Cover and refrigerate for at least 6 hours or overnight.

3 Preheat the grill to high. Grill the chicken on both sides, about 12 minutes in all, until chicken springs back when touched. Brush each chicken breast with plum sauce and grill 1 minute more.

4 Serve warm with steamed rice and stir-fried vegetables.

SERVES: 4 to 6

2 pounds boneless skinless chicken breasts

2 tablespoons balsamic vinegar

2 teaspoons Dijon mustard

½ teaspoon salt

⅛ teaspoon coarsely ground black pepper

⅓ cup olive oil

½ cup plum sauce*

*plum sauce is available in jars in the Asian section of the supermarket

New Albany on a spring day

COURTESY TIM FABER

Kung Pao Chicken

A CHINESE CLASSIC BEST EATEN WITH STEAMED RICE. THIS TAKE-OUT STAPLE IS TYPICALLY FLAMING HOT; FEEL FREE TO NOTCH IT UP WITH THE CHILI SAUCE.

1 In a medium bowl, stir together all the marinade ingredients. Add the chicken pieces and stir to coat well.

2 Heat 2 tablespoons of the oil in a wok over medium-high heat. Swirl the oil around the pan. Toss in the pepper squares and water chestnuts. Stir-fry until the pepper is tender but still crispy. Remove from the pan and set aside.

3 Heat the remaining 3 tablespoons oil in the wok. Toss in the ginger. Stir-fry until lightly browned. Add the garlic and green onion; stir-fry briefly. Add the marinated chicken. Stir-fry until the chicken is cooked through.

4 Return the green peppers and water chestnuts to the wok. Add the hoisin sauce, chili sauce, and the cornstarch mixture. Stir-fry until the ingredients are well mixed and the sauce is thickened and translucent. Add peanuts and toss to mix. Serve immediately.

SERVES: 4

Marinade:

1 tablespoon dry sherry

2 teaspoons soy sauce

1 teaspoon cornstarch

½ teaspoon salt

¼ teaspoon pepper

1 egg white, lightly beaten

4 boneless skinless chicken breasts (about 2 pounds), cut into bite-sized pieces

5 tablespoons peanut or canola oil

1 green bell pepper, cut into ½-inch squares

1 (8-ounce) can sliced water chestnuts, drained

1-inch piece peeled fresh ginger, julienned

1 clove garlic, minced

1 green onion, sliced

½ cup hoisin sauce

1 teaspoon Chinese chili sauce

2 teaspoons cornstarch dissolved in 2 tablespoons water

¾ cup roasted skinless peanuts

Chicken with Snow Peas

THIS CLASSIC CHINESE STIR-FRY CAN EASILY BE TURNED INTO A VEGETARIAN DISH BY SUBSTITUTING BITE-SIZED CUBES OF FRIED TOFU FOR THE CHICKEN.

1   Trim the snow peas by cutting the tips from both ends of the pod and pulling away the string that runs the length of the peas. Blanch the snow peas in boiling water for 1 minute, transfer to a basin of ice-cold water to stop the cooking, then drain and set aside.

2   To make the marinade, in a medium bowl stir together the wine, cornstarch, white pepper, and ½ teaspoon of the salt. Add the chicken and stir to coat. Marinate for 10 minutes.

3   Heat the oil in a wok or large sauté pan over medium-high heat. Stir-fry the garlic until it is fragrant. Add the chicken and stir-fry until it is no longer pink inside; remove from the pan and set aside. Add the snow peas and mushrooms to the wok; sauté for 1 minute. Add the chicken, the remaining 1 teaspoon salt, a pinch of sugar, and the cashews. Stir. Serve immediately with steamed white rice.

SERVES: 8

½ pound snow peas

1½ pounds boneless skinless chicken breasts, cut into bite-sized pieces

5 tablespoons cooking oil

1½ tablespoons chopped garlic

1 (8-ounce) can straw mushrooms, drained

Pinch of sugar

½ cup cashews

Marinade:

1 tablespoon dry white wine or dry vermouth

1 tablespoon cornstarch

White pepper to taste

1½ teaspoons salt

Chicken Clemenceau

THIS IS A CLASSIC CREOLE DISH NAMED FOR GEORGES CLEMENCEAU, WHO BECAME THE FRENCH PREMIER IN 1906.

NEW ALBANY AREA CHAMBER OF COMMERCE

The New Albany Chamber of Commerce was established in 1996 by a group of business and civic leaders to encourage business expansion in the community. The Chamber is a private non-profit corporation whose mission is to promote the success and growth of the business and civic community in the Village of New Albany.

The Chamber has a wide spectrum of businesses, services, churches, and civic groups among its membership and it is one of the fastest growing Chambers of Commerce in Central Ohio.

New Albany has experienced rapid growth in residential communities and corporate employers. Its accessible office parks, attractive commercial centers, variety of housing options, and a pedestrian-friendly environment have resulted in a thriving local economy.

A high level of entrepreneurial spirit is prevalent in New Albany and is supported by the Chamber. In addition, trendy retail clusters showcase boutique-style shops where personal attention is the custom. Business and civic leaders from all fields are actively engaged in advancing economic growth through direct involvement in preserving the competitive enterprise system.

The community is home to Fortune 500 companies as well as sole proprietors who relish living and working where continuous improvement and lifestyle enjoyment are part of the culture.

— *Eileen Leuby on behalf of New Albany Chamber of Commerce*

1 Fill a wide, deep saucepan or a 6-quart sauté pan with 2 inches of the vegetable oil and heat on medium-high heat. When the oil is hot, add the potatoes and fry until cooked through and lightly browned. Drain on paper towels. Set aside.

2 Discard the vegetable oil, and in the same pan, heat the olive oil and butter on medium-high heat. Add the chicken and sauté until browned. Add the garlic and sauté until aromatic. Stir in the vermouth and cook for 2 minutes, scraping up any browned bits from the bottom of the pan. Add the mushrooms, peas, salt, and pepper. Cook until the mushrooms are tender. Add ¼ cup water if the mixture looks dry. Stir in the fried potatoes and parsley and cook until heated through. Serve immediately.

SERVES: 8

Vegetable oil for frying

8 small potatoes, peeled and cut in ¾-inch cubes

2 tablespoons olive oil

2 tablespoons unsalted butter

2 pounds boneless skinless chicken breasts, cut into bite-sized pieces

1½ heads garlic, peeled and coarsely chopped

½ cup dry vermouth

8 ounces shiitake mushrooms, thickly sliced

1½ cups fresh, frozen, or canned sweet green peas

1 teaspoon salt

Pepper to taste

¼ cup chopped fresh parsley

NEW ALBANY CLASSIC SIGNATURE SERIES PHOTOS
COURTESY DANIEL W. FLOSS & ASSOCIATES PHOTOGRAPHY

Chamber of Commerce's "A Taste of New Albany"

Chicken Sautéed with Curried Pear Sauce

THIS CHICKEN DISH HAS AN UNUSUAL SWEET FLAVOR AND IS GREAT SERVED WITH STEAMED LONG-GRAIN OR WILD RICE AND ASPARAGUS.

1 Slice each chicken breast lengthwise. Season both sides with salt and pepper. In a 12-inch heavy skillet, heat the oil over medium-high heat. Working in two batches, add the chicken and sear until well browned on both sides, about 3 minutes per side. Transfer chicken to a plate and tent with foil.

2 To make the sauce, reduce the heat to medium. Add the oil. When the oil is hot, add the pears, shallots, and curry powder. Cook, stirring, until the pears are softened, about 4 minutes. Add the wine and simmer until the sauce is slightly thickened, another 2 minutes. Return the chicken and any juices to the skillet; reduce the heat to low. Stir in the coconut milk. Simmer until the chicken is cooked through, about 4 minutes. Stir in the mint and cilantro.

3 Transfer the chicken to a warmed platter and spoon the sauce over it. Serve immediately.

SERVES: 8

2 pounds boneless skinless chicken breasts

Salt and pepper to taste

2 teaspoons olive or canola oil

Curried Pear Sauce:

2 teaspoons olive or canola oil

3 firm but ripe pears, peeled, cored, and thickly sliced

¼ cup finely chopped shallots

1 teaspoon curry powder

⅓ cup dry white wine

⅓ cup coconut milk

1 tablespoon chopped fresh mint

1 tablespoon chopped fresh cilantro

Chicken Paprikash

This is Zsuzsa Bocsardy's version of a traditional Hungarian dish. It is very satisfying, especially on cold days served with spaetzle dumplings.

1 Heat the oil in a large saucepan over low heat. Add the onions and green pepper and cook, stirring occasionally, until the onions are golden, about 10 minutes. Add the chicken, tomato, garlic, salt, and pepper; cook slowly, uncovered and stirring occasionally, until the chicken is tender, 30 to 40 minutes. Stir in the paprika.

2 Stir the sour cream until it turns into a smooth paste; stir in some of the hot liquid from the chicken stew. Stir the sour cream into the stew. Bring it to nearly to the boiling point, stirring all the time. Do not let it boil.

3 Serve with spaetzle dumplings (see recipe below) or hot cooked egg noodles.

SERVES: 6

CHEF TIP: You may substitute Hungarian hot paprika for the sweet paprika for a more authentic piquant taste.

3 tablespoons vegetable oil

2 medium onions, chopped

⅔ cup chopped green bell pepper

1 (3 to 4-pound) chicken, cut into 12 pieces

1 small ripe tomato, chopped

1 clove garlic, minced (optional)

Salt and pepper to taste

2 tablespoons Hungarian sweet paprika*, or to taste

½ cup sour cream

*available in the ethnic section of large supermarkets

SPAETZLE DUMPLINGS

1 In a medium bowl, combine the eggs, water, and flour. Beat with a wooden spoon until smooth. Drop teaspoons of the batter into boiling salted water and cook until the dumplings rise to the top, about 10 minutes. Drain.

3 eggs
⅓ cup water
2½ cups all-purpose flour, sifted

Chicken Adobo (Adobong Manok)

Adobo is considered the Philippine national dish. Many variations of adobo exist, using chicken and pork, chicken alone, pork alone, or squid. The dish should have a subtle sourness from the vinegar, which also acts as a preservative.

1 Combine all the ingredients in a covered pot large enough to hold the chicken in one layer. Bring to a boil over high heat; reduce the heat to medium-low or low (you want a slow simmer, nothing more). Cook, covered, about 30 minutes, turning once or twice, until the chicken is cooked through. (You may prepare the recipe in advance up to this point; refrigerate the chicken, in the liquid, for up to 1 day before proceeding.)

2 Remove the chicken from the liquid and pat it dry with paper towels. Boil the liquid over high heat until it is reduced to about 1 cup. Remove from the heat, discard the bay leaves, and keep the sauce warm.

3 Meanwhile, position a rack 3 or 4 inches from the heat source and preheat the grill or broiler.

4 Grill or broil the chicken until brown and crisp, about 5 minutes per side. Pour the sauce over the chicken and serve with white rice.

SERVES: 4

CHEF TIPS: Adobo is best served the day after cooking, when the sauce has thoroughly infused the meat. Simply reheat in the microwave before serving.

Instead of a whole chicken, you may use 4 pounds of bone-in thighs and drumsticks. Filipinos find dark meat more flavorful and suitable for this dish.

1 (3 to 4-pound) chicken, cut into 12 pieces

1 cup water

¾ cup white or rice vinegar

½ cup soy sauce

3 tablespoons chopped garlic

2 bay leaves

½ teaspoon freshly ground black pepper (or 1 teaspoon whole black peppercorns)

Chicken Mediterranean (Pollo Mediterraneo)

THIS INCREDIBLY TASTY ENTRÉE GOES WELL WITH COUSCOUS OR WITH SAFFRON RICE PILAF (SEE PAGE 149). CHOCK-FULL OF FLAVORS, THIS CHICKEN DISH IS A FAVORITE AMONG COOKING WITH FRIENDS MEMBERS YEAR-ROUND.

1 Stir together all the marinade ingredients. Put the chicken in a 2-gallon resealable plastic bag and pour in the marinade. Marinate overnight in the refrigerator, turning several times to coat the chicken.

2 Preheat the oven to 350°F.

3 Arrange the chicken in a single layer in 2 large, shallow baking pans and spoon the marinade evenly over it. Sprinkle the chicken with the brown sugar and pour the wine around it. Bake for 50 minutes to 1 hour, basting frequently with the pan juices. The chicken is done when thigh pieces yield clear yellow juice when pricked with a fork at their thickest point. Discard the bay leaves.

4 To serve hot, with a slotted spoon, transfer chicken, prunes, olives, and capers to a serving platter. Moisten with a few spoonfuls of the pan juices and sprinkle generously with the parsley. Pass remaining pan juices in a gravy boat.

5 To serve cold, cool to room temperature in the cooking juices before transferring to a serving platter. Spoon some of the reserved juice over the chicken and sprinkle with the parsley.

SERVES: 12

Marinade:

1 medium head garlic, peeled and mashed

1 cup pitted prunes

½ cup pimiento-stuffed Spanish green olives

½ cup capers with 1 teaspoon of their brine

½ cup olive oil

⅓ cup red wine vinegar

⅓ cup dried oregano

5 bay leaves

Kosher salt and freshly ground black pepper to taste

3 (3-pound) chickens, each cut into 8 pieces, breast bones removed

1 cup light brown sugar

1 cup dry white wine

¼ cup minced fresh parsley

Deep-fried Turkey

THIS SOUTHERN DELICACY CAME FROM JAKKI ALLEN'S FAMILY. DEEP-FRIED TURKEY IS GAINING IN POPULARITY. THE TURKEY COMES OUT VERY MOIST AND TASTY WITH DARK, CRISPY SKIN. IT'S PERFECT FOR BARBECUES, BLOCK PARTIES, AND HOLIDAY FEASTS.

1 Stir together all the seasoning mix ingredients; set aside. Process all the marinade ingredients in a food processor. Using a kitchen syringe or Cajun Injector (a popular brand of marinade injector), inject all the marinade into the turkey breasts, wings, drumsticks, thighs, and back. Rub the turkey all over with the seasoning mix. Seal in a large plastic bag for 12 to 24 hours.

2 It is recommended that you do the deep-frying outdoors, using a propane burner and a heavy 40 to 60-quart pot fitted with a metal basket. Be sure to place newspapers or cardboard around the cooking area to protect everything from the hot splattering oil.

3 Heat the oil until a candy/fat thermometer reads 350°F and maintain that temperature. A heavy wire coat hanger hooked to the wire band that secures the turkey's legs will help when lowering the turkey into the hot fat and lifting it when done. Alternatively, you may use a sturdy cooking spoon, tongs, or a large fork for extra support. Wearing long oven mitts, very slowly and carefully lower the turkey all the way into the hot oil. Deep-fry the turkey for 50 to 60 minutes (about 4 minutes per pound).

4 Have ready a large cutting board padded with paper towels. Carefully remove the turkey from the oil by lifting it with the hanger hook. Hold the turkey over the pot, allowing excess oil to drain, before transferring it to the cutting board. Stand the turkey upright on its legs so excess oil will drain from the cavity. Test for doneness by making a small cut at the bone in the thigh joint and checking to see that juices run clear. Let rest for 10 minutes before carving.

SERVES: 12

VARIATION: Clem Greene, Jakki's father, fries the turkey in the same manner as above but he uses a simple seasoning of salt and pepper inside and outside of the turkey and skips the marinating.

Seasoning Mix:

1 cup salt

1 tablespoon cayenne

1 tablespoon freshly ground black pepper

Marinade:

1 (12-ounce) bottle beer

¾ cup honey

¼ cup fresh apple cider

2 tablespoons Worcestershire sauce

½ cup Emeril's Original Essence*

1 tablespoon liquid concentrated crab and shrimp boil**

1 tablespoon salt

1 tablespoon ground allspice

¼ teaspoon cayenne

*a blend of spices and herbs including salt, paprika, black pepper, granulated garlic, and onion powder

**spicy Cajun seasoning; a recommended brand is Zatarain's

1 (10 to 12-pound) turkey, giblets removed, washed and patted dry (do not undo the wire band that secures the legs)

5 gallons peanut oil

Grilled Beef Tenderloin with Oriental Seasonings

THIS INTENSELY FLAVORED FUSION DISH TASTES WONDERFUL SERVED WARM AS A MAIN COURSE OR SERVED COLD AS A LUNCHEON SANDWICH OR OPEN-FACED SANDWICH USING THE BRUSCHETTA ON PAGE 54 AS A BASE.

1 Using a sharp knife, remove the layers of outer fat from the tenderloin. The layers should pull away easily after a knife has been inserted between the fat and the meat. The silverskin, which is a tough, silver-colored membrane, should also be completely removed. Cut the tenderloin in half crosswise.

2 Combine the marinade ingredients. Put the tenderloin in a 2-gallon resealable plastic bag, add the marinade, and marinate, refrigerated, for at least 3 hours; overnight is even better.

3 Preheat the grill to high the oven to 450°F.

4 Grill the tenderloins until crusty on all sides, about 12 minutes. Transfer to the oven and roast for 5 minutes for rare, 10 minutes for medium, or 15 minutes for well done. Let the meat stand for 5 to 10 minutes before slicing. Serve garnished with watercress greens.

SERVES: 10

CHEF TIP: To save on preparation time, have a butcher trim and cut the tenderloin for you.

1 (5 to 7-pound) beef tenderloin

Watercress leaves for garnish

Marinade:

½ cup hoisin sauce

⅓ cup medium-dry sherry

¼ cup dark soy sauce

¼ cup American chili sauce

2 tablespoons plum sauce*

2 tablespoons dark rice miso

1 tablespoon minced fresh ginger

2 teaspoons minced garlic

3 green onions, sliced ⅛-inch thick

*plum sauce is available in jars in the Asian section of the supermarket

Flank Steak with Papaya-Kiwi Marinade

FLANK STEAK IS AN IDEAL CUT FOR MARINATING BECAUSE IT IS RELATIVELY THIN AND POROUS. PAPAYA IS USED BY TROPICAL CULTURES AS A NATURAL MEAT TENDERIZER. THIS RECIPE DELIVERS A TENDER, EXOTIC-FLAVORED ENTRÉE IF COOKED QUICKLY TO RARE OR MEDIUM-RARE AND SLICED VERY THINLY ON THE BIAS.

1 Put the papaya and kiwis in a food processor and pulse until just finely chopped but not puréed. Transfer the mixture to a saucepan and add the vinegar and sugar. Cook over medium heat for 5 minutes, stirring often. Remove from the heat and let cool. Set aside ⅔ cup.

2 In a shallow nonreactive dish just large enough to hold the steak, stir together the remaining papaya-kiwi mixture, the shallots, olive oil, lemon juice, honey, parsley, garlic, pepper, and salt. Add the steak and turn to coat with the marinade. Marinate, covered and refrigerated, at least 5 hours and up to 24, turning the steak occasionally.

3 Broil or grill the steak (discarding the marinade) on high to the desired doneness, about 4 minutes per side for medium-rare, 5 minutes for medium. Thinly slice the steak against the grain on the diagonal. Drizzle the reserved fruit mixture over the meat and serve.

SERVES: 6

CHEF TIPS: The longer you marinate your flank steak, the more tender and flavorful it will be.

Use a ripe papaya: it should have a bright yellow-orange skin and give slightly to palm pressure. A Hawaiian papaya is the type commonly found in supermarkets; it is pear-shaped, bright yellow when ripe, and generally weighs about 1 pound.

1 ripe Hawaiian papaya (1 to 1½ pounds), peeled, seeded and sliced (see Chef Tips)

3 ripe kiwi fruits, peeled and sliced

2 tablespoons balsamic vinegar

1 tablespoon light brown sugar

2 large shallots, finely chopped

2 tablespoons olive oil

2 tablespoons fresh lemon juice

1½ teaspoons honey

2 tablespoons chopped fresh parsley

1 tablespoon minced garlic

2 teaspoons freshly ground black pepper

1½ teaspoons salt

1 (2-pound) flank steak, trimmed

Grilled Flank Steak with Far East Seasonings

Zsuzsa Bocsardy shared this recipe at the first Cooking with Friends spring dinner, the first time members' husbands were invited. This has been one of the most passed-around recipes in the club because it is so easy to do and is great for when you have company over for a cook-out. Leftovers make delicious sandwiches.

THE NORTH MARKET

The historic North Market in the heart of downtown Columbus has been home to butchers, bakers, fishmongers, greengrocers, and farmers since 1876. Over the years, the offerings have expanded to include a tremendous selection of ethnic food specialties, gourmet groceries, and distinctive gifts. The North Market is the only remaining public market in Central Ohio and it is visited by more than one million customers every year. In the 1980s a not-for-profit group called the North Market Development Authority (NMDA) was established "to preserve and promote the traditional and cultural aspects of the historic North Market" and to administer the daily operations.

Throughout the year, the market hosts a variety of festivals, activities, and entertainment to make visiting even more of an experience. The Saturday Farmer's Market is held from May through October. The North Market Apron Gala is a beloved spring tradition that offers food enthusiasts and public-market supporters an insider's view of the market after-hours while enjoying great food samples prepared by the merchants. The Harvest Festival and Scarecrow Affair takes place in the fall, and the Holiday Open House and Craft Extravaganza caps the year. Other events include a Microbrew Festival, a Grillmasters Festival, and the Annual North Market Food and Ohio Wine Festival. Visit **www.northmarket.com** for more information. — *Marilu Faber*

---

1 Stir together the oil, kecap manis, honey, vinegar, ginger, and garlic. Put the steak in a 1-gallon resealable plastic bag and add the marinade. Marinate the steak, refrigerated and turning occasionally, for at least 24 hours.

2 Grill the steak (discarding the marinade) on high until medium-rare, about 8 minutes on each side. Let the steak stand for 10 minutes, then slice thinly against the grain on the diagonal. Serve with your favorite green salad.

SERVES: 6

½ cup salad or vegetable oil

¼ cup kecap manis* or soy sauce

2 tablespoons honey

2 tablespoons red wine vinegar

1 teaspoon ground ginger

2 cloves garlic, mashed

1 (2-pound) flank steak, trimmed

*Indonesian condiment that is sweeter, thicker, and more complexly flavored than soy sauce; found in Asian groceries and Dutch specialty stores

COURTESY RANDALL LEE SCHIEBER / EXPERIENCE COLUMBUS

The historic North Market in the Short North area of downtown Columbus

Stuffed Flank Steak

HERE IS A DISH THAT CAN BE PREPARED AHEAD OF TIME, LOOKS ELEGANT, AND IS FULL OF FLAVOR.

1 Pound both sides of the flank steak to tenderize. Season with salt and pepper. Layer the prosciutto over the steak. Set aside.

2 Squeeze all the excess water from the spinach. In a food processor, combine the spinach, bread crumbs, cheese, oil, and garlic. Process to a smooth paste. Spread the spinach mixture over the steak. Starting at one of the narrow ends, roll the steak into a log. Tie with kitchen string. (Can be prepared 1 day ahead. Cover and refrigerate. Bring to room temperature before baking.)

3 Preheat the oven to 375°F. Oil a small baking dish.

4 Place the steak in the baking dish; brush with additional olive oil. Bake, uncovered, for 40 minutes. Let the meat stand for 10 minutes. Remove the string and slice about 1 inch thick.

SERVES: 4

1 (1½-pound) flank steak, trimmed

Salt and pepper to taste

¼ pound very thinly sliced prosciutto

1 (10-ounce) package frozen chopped spinach, thawed

½ cup dry bread crumbs

½ cup freshly grated Parmesan cheese

¼ cup olive oil, plus more for brushing

2 cloves garlic, chopped

Rolled Stuffed Beef, Calabrian Style (Braciole di Manzo alla Calabrese)

Braciole is a traditional Calabrian Christmas dish. With its flavorful stuffing it makes a scrumptious entrée.

1 Cut the top round into 9 pieces, each about ¼ inch thick, 2 to 3 inches wide, and 8 inches long. Pound the slices with a meat pounder to tenderize, being careful not to tear the slices. Spread them out flat on a work surface.

2 In a medium bowl, mix the eggs, bread crumbs, cheese, parsley, garlic, olive oil, salt, and pepper. Spread the mixture evenly over the meat slices. Starting at a short end, gently roll up each slice, jelly-roll fashion. Tie the rolls securely in several places with kitchen string.

3 To make the sauce, in a large, heavy skillet, heat the oil over medium heat. Cook the onion, stirring frequently, for 3 to 4 minutes until it is translucent. Add the garlic and sauté for 1 to 2 minutes, until it is light golden brown. Transfer the onion and garlic mixture to a small bowl.

4 Raise the heat to medium-high. Using tongs, put the meat rolls in the skillet. Do not crowd the pan. Sauté for 6 to 8 minutes, turning to brown all sides. Add the onion and garlic mixture, the tomatoes, basil, parsley, and salt. Lower the heat, cover and simmer gently, turning occasionally, for 1 hour or until the meat is tender when pierced with a fork. Transfer to a platter, remove the string, and cut into 2-inch slices. Serve immediately with the sauce.

SERVES: 8

CHEF TIP: Have a butcher slice the meat with a machine for uniform slicing. Butchers at Italian groceries will know how to cut the meat if you specify *braciole* cut.

2 pounds top round steak

2 hard-boiled eggs, finely chopped

½ cup coarse dry bread crumbs

⅓ cup freshly grated pecorino or Parmesan cheese

¼ cup finely chopped fresh parsley

3 cloves garlic, minced

1 tablespoon olive oil

1 teaspoon salt

½ teaspoon freshly ground black pepper

Sauce:

2 tablespoons olive oil

1 small onion, coarsely chopped

1 clove garlic, finely minced

1 (16-ounce) can Italian plum tomatoes, coarsely chopped, with their juice

2 tablespoons coarsely chopped fresh basil

2 tablespoons coarsely chopped fresh parsley

¼ teaspoon salt

Korean Barbecued Beef with Asian Pear Dipping Sauce (Bulgogi)

The recipe calls for the meat to be wrapped in crisp, crunchy lettuce. Traditional bulgogi is wrapped in thin bread similar to mu shu pancakes, but you can use tortillas or pile it on hot steamed rice.

1 Slice the beef diagonally against the grain into ¼-inch-thick strips. Put the beef in a large resealable plastic bag.

2 Mince 4 of the green onions (white and green parts). In a small bowl, combine the minced green onions with all the marinade ingredients; stir well. Pour over the beef, seal the bag and toss the bag lightly back and forth to coat the beef. Refrigerate overnight. Half an hour before grilling, remove the beef from the refrigerator. Drain the beef, reserving the marinade.

3 Preheat an indoor or outdoor grill to medium-high. If an outdoor grill is used, place a mesh screen on the rack to keep the meat slices from falling into the fire. Spray the grill generously with vegetable oil before cooking.

4 With tongs, carefully place the beef slices on the hot grill. Baste with the reserved marinade, turning once to prevent burning, until slightly charred and medium-rare, 3 to 4 minutes. Transfer to a cutting board and tent with foil.

5 Grill the remaining 10 green onions, turning frequently, until slightly charred, about 2 minutes. Transfer to a plate and keep warm. Cut the beef into thin shreds. Chop the green onions into bite-sized chunks.

6 To eat, place 3 to 4 tablespoons of the shredded meat and 2 or 3 chunks of green onion on a lettuce leaf. Fold over all 4 sides to make a bundle.

SERVES: 8 to 10

CHEF TIP: High-quality pre-sliced beef, usually labeled sukiyaki beef, is available at most Japanese groceries. This makes the best bulgogi.

2 pounds beef sirloin

14 green onions

10 romaine lettuce leaves

Asian Pear Dipping Sauce (recipe on page 192)

Marinade:

¼ cup fresh lemon juice

¼ cup soy sauce

3 tablespoons sugar

2 tablespoons minced fresh ginger

2 tablespoons minced garlic

2 tablespoons toasted sesame seeds

2 tablespoons dark sesame oil

1 tablespoon molasses

1 teaspoon ground black pepper

1 teaspoon cayenne

Continued on next page

ASIAN PEAR DIPPING SAUCE

1 Combine all the ingredients in a bowl and stir until the sugar dissolves. Divide the sauce among as many small bowls as there are people, so each person has a dipping sauce for their bulgogi.

YIELD: 1½ cups

½ cup soy sauce

½ cup sake, Chinese rice wine, or dry sherry

¼ cup sugar

¼ cup finely chopped onion

2 tablespoons toasted sesame seeds

1 small Asian pear, peeled, cored, and finely chopped

4 green onions (white and green parts), finely chopped

New Albany residence

Fragrant Beef Curry

THIS CURRY WITH A SWEET-SPICY FLAVOR KEEPS WELL AND TASTES BETTER A DAY OR TWO AFTER. SIMPLY REHEAT IN THE MICROWAVE. THE CARDAMOM PODS LEND THE DISH A PERFUMY FRAGRANCE.

1   In a large pressure cooker (at least 6-quart capacity) over medium heat, cook the onions in the oil, stirring occasionally, for at least 10 minutes, until transparent. Add the garlic and fry for 1 minute. Add the curry mix and ginger; fry until the oil starts to separate. Add the tomato purée, beef, lemon juice, and cardamom pods. Cover and pressure-cook over low heat for at least 35 minutes after it starts to steam. Stir and check if the meat is tender; if it isn't, continue to pressure-cook, checking the meat every 5 minutes, until desired tenderness is reached. Uncover, increase heat to medium, and boil the stew until the juices are slightly thickened, about 5 minutes. Stir in the chutney. Taste and adjust seasoning with salt. Discard the cardamom pods. Serve with hot rice.

SERVES: 10

CHEF TIP: Wrap the cardamom pods in a cheesecloth pouch tied with string. This will make it easy to remove the pods after cooking.

2 pounds onions, chopped

3 tablespoons vegetable oil

2 cloves garlic, minced

½ cup curry powder mix*

3 tablespoons minced fresh ginger

6 ounces (¾ cup) tomato purée or paste

4 pounds beef round steak or stewing beef, cut into 1½-inch cubes

Juice of 1 lemon

8 green cardamom pods

⅓ cup Major Grey mango chutney

Salt to taste

Hot cooked rice

*curry powder mix, available at South Asian groceries, is recommended for this recipe; it is not the same as curry powder

Malaysian Beef Stew (Rendang)

THIS MALAYSIAN DISH, WITH ITS COMPLEX SEASONING, IS EASY TO PREPARE. SIMMER ALL THE INGREDIENTS IN ONE POT UNTIL RICH, THICK, AND AROMATIC.

1 Place the onions, garlic, chiles, ginger, and 2 tablespoons of the coconut milk in a food processor and process to a smooth paste.

2 Heat the oil in a large skillet over medium heat. Add the paste, coriander, cumin, turmeric, cinnamon, cloves, chili powder, lemon rind, and the steak; stir until the meat is well coated with the spice mixture. Add the remaining coconut milk and bring to a boil, then reduce heat to low, cover and simmer, stirring occasionally, for 1½ hours or until the meat is tender and the mixture is almost dry. (You may use a pressure cooker to cut the tenderizing time; cook for 30 minutes on medium heat.)

3 When the oil starts to separate from the sauce, add the sugar, lemon juice, and tamarind; stir until heated through. Adjust seasonings. Serve with hot steamed rice.

SERVES: 6

CHEF TIPS: This recipe produces a "dry" curry, which does not have much liquid. The meat absorbs the spicy flavors as it cooks. It tastes even better if it is made a day in advance.

Tamarind is a souring agent commonly used in South Asian curries and chutneys much like lemon juice is in Western cuisine. It is also popular in Thai, Mexican, and Mediterranean cooking and can be found in Asian groceries in various forms: jars of concentrated pulp with seeds, canned paste, whole pods dried into "bricks," ground into powder, or fresh. If you have no tamarind, use extra lemon juice.

2 large onions, chopped

4 cloves garlic, crushed

5 red chiles, seeded

1 tablespoon grated fresh ginger

2 cups coconut milk

1 tablespoon vegetable oil

1 tablespoon ground coriander

1 tablespoon ground cumin

1 teaspoon ground turmeric

1 teaspoon cinnamon

¼ teaspoon ground cloves

¼ teaspoon chili powder

1 large strip lemon rind

2 pounds chuck or skirt steak, cut into 1½-inch cubes

1 tablespoon brown sugar

1 tablespoon lemon juice

1 teaspoon tamarind concentrate (see Chef Tips)

Lemon slices and cilantro sprigs for garnish

Moroccan Meat-filled Phyllo Pastry (Briouat Bil Kefta)

MARILU FABER ADAPTED THIS IMAGINATIVELY PREPARED MEAT PIE FROM A HANDOUT AT A CULINARY INSTITUTE OF AMERICA WEEKEND COURSE. THE IDEA OF MEAT MIXED WITH SPICES AND ENCASED IN PASTRY WAS BROUGHT TO MOROCCO FROM THE MIDDLE EAST; THE DELICATE PASTRY SHEETS, IT IS THOUGHT, CAME SPECIFICALLY FROM PERSIA.

1 To make the meat filling, heat the oil in a large skillet over medium heat. Cook the onions, stirring occasionally, for 7 minutes. Stir in the parsley, cilantro, cumin, paprika, cinnamon, and cayenne; cook 2 minutes longer. Add the meat and cook quickly until it loses its raw color. Pour the eggs over the meat, stir well and cook, stirring constantly, until the eggs are set, 3 to 4 minutes. Adjust seasoning with salt and pepper. Remove from the heat and let cool.

2 To make the potato filling, cook the potatoes in boiling salted water until they are soft. Drain well and mash; set aside. Heat the oil in small skillet over medium heat. Cook the onions, stirring frequently, for 7 minutes. Add the garlic, salt, and pepper; cook for 2 minutes. Remove from the heat and stir in the parsley and mint. Add the onion mixture to the potatoes; season to taste with salt and pepper. Stir in the beaten egg to bind the mixture. Stir in the hard-boiled eggs.

3 Preheat the oven to 375°F.

4 Fit 1 sheet of phyllo in a 10-inch springform pan, letting the excess hang over the edge, and brush all over with clarified butter. Arrange another sheet on top with the corners 1 inch beyond the corners of the previous sheet; brush with butter. Repeat, using 7 sheets in all.

5 Spread the potato filling in the phyllo shell. Spread the meat filling on top. Lay 1 sheet of phyllo over the filling and brush with clarified butter. Arrange another sheet on top with the corners 1 inch beyond the corners of the previous sheet; brush with butter. Repeat, using 4 sheets in all. Fold all the overhanging pastry over the top of the pie and press down lightly. Brush top with butter.

6 Bake until golden, about 20 minutes. Let cool in the pan for 10 minutes. Release pie from springform pan. Serve warm.

SERVES: 6

Meat Filling:

2 tablespoons olive oil

½ cup diced onion

3 tablespoons chopped fresh parsley

2 tablespoons chopped fresh cilantro

1 teaspoon ground cumin

1 teaspoon paprika

1 teaspoon cinnamon

½ teaspoon cayenne

8 ounces ground beef or lamb

3 eggs

¾ teaspoon salt

Black pepper to taste

Potato Filling:

14 ounces potatoes, peeled and cubed

2 tablespoons olive oil

½ cup diced onion

1 tablespoon minced garlic

1 teaspoon salt

½ teaspoon freshly ground black pepper

¼ cup minced fresh parsley

3 tablespoons minced fresh mint

1 egg, lightly beaten

2 hard-boiled eggs, chopped

11 sheets phyllo dough

½ cup clarified butter, melted

Veal Braciola

THIS SKILLET VEAL IS TOPPED WITH CRUNCHY FRESH VEGETABLES. YOU CAN ALSO PREPARE IT USING CHICKEN.

1   Pound the veal with a meat pounder until ¼-inch thick. (If you are using scaloppine, leave them as is.) Cut into serving-size pieces. Soak the veal in the beaten eggs for 30 minutes.

2   Meanwhile, in a bowl stir together the tomatoes, celery, and zucchini; set aside. Spread the bread crumbs on a plate.

3   In a large skillet, heat ¼ cup oil over high heat until hot. Working in batches so you don't crowd the pan, remove the veal from the egg, letting the excess egg drip off, and dredge in the bread crumbs, pressing down hard with your hands to make sure the crumbs stick. Fry the veal until golden brown on both sides, about 4 minutes on each side. Drain on paper towels and sprinkle with salt and pepper. Replenish the oil as needed to fry the remaining veal.

4   Transfer the veal to a platter or plates. Spoon the vegetable mixture over the veal and drizzle with the olive oil. Garnish with basil leaves and serve warm.

SERVES: 4 to 6

CHEF TIP: Scaloppine is the thinnest piece of veal you can buy. It's so tender it saves you the time and effort of pounding the veal.

2 pounds sliced veal top round or scaloppine (or boneless skinless chicken breasts)

2 eggs, beaten

4 large ripe tomatoes, diced

2 celery stalks, cut into ¼-inch slices

2 medium zucchini, grated on the large holes of a grater

¾ cup fine dry bread crumbs

¼ cup peanut or vegetable oil for frying (approx.)

Salt and pepper to taste

Extra virgin olive oil for drizzling

12 large basil leaves

Osso Buco (Braised Veal Shanks)

THIS VELVETY-TENDER BRAISED VEAL WITH A TOMATO SAUCE AND LEMONY GARNISH IS A PERFECT DISH FOR A COOL NIGHT. THIS HEARTY ITALIAN ENTRÉE IS GREAT SERVED WITH PASTA WITH GRATED PARMESAN OR GRUYÈRE CHEESE.

1   Dredge the veal shanks in the flour and shake off excess. Heat the butter and oil in a wide 5-quart pot over medium-high heat; when the foam subsides, add the meat, in batches if necessary, and brown on both sides. Set meat aside. Into the pot add the onions, carrot, celery, and garlic; brown lightly. Reduce the heat to medium and stir in the marjoram, rosemary, lemon zest, salt, and pepper. Pour in the wine and cook for a few minutes, stirring to scrape up any brown bits from the bottom of the pan. Add the tomatoes, tomato paste, and stock; stir. Put the veal back into the pot. Cover and simmer for 1½ to 1¾ hours, until the meat is starting to fall off the bone. Check periodically, and if the sauce is too thick, add a bit more stock or water.

2   Meanwhile, stir together the garnish ingredients. A few minutes before the meat and sauce are done, sprinkle with the garnish and simmer for another few minutes. Taste and adjust seasonings.

SERVES: 6 to 8

3 pounds veal shanks (6 to 8 slices, each 1½ to 2 inches thick)

⅓ cup all-purpose flour

2 tablespoons unsalted butter

2 tablespoons olive oil

1 cup chopped onion

1 carrot, diced

1 stalk celery, diced

1 clove garlic, crushed

Minced fresh (or crumbled dried) marjoram and rosemary, to taste

Grated zest of 1 lemon

Salt and pepper to taste

¼ cup dry white wine

2 ripe tomatoes, peeled, seeded, and chopped (1 cup)

2 tablespoons tomato paste

¼ cup beef stock or more as needed

Garnish:

2 tablespoons finely chopped fresh parsley

2 tablespoons unsalted butter, cut into small pieces

1 teaspoon grated lemon zest

1 clove garlic, minced

Barbecued Ribs with Spicy Lime Sauce

These ribs are fragrant with exotic Far East spices. They can be served as the main event at a dinner party or can be carved into individual ribs and offered as cocktail appetizers.

1   Trim fat from the ribs and remove the thin, papery skin from the back of each rack. Put the ribs in a roasting pan.

2   Combine all the ingredients for the spice rub; rub the spice mix all over the ribs. Cover tightly with foil and refrigerate for 1 hour.

3   Meanwhile, preheat the oven to 250°F. Roast the ribs, covered tightly with foil, for 3 hours.

4   Preheat the grill to medium-high.

5   Stir together all the sauce ingredients until the sugar has dissolved. Set aside 1 cup of the sauce. Brush the remaining sauce on both sides of the roasted ribs. Grill the ribs, turning once, for a total of 15 minutes. Serve with the reserved sauce and Thai Cucumber Relish (see page 82).

SERVES: 10

4 racks pork spareribs
(about 6 pounds)

Spice Rub:

2 tablespoons cinnamon

2 tablespoons kosher salt

2 tablespoons ground black pepper

1 tablespoon ground coriander

1 tablespoon ground cloves

Spicy Lime Sauce:

½ cup chopped fresh cilantro

3 tablespoons coarsely chopped fresh ginger

2 tablespoons coarsely chopped garlic

¾ cup rice vinegar

½ cup soy sauce

½ cup ketchup

⅓ cup dark brown sugar

⅓ cup fresh lime juice

¼ cup hoisin sauce

2 tablespoons dark sesame oil

1 tablespoon Sichuan peppercorns or red pepper flakes

Stir-fried Bean Curd and Pork
(Ma-Po Tofu)

A SPICY SZECHUAN RECIPE, THE NAME REFERS TO THE GRANDMOTHER WHO SUPPOSEDLY INVENTED THE DISH.

1 Combine the ground pork, soy sauce, sherry, and sugar. Mix well.

2 In a wok or large skillet over medium-high heat, heat 1 tablespoon of the oil until hot. Drop in the ginger slices and stir-fry until slightly browned. Add the minced garlic and then the pork mixture and stir-fry until pork is cooked through. Remove from the pan and set aside.

3 Dissolve the cornstarch in the water; set aside. Heat the remaining 2 tablespoons oil in the wok until hot. Swirl the oil in the pan. Add the tofu cubes. Stir-fry until hot. Stir in the green onions, oyster sauce, and chili sauce. Add the cooked pork mixture. Cook until heated through. Give the cornstarch mixture a stir and add to the pan. Cook, stirring, until the sauce is lightly thickened and clear. Remove from the heat. Add the sesame oil and give it a quick stir to combine. Serve immediately (or, to serve later, reheat in microwave just until hot) with steamed rice.

SERVES: 4

½ pound (or more to taste) ground pork

1 tablespoon soy sauce

1 tablespoon dry sherry

½ teaspoon sugar

3 tablespoons peanut or canola oil

2 thin slices fresh ginger

1 clove garlic, minced

2 teaspoons cornstarch

1 tablespoon water

2 (14-ounce) packages firm tofu, drained and cut into ¾-inch cubes

2 green onions, finely chopped

3 tablespoons oyster sauce or to taste

½ teaspoon chili sauce or to taste

2 teaspoons sesame oil*

*dark sesame oil typically found in Asian groceries is recommended

Cantonese Pork Tenderloin (Char Siu)

A DELICIOUS ENTRÉE. THE DISH CAN ALSO BE USED TO GARNISH VEGETABLE DISHES, MUCH AS ONE WOULD USE BACON BITS AS FLAVORING.

1 Fold the thin ends of the tenderloins under so the meat is an even thickness; tie ends with kitchen string.

2 In a resealable plastic bag, combine all the marinade ingredients. Mix well. Add the pork, seal well and marinate at room temperature for at least 3 hours or refrigerated overnight. Turn pork occasionally.

3 Stir together the honey and sesame oil. Set aside.

4 To roast: Preheat the oven to 375°F. Remove the tenderloins from the marinade (discard the marinade). Place on a rack in a roasting pan above about 1 inch of hot water. Roast for 30 minutes. Increase oven temperature to 450°F. Brush the meat with the honey mixture. Roast for another 6 to 8 minutes or until a meat thermometer registers 150°F.

5 To grill: Preheat the grill to high. When hot, sear both sides of the pork, then grill for 30 minutes over indirect flame, turning once. Brush with the honey mixture and grill for a few more minutes, until a meat thermometer registers 150°F.

6 Let the pork stand for 10 minutes before slicing.

SERVES: 8

CHEF TIP: This recipe can be prepared in advance and can be frozen for several months.

2 pounds pork tenderloin, trimmed of fat and silverskin

½ cup honey

2 tablespoons sesame oil

Marinade:

2 cloves garlic, crushed

¼ cup sugar

¼ cup dry sherry

3 tablespoons soy sauce

2 tablespoons brown bean paste*

2 tablespoons hoisin sauce

1 tablespoon sesame paste*

1 teaspoon salt

½ teaspoon Chinese five-spice powder

*found in Asian grocery stores

Pork Medallions in Crème Fraîche

THIS DELICIOUS CASSEROLE WAS CREATED BY ROSE-MARIE SVENSSON IN LINKÖPING, SWEDEN. IT IS A FAMILY FAVORITE IN THE SUMMER WHEN THERE IS FRESH PARSLEY IN THE GARDEN. IT CAN EASILY BE PREPARED AHEAD OF TIME AND POPPED IN THE OVEN WHEN COMPANY ARRIVES.

1 Preheat the oven to 375°F. Butter a 2-quart casserole dish.

2 Cut the tenderloin crosswise into 1-inch slices. Heat the butter and olive oil in a large skillet over medium-high heat; sauté the pork until just cooked through. Season with salt and pepper. Arrange the pork in the casserole dish and sprinkle ham on top.

3 In a bowl mix together the crème fraîche, whipping cream, mustard, and parsley. Evenly pour over the pork and ham. Sprinkle with the cheese.

4 Bake for 20 to 30 minutes, until the cheese is melted and golden and the pork is heated through.

SERVES: 8

CHEF TIP: Instead of parsley you may use tarragon, dill, or other fresh herbs. You may use boneless skinless chicken instead of pork.

2 pounds pork tenderloin, trimmed of fat and silverskin

2 tablespoons unsalted butter

1 tablespoon olive oil

Salt and pepper to taste

1 cup diced thinly sliced smoked ham

1¾ cups crème fraîche*

2 cups whipping cream

3 tablespoons Dijon mustard

1 cup chopped fresh parsley

1 cup mixed grated Romano and Parmesan cheese

*crème fraîche and sour cream can be used interchangeably in most recipes, but crème fraîche is less sour and thinner than sour cream and it will not curdle if boiled

Pork Tenderloin in Baguette (Porc en Baguette)

THIS RECIPE WAS BROUGHT BACK FROM MAS DU CORNUD COOKING SCHOOL IN PROVENCE BY COOKING WITH FRIENDS MEMBER SHERYL ZANGARDI. IT IS A GREAT PICNIC ENTRÉE.

1 Preheat the oven to 350°F.

2 Slice the tenderloin in half lengthwise. Slice the bread in half lengthwise but do not cut all the way through. Hollow out most of the bread from both halves (save it to make bread crumbs), leaving a ½-inch lining of bread. Brush the bread shell with the olive oil. Sprinkle with garlic and herbs. Lay the tenderloin inside the bread, tucking under the thin end so all of the pork is of about the same thickness. Close the loaf and wrap tightly in foil. Bake for 1 hour and 5 minutes. Let stand for 10 minutes before unwrapping and slicing. May be served hot, warm, or at room temperature.

SERVES: 6

1½ pounds pork tenderloin (about 2), trimmed of fat and silverskin

1 (1-pound) baguette

¼ cup olive oil

2 teaspoons minced garlic

1 tablespoon herbes de Provence

New Albany Leisure Trail

COURTESY TIM FABER

Pork Tenderloin with Shallot Sauce

HERE'S A GOOD CHOICE WHEN COOKING FOR A CROWD. THE AROMA OF THE MEAT ROASTING IN THE OVEN WILL MAKE EVERYONE HUNGRY. THE SWEET INTENSITY OF THE SHALLOT SAUCE MAKES THIS A MEMORABLE DISH.

1 Preheat the oven to 500°F. Lightly oil a large roasting pan. Toss the shallots with 2 tablespoons of the oil, ¾ teaspoon of the salt, and ½ teaspoon of the pepper. Set aside.

2 Stir together the remaining 1 teaspoon salt, 1½ teaspoons of the pepper, the onion powder, garlic powder, and thyme. Rub tenderloins with the remaining ¼ cup oil and sprinkle the seasonings over the top and sides of the tenderloin, pressing gently so the seasonings adhere. Place the tenderloins in the roasting pan; arrange shallots around them. Roast, uncovered, for 25 minutes. Reduce oven temperature to 375°F and bake 10 to 15 minutes or until the meat reaches 160°F. Do not overcook.

3 Meanwhile, combine the chicken stock and Marsala in a large skillet. Boil until reduced by half, 6 to 8 minutes.

4 Transfer tenderloins to a platter and cover with foil. Leave the shallots and drippings in the pan. Add the stock reduction; cook over medium heat, stirring to scrape up the brown bits from the pan.

5 Whisk the flour with the water until smooth. Stir into the roasting pan. Cook, stirring constantly, until slightly thickened. Add the butter and stir until melted. Stir in the remaining ¼ teaspoon pepper. Strain the sauce into a gravy boat. Thinly slice the tenderloins on the diagonal and serve with the sauce.

SERVES: 8 to 10

1 pound shallots, peeled and halved

¼ cup plus 2 tablespoons olive oil

1¾ teaspoons salt

2¼ teaspoons pepper

1½ teaspoons onion powder

1½ teaspoons garlic powder

½ teaspoon dried thyme

4 (1-pound) pork tenderloins, trimmed of fat and silverskin

3 cups chicken stock

1 cup dry Marsala

2 tablespoons all-purpose flour

3 tablespoons water

3 tablespoons unsalted butter

Spicy Grilled Pork Tenderloin

FEAST ON THIS INTENSELY FLAVORED PORK TENDERLOIN. IT DISAPPEARS FROM THE BUFFET TABLE BEFORE YOU CAN RETURN FOR A SECOND SERVING.

1   Combine the soy sauce, brown sugar, cumin, mustard, paprika, garlic, and cilantro in a resealable plastic bag. Mix well.

2   Fold under the thin ends of the tenderloins so the meat is an even thickness; tie with kitchen string. Add the pork to the marinade, seal well and refrigerate overnight.

3   Preheat the grill to medium-high. Grill the pork (reserving the marinade) for 5 minutes. Baste with reserved marinade. Turn and grill 5 minutes longer. Let stand 5 minutes. Discard leftover marinade.

4   Thinly slice the tenderloins crosswise. Serve warm or at room temperature.

SERVES: 6 to 8

½ cup soy sauce

¼ cup plus 2 tablespoons brown sugar

2 teaspoons ground cumin

2 teaspoons dry mustard

1 teaspoon sweet paprika

8 cloves garlic, sliced

¼ cup chopped fresh cilantro or parsley

2 (12-ounce) pork tenderloins, trimmed of fat and silverskin

Rum-glazed Smoked Easter Ham

A MAGNIFICENT CENTERPIECE FOR EASTER DINNER. THIS VERSION, CREATED BY COOKING WITH FRIENDS MEMBER JAKKI ALLEN, ADDS THE WONDERFUL FLAVORS OF GRILLED HICKORY OR MESQUITE.

1   In a small saucepan combine the sugar, peppercorns, rum, molasses, butter, and mustard. Over low heat, stir until the sugar has dissolved and the butter is melted. Pour a third of the mixture over the ham, spreading the spiral cuts to allow the glaze to penetrate.

2   Preheat the grill to high. Place hickory or mesquite chunks in a disposable aluminum pan. Add about 1 inch of water. Place the pan on one side of the grill. Place the ham on the other side, close the lid and smoke the ham for 1 hour and 15 minutes. During the last 30 minutes of cooking, baste the ham several times with the remaining glaze.

SERVES: 8 to 10

¼ cup brown sugar

¼ cup 4-color peppercorn blend, roughly ground

¼ cup dark rum

¼ cup molasses (preferably mildly flavored)

4 tablespoons unsalted butter

1 tablespoon Dijon mustard

1 (8 to 9-pound) cooked spiral-sliced ham

Hickory or mesquite wood chunks

Desserts, Cookies, and Cakes

Columbus skyline

ONLY a short drive from New Albany is the Ohio state capital, Columbus. It is the fifteenth largest city in the United States and the second-fastest-growing major metropolitan area in the Midwest. Its residents and businesses get to experience the best of both worlds—cosmopolitan city living and midwestern values of friendliness and tolerance. Residents in and around Columbus enjoy easy commute times, neighborhood variety, and a vibrant downtown that helps them strike a special balance between work and play all in the same day.

The community's workforce of roughly 927,000 people has strong employment in finance and insurance, transportation and warehousing, professional services, and education, health, and social services. Six Fortune 500 companies, including Abercrombie & Fitch, American Electric Power, Cardinal Health, Limited Brands, Nationwide, and Wendy's International are headquartered in Columbus and its suburbs. The central location of Columbus makes it ideal for distribution, with easy access to all major U.S. cities. Entrepreneurs and small business owners are at home here too, which adds to the diversity of this ever-expanding city.

Educational attainment in Columbus exceeds state and national levels. Families find a diverse range of school districts; three local high schools are listed on *Newsweek* magazine's top 1,000 list. With 20 colleges and universities in the region, opportunities for continued learning are abundant, and the workforce—built in part by local graduates—is strong. These institutions of higher learning include private liberal arts colleges, community colleges, business schools, a college of arts and design, and of course the Ohio State University, the nation's third-largest campus.

Ranked among the best in the country by *U.S. World News & World Report,* Columbus's four health-care systems keep our community healthy with world-class heart, cancer, and pediatric care. Friendly competition among the four systems creates incentives for innovative patient treatment and efficient operations that keep area health-care costs below the national average.

After work, Columbus residents take part in a wide variety of cultural, entertainment, sporting, and recreational activities. The city boasts professional teams in hockey, soccer, and arena football. World-class shopping and dining, a nationally recognized zoo and aquarium, and six state parks offer a range of enticing options. The Columbus region is rich in arts, with a full-time symphony orchestra, a jazz orchestra, a grand opera, one of the top ballet companies in the country, 20 theater companies, and more than 100 art galleries and dealers.

— *Susan Merryman on behalf of Columbus Chamber of Commerce*

Vanilla Cream Wafers 209

Scandinavian Almond Wedges with Cointreau 210

Biscotti di Prato
(Bite-sized Almond Biscotti from Prato) 212

Dried Cranberry Biscotti 213

Brown Sugar Ginger Crisps 214

Crispy Thin Oatmeal Cookies 215

Mint Chocolate Chip Cookies 216

Grand Marnier Madeleines 217

Peach Currant Rugelach 218

Lemon Squares 219

Mexican Truffles 220

Raspberry-topped Chocolate Tart with Pecan Crust 221

Strawberry Cream Tart 222

Bananas Foster 223

Crème Caramel Filipino Style (Leche Flan) 224

Coconut Flan 225

Ginger and Vanilla Crème Brûlée 226

Apple Clafoutis 227

Mexican Sundae with Tortilla Crisps 228

White Chocolate Bread Pudding with
White Chocolate Sauce 229

Blueberry and Nectarine Crisp 230

Tiramisù with Kahlua and Amaretto 231

Mormor's Meringue and Cream Torte 232

Fresh Berry Cake with Raspberry Glaze 233

Golda's Hungarian King's Cake 234

Black Russian Cake 235

Sally's Orange Almond Cake 236

Chocolate Almond Pound Cake 237

Black Forest Cupcakes 238

Chocolate and Port Gâteau with Chocolate Icing 239

Flourless Chocolate Torte with
Toffee and Amaretto Cream 240

Vanilla Cream Wafers

LINDY TURNBULL'S DELICATE MELT-IN-YOUR-MOUTH BUTTER WAFERS CAN BE PRESENTED IN VARIOUS COLOR COMBINATIONS DEPENDING ON THE OCCASION.

1 To make the cookies, blend the butter and cream with an electric mixer until light and fluffy. Beat in the flour and mix until incorporated into a dough. Be careful not to over-mix. Divide the dough into 3 pieces, gently shape each piece into a disk, wrap in plastic wrap, and chill for 1 hour.

2 Preheat the oven to 375°F. Fill a plate with granular sugar.

3 Working with one piece of dough at a time (keep the rest chilled), place the dough on a generously floured surface and roll out to ⅛-inch thickness. Cut out cookies using a 1-inch round cookie cutter. Press each round lightly in the sugar to coat both sides. Place rounds 1½ inches apart on an ungreased cookie sheet and prick the top of each round twice with a fork, making two rows of "dots." Bake for 5 to 7 minutes, until the cookies are very light golden around the edge; don't let the cookies brown on the bottom. Cool cookies on the cookie sheet for 15 minutes, then transfer to a rack to cool completely. Repeat with the remaining dough.

4 To make the frosting, beat the butter and sugar with an electric mixer until light in color. Beat in the egg yolk and vanilla. Beat in food coloring, if desired. Place ½ teaspoon of frosting on the bottom of a cookie, then make a sandwich by placing the bottom of another cookie on top and pressing gently. Chill for about an hour to set the frosting.

YIELD: 3 dozen

CHEF TIP: Cookies will keep in the freezer for 2 weeks. Thaw cookies for an hour before serving.

Cookies:

1 cup unsalted butter, at room temperature

⅓ cup whipping cream

2 cups sifted all-purpose flour

Granular sugar for coating

Frosting:

¼ cup unsalted butter, at room temperature

¾ cup sifted confectioners' sugar

1 egg yolk, beaten

1 teaspoon vanilla

Food coloring of choice (optional)

Scandinavian Almond Wedges with Cointreau

THIS SCANDINAVIAN TREAT, A JOHANSSON FAMILY CHERISHED RECIPE, IS PERFECT FOR AN AFTERNOON TEA PARTY OR OTHER FESTIVE OCCASIONS. WRAP SEVERAL WEDGES IN CELLOPHANE AND TIE WITH AN ORANGE BOW FOR A CHARMING HOSTESS GIFT.

1 Preheat the oven to 350°F. Butter a 12 by 9-inch baking pan.

2 To make the bottom crust, combine the flour, butter, sugar, and egg yolks in a bowl. Using a wooden spoon, mix until all ingredients are just combined into a dough. Knead dough on a floured surface until smooth. Working quickly so the dough does not stick to the counter, roll out the dough to the size of the baking pan and press it into the bottom of the pan.

3 To make the filling, crumble the almond paste into a bowl. Add the eggs and butter and beat well. Beat in the flour and baking powder until smooth. Beat in the Cointreau. Pour the filling onto the bottom layer. Bake for 30 to 40 minutes or until the filling is light brown and set (a toothpick inserted into the filling should come out dry). Let cool in the pan for 10 minutes. Cut into 2-inch triangles, transfer to a rack and let cool completely.

4 To make the glaze, beat together the confectioners' sugar, Cointreau, and vegetable oil. Beat in the orange juice to make the glaze smooth and thin. Add a drop of orange food coloring and beat again.

Bottom Crust:

1¼ cups all-purpose flour

1 stick unsalted butter (½ cup), at room temperature

¼ cup sugar

1 to 2 egg yolks

Filling:

7 ounces almond paste* (store-bought or see recipe opposite), at room temperature

2 eggs

1 tablespoon unsalted butter, at room temperature

3 tablespoons all-purpose flour

1 teaspoon baking powder

½ teaspoon Cointreau or other orange liqueur

*a smooth blend of ground almonds and sugar, typically packed in cans and found in the baking aisle of a supermarket or at specialty nut stores. Do not use marzipan.

Glaze:

1 cup confectioners' sugar

1 tablespoon Cointreau or other orange liqueur

½ teaspoon vegetable oil

⅛ teaspoon orange juice

Orange food coloring

Finely chopped candied orange peel

Spread the glaze thinly over the top and sides of the wedges. Sprinkle with candied orange peel. Refrigerate until the glaze hardens.

YIELD: 20 cookies

CHEF TIP: Almond wedges will keep for 1 week in the refrigerator or 4 weeks in the freezer, stored in airtight plastic containers. If frozen, thaw for at least 2 hours before serving.

ALMOND PASTE

1 Blend the butter and sugar with a wooden spoon until well mixed. Add the eggs and ground almonds and stir until everything is mixed thoroughly.

6 tablespoons unsalted butter, at room temperature

¾ cup confectioners' sugar

2 large eggs

1 cup ground almonds

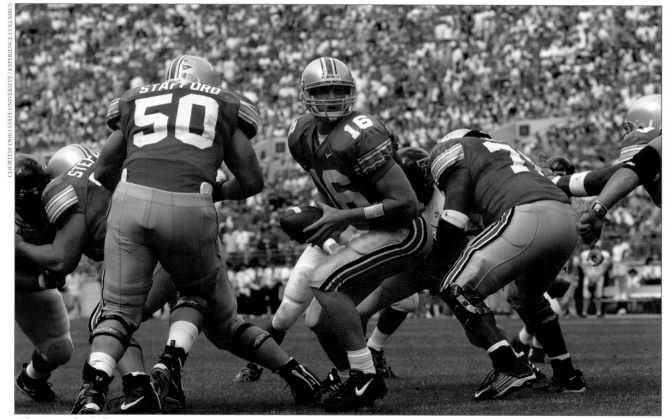

Ohio State football

Biscotti di Prato
(Bite-sized Almond Biscotti from Prato)

These irresistible almond cookies are traditionally dunked in a glass of Vin Santo dessert wine to finish off a celebratory meal.

1 Set oven racks in the top third and lower third of the oven and preheat the oven to 350°F. Line 2 heavy baking sheets with parchment paper or silicone baking mats.

2 Place the flour in a mound on your work surface and make a well in the center. Put the sugar, 4 of the eggs, the egg yolk, baking powder, salt, saffron, and melted butter in the well, and, using the fingers of one hand, stir them together. Begin to mix in flour from the sides of the well, gradually forming a dough. The dough will be soft and sticky but hold its shape when you drop it from a spoon. Knead in the almonds. Dust your hands with flour anytime the mixture gets sticky. Shape the dough into 4 logs about 2½ inches wide and ½ inch high.

3 Place 2 logs on each baking sheet, spacing them 3 inches apart, as they will expand. Beat the remaining egg and brush the logs with it. Bake the logs for 35 to 40 minutes or until they are light brown, switching racks midway. Remove from the oven and let cool 15 minutes on the baking sheets on a rack. Do not turn off the oven.

4 Transfer the logs to a work surface. Discard parchment paper. Using a serrated knife, cut logs on the diagonal into ½-inch slices. Place the slices cut side up on the same baking sheets and bake again for 10 minutes. Turn slices over and bake an additional 5 minutes or until crisp. Transfer to a rack to cool completely.

YIELD: 6 dozen

CHEF TIP: Biscotti can be prepared one week ahead. Store in an airtight container at room temperature.

3½ cups all-purpose flour

2 cups sugar

5 large eggs

1 egg yolk

1 teaspoon baking powder

½ teaspoon salt

½ teaspoon crushed saffron threads

6 tablespoons unsalted butter, melted and slightly cooled

1½ cups whole almonds with skins, toasted and coarsely chopped

Dried Cranberry Biscotti

THESE BISCOTTI ARE MORE AMERICAN-STYLE THAN THE PRECEDING TRADITIONAL ITALIAN COUNTERPART. USING MORE BUTTER PRODUCES A SOFTER, CRUNCHIER, RICHER, MORE COOKIE-LIKE TEXTURE. THERE IS NO NEED TO DUNK THEM IN COFFEE OR WINE.

1 Preheat the oven to 350°F. Line a heavy baking sheet with parchment paper or a silicone baking mat.

2 Combine the flour, baking powder, and salt. In a large bowl using an electric mixer, beat together the sugar, butter, 2 eggs, and almond extract until well blended. Beat in the flour mixture, then stir in the cranberries and almonds.

3 Divide the dough in half. Using floured hands, shape each piece into a log 2½ inches wide, 9½ inches long, and 1 inch high. Transfer the logs to the baking sheet, spacing evenly. Whisk the egg white in a small bowl until foamy; brush over top and sides of each log. Sprinkle with turbinado sugar, if using.

4 Bake the logs until golden brown (logs will spread), about 40 minutes. Cool 10 minutes on the baking sheet on a rack. Do not turn off the oven.

5 Transfer the logs to a work surface. Discard parchment paper. Using a serrated knife, cut logs on the diagonal into ½-inch slices. Arrange slices cut side up on the baking sheet. Bake for 8 minutes, until just beginning to color, then turn over and bake an additional 5 minutes. Transfer biscotti to racks to cool completely.

YIELD: about 4 dozen

2½ cups all-purpose flour

1 teaspoon baking powder

½ teaspoon salt

1½ cups sugar

½ cup (1 stick) unsalted butter, at room temperature

2 large eggs

½ teaspoon almond extract

1½ cups dried cranberries (about 6 ounces)

½ cup toasted whole almonds

1 egg white for egg wash

2 to 3 tablespoons turbinado sugar (optional)*

*turbinado is what remains after raw sugar is washed; it can be found in the baking section or organic section of the supermarket.

Brown Sugar Ginger Crisps

A GREAT ADDITION TO A COOKIE GIFT TIN FOR HOLIDAY GIFT-GIVING. THE BUTTERY GINGER TASTE IS SIMPLY DIVINE!

1 Preheat the oven to 350°F. Lightly grease (or line with parchment paper or silicone baking mats) 2 cookie sheets.

2 Sift together the flour, baking powder, and salt. In a large bowl, cream together the butter and brown sugar until pale and fluffy, about 3 minutes. Beat in the egg yolk, vanilla, crystallized ginger, and ground ginger until well combined. Beat in the flour mixture until just combined.

3 Drop heaping teaspoons of dough about 3 inches apart onto the cookie sheets. Bake one sheet at a time in the middle of the oven until golden, 13 to 15 minutes. Do not bake more than one sheet at a time or the cookies will not cook through and brown evenly. Cool on cookie sheets on a rack for 5 minutes, then transfer to racks to cool completely.

YIELD: about 4 dozen

CHEF TIPS: Cookies can be kept in an airtight container at room temperature for 3 weeks.

Silpat or other silicone nonstick baking sheet liners make clean-up a breeze and save on paper over the long term.

1½ cups all-purpose flour

¾ teaspoon baking powder

½ teaspoon salt

1 cup (2 sticks) unsalted butter, softened

1 cup packed light brown sugar

1 large egg yolk

1 teaspoon vanilla

½ cup finely chopped crystallized ginger

½ teaspoon ground ginger

Crispy Thin Oatmeal Cookies

KIDS AND ADULTS ALIKE LOVE THESE DELICATE AND DELICIOUS COOKIES. THIS DESSERT WILL BE A STAR IF YOU SERVE THESE WITH FRUIT-TOPPED ICE CREAM AT YOUR NEXT DINNER PARTY.

1 Preheat the oven to 350°F. Line 4 baking sheets with parchment paper or silicone baking mats.

2 In a large bowl, stir together the oats, sugar, flour, salt, and baking powder. In a small bowl beat the egg and vanilla with a fork until just blended. Add egg mixture to the oat mixture and blend thoroughly. Add the butter and stir until just combined. The batter will be moist. Let batter rest for 20 minutes, stirring occasionally.

3 Drop batter 1 teaspoon at a time onto prepared baking sheets, leaving 2½ inches between cookies as they will spread to a 3-inch diameter. Bake one sheet at a time until cookies are golden, 8 to 10 minutes, watching carefully and rotating the cookie sheet if necessary for even baking. Slide parchment with cookies onto a rack. Let cookies cool completely. Gently peel cookies from parchment and store in an airtight container.

YIELD: 4 dozen

1 cup old-fashioned or quick-cooking rolled oats

1 cup sugar

2 tablespoons plus 2 teaspoons all-purpose flour

½ teaspoon salt

½ teaspoon baking powder

1 large egg

1 teaspoon vanilla

½ cup (1 stick) unsalted butter, melted

COURTESY ROD BERRY / EXPERIENCE COLUMBUS

Short North Gallery Hop

HIGH STREET HIGHLIGHTS

Whether you want to wander charming historical areas, peruse sophisticated art galleries, browse one-of-a-kind boutiques or savor a gourmet meal, you can find it in and around High Street.

The Short North is a popular area centered on High Street that is packed with trendy bars, fine dining, intriguing boutiques, and an array of unique art galleries. The area is at its liveliest during Gallery Hop, a bustling neighborhood-wide open house held the first Saturday of every month. It's the best time to people-watch and browse the area's galleries, which offer everything from contemporary photography to African-American sculpture.

Located just a block west is the historic Victorian Village, a quaint neighborhood full of beautifully restored Victorian mansions. This area also features Goodale Park, one of the oldest urban green spaces in the country.

German Village is east of High Street. It is a traditional European neighborhood featuring cobblestone streets, gorgeous restored homes in classic Dutch, Italianate, and Queen Anne designs and the 23-acre Schiller Park.

The Ohio State University sits farther north on High Street. Its famous Oval, the park-like heart of the campus, was designed by Central Park architect Frederick Law Olmsted. A new $150-million development called South Campus Gateway features shops, bars, restaurants, shops, and a deluxe seven-screen movie theater.

— *Information courtesy Experience Columbus*

Mint Chocolate Chip Cookies

IF YOU LOVE THOSE IRRESISTIBLY DELICIOUS THIN MINT GIRL SCOUT COOKIES THAT COME TO YOUR DOOR ONCE A YEAR, THEN YOU WILL LOVE THESE COOKIES.

1 Preheat the oven to 350°F. Line a cookie sheet with parchment paper or a silicone baking mat.

2 Place peppermint candies in a resealable plastic bag and crush with a rolling pin. Set aside. Later you will sprinkle this on top of each frosted cookie.

3 In the bowl of an electric mixer, cream the butter and both sugars until light and fluffy. Beat in the vanilla. Beat in the eggs, one at a time, and mix well. Beat in the cocoa. Sift together the flour, baking soda, and salt and add to the butter mixture with the mixer on low speed. Stir until just combined. Fold in the chocolate chunks and baking chips.

4 Drop tablespoons of dough onto the cookie sheet. Dampen your hands and flatten the dough slightly. Bake for 15 minutes or until the cookies are set on top but give easily when touched; the cookies should seem a little under-done. Cool slightly on the pan, then transfer to a rack to cool completely.

5 To make the frosting, beat together the confectioners' sugar and butter. Add vanilla and beat until smooth. Add 5 to 6 drops of food coloring and beat to make pink frosting.

6 Spread frosting on the top of each cookie and sprinkle with the crushed peppermint candy.

YIELD: about 4 dozen cookies

CHEF TIP: We have found that an excellent choice for good unsweetened cocoa is Dutch Cocoa from Penzeys.

12 hard peppermint candies or 5 candy canes

1 cup unsalted butter, at room temperature

1 cup packed light brown sugar

1 cup granulated sugar

2 teaspoons vanilla

2 large eggs, at room temperature

⅔ cup cocoa powder

2 cups all-purpose flour

1 teaspoon baking soda

1 teaspoon kosher salt

8 ounces semisweet chocolate, cut into chunks

10 ounces Andes crème de menthe baking chips*

Butter frosting (recipe below)

*if you can't find the baking chips, just cut up Andes chocolate mint candies

Butter Frosting:

4 cups confectioners' sugar, sifted

1 cup unsalted butter, at room temperature

2 teaspoons vanilla

Red food coloring (optional)

Grand Marnier Madeleines

A TWIST ON THE FAMOUS SPONGE CAKE IMMORTALIZED BY THE FRENCH NOVELIST MARCEL PROUST. THEY ARE A PERFECT ENDING TO ALMOST ANY DINNER PARTY OR AN ACCOMPANIMENT TO AFTERNOON TEA.

1   Preheat the oven to 375°F. Using a pastry brush, thoroughly grease 3 madeleine pans with the melted butter, making sure you grease the many indentations of the seashell-like molds. Sprinkle the molds with flour and shake off the excess.

2   In a medium bowl, combine the eggs, salt, orange zest, and sugar; beat until thick, 6 to 8 minutes. Add Grand Marnier and mix gently. With a rubber spatula fold in the flour quickly and gently. Fold in the melted butter gently, making sure that it does not settle on the bottom. Working rapidly, gently spoon the batter into the madeleine pans, filling each indentation about three-quarters full. Bake until golden brown, about 10 minutes. Remove from pans and cool on racks.

3   Madeleines may be dusted with confectioners' sugar after they have cooled.

YIELD: 3 dozen

CHEF TIP: Dipping the madeleines halfway in melted chocolate makes for a spiffy presentation.

4 tablespoons melted butter for greasing pans

4 large eggs

Pinch of salt

Grated zest of 1 orange

⅔ cup sugar

1 teaspoon Grand Marnier or other orange liqueur

1 cup sifted all-purpose flour

½ cup (1 stick) unsalted butter, melted and cooled

Confectioners' sugar for dusting

Peach Currant Rugelach

RUGELACH ARE WONDERFUL ROLLED CREAM CHEESE COOKIES SOMETIMES CALLED RUSSIAN TEA BISCUITS AND TRADITIONALLY BAKED FOR JEWISH HOLIDAYS. THEY ARE WONDERFUL SERVED AT AFTERNOON TEA OR AFTER DINNER WITH ICE CREAM AND COFFEE.

1 To make the pastry, place the cream cheese and the butter in the bowl of an electric mixer and beat until light. Add the sugar, salt, lemon zest, and vanilla. With the mixer on low speed, add the flour and mix until just combined. Transfer the dough to a lightly floured surface, shape it into a ball and flatten it slightly. Cut the ball into quarters, shape each quarter into a ball, then wrap each ball in plastic wrap and chill overnight.

2 To make the filling, combine the sugars, cinnamon, pecans, and currants. Set aside.

3 Line 2 cookie sheets with parchment paper or a silicone baking mat. Remove one piece of pastry from the refrigerator (keep the remaining dough chilled) and on a well-floured surface roll the dough into a 9-inch circle. Spread 2 heaping tablespoons of the preserves onto the dough, keeping a ½-inch border clear. Sprinkle with ½ cup of the filling. Press the filling lightly into the dough by rolling over it gently with a rolling pin. Cut the circle into quarters, then cut each quarter into thirds to make 12 equal wedges. Starting at the widest edge, roll up each wedge. Curve each cookie slightly to form an arc and place on the cookie sheet. Repeat with the remaining dough, preserves, and filling. Chill for 30 minutes.

4 Meanwhile, preheat the oven to 350°F.

5 Brush each cookie with the egg wash. Sift the cinnamon sugar over the cookies. Bake for 15 to 20 minutes, until lightly browned. Transfer to racks to cool.

YIELD: 4 dozen

Pastry:

8 ounces cream cheese, at room temperature and cut in 4 pieces

1 cup (2 sticks) unsalted butter, at room temperature

¼ cup sugar

Pinch of kosher salt

Grated zest of 1 lemon

1 teaspoon vanilla

2 cups unbleached all-purpose flour, sifted

Filling:

¼ cup firmly packed light brown sugar

6 tablespoons granulated sugar

½ teaspoon ground cinnamon

1 cup pecans, toasted and finely chopped

¾ cup currants

¾ cup peach, apricot, or raspberry preserves, puréed in a food processor

Topping:

1 egg beaten with 1 tablespoon milk, for egg wash

3 tablespoons sugar mixed with 1 teaspoon cinnamon

Lemon Squares

THESE ATTRACTIVE LEMON SQUARES, WITH THEIR BRIGHT YELLOW FILLING PEEKING OUT FROM UNDER A LAYER OF CONFECTIONERS' SUGAR, ARE A WONDERFUL ADDITION TO A PASTRY TRAY FOR A BUFFET DINNER.

1. To make the crust, in the bowl of an electric mixer, cream the butter with the confectioners' sugar until light. Mix the flour and salt; add to the butter mixture and beat until just mixed. Turn the mixture out onto a floured surface and gather it into a ball. With floured hands, flatten the dough into a rectangle, then press it over the bottom and ½ inch up the sides of a 13 by 9-inch baking pan. Chill for at least 30 minutes.

2. Preheat the oven to 350°F. Bake the crust for 15 to 20 minutes, until lightly browned. Cool on a rack while you make the filling. Do not turn off the oven.

3. To make the filling, whisk together the eggs, granulated sugar, flour, lemon juice, and lemon zest until well combined. Pour the mixture over the baked butter crust and bake for 30 to 35 minutes, until the filling is set. Let cool on a rack. When cool, dust with confectioners' sugar and cut into 2-inch squares.

YIELD: 24 squares

Crust:

1 cup unsalted butter, at room temperature and cut into small pieces (½ pound)

½ cup confectioners' sugar

2 cups unbleached all-purpose flour, sifted

Pinch of kosher salt

Filling:

6 large eggs, at room temperature

2¾ cups granulated sugar

1 cup unbleached all-purpose flour

1 cup freshly squeezed lemon juice

1½ tablespoons grated lemon zest

Confectioners' sugar for dusting

Mexican Truffles

CINNAMON AND KAHLUA COMBINE WITH THE CHOCOLATE AND MILK IN THIS TRUFFLE TO CREATE A DISTINCTIVE FLAVOR, SPICY BUT NOT HOT. YOU MAY, HOWEVER, NOTCH UP THE HEAT BY ADDING CAYENNE.

1 In a heavy saucepan over low heat, combine the chocolate chips, condensed milk, and cinnamon. Stir until all the chips are melted and the mixture is smooth. Remove from the heat and stir in the Kahlua. Chill for 2 hours or until the mixture is firm enough to work with. Shape into whatever size truffle you prefer and then roll the truffles in the cookie crumbs. Chill the finished truffles for 1 hour before serving.

2 The truffles will keep, refrigerated, about 3 weeks.

YIELD: 2 dozen

VARIATIONS: Roll truffles in a good-quality cocoa powder or confectioners' sugar to make a pretty platter with various coatings.

For different flavors, add a pinch of cayenne when melting the chocolate and/or use a liqueur or extract such as framboise (raspberry), amaretto (almond), kirsch (cherry), or Grand Marnier (orange).

Use a mixture of semisweet and milk chocolate chips for a lighter truffle.

3 cups (18 ounces) semisweet chocolate chips

1 (14-ounce) can sweetened condensed milk

1 teaspoon cinnamon

¼ cup Kahlua

Chocolate wafer cookie crumbs (see variations below)

Raspberry-topped Chocolate Tart with Pecan Crust

THE PECAN PIE CRUST PROVIDES A NICE CONTRAST TO THE SMOOTH AND CREAMY CHOCOLATE FILLING. THE RASPBERRY TOPPING MAKES A VERY STRIKING PRESENTATION.

1 Preheat the oven to 325°F.

2 To make the crust, finely grind the pecans, sugar, and cinnamon in a food processor. Add the butter and process until moist clumps form. Press the dough over the bottom of a 9-inch tart pan with removable bottom. Bake the crust until golden brown and firm to the touch, about 30 minutes. Transfer to a rack to cool completely.

3 To make the filling, bring the cream to a simmer in a medium, heavy saucepan. Remove from the heat. Add the chocolate and stir until melted and smooth. Pour the chocolate over the cooled crust and let cool 15 minutes. Arrange raspberries decoratively over the top, pressing each one lightly into the chocolate. Chill until set, about 1 hour. (The tart can be made up to this point 1 day ahead.)

4 Just before serving, brush the jam over the berries.

SERVES: 8 to 10

Crust:

2 cups pecans

6 tablespoons packed light brown sugar

¼ teaspoon cinnamon

4 tablespoons (½ stick) unsalted butter, melted

Filling:

¾ cup whipping cream

6 ounces bittersweet chocolate, chopped

Topping:

1 pint fresh raspberries

¼ cup seedless raspberry jam, puréed in a food processor

COLUMBUS'S LIVELY PERFORMING ARTS SCENE HAS IT ALL

For superb song, dance, and drama direct from the Big Apple, catch a Broadway Across America–Columbus production at the historic Ohio and Palace theaters downtown. Enjoy a play by the Contemporary American Theatre Company (CATCO), Columbus's resident professional theater group, downtown at the Riffe Center's Studio One Theatre. Shadowbox Cabaret at Easton Town Center offers a mix of one-act plays, wacky sketch comedy, and live rock 'n' roll. The Ohio State University's Wexner Center for the Arts offers world-class modern dance, including cutting-edge contemporary fare you won't see anywhere else. And the Columbus Children's Theatre and Phoenix Theatre for Children produce an array of fun and family-oriented fare.

On the music front, the seasonal lineups for the Columbus Symphony Orchestra and ProMusica Chamber Orchestra are always packed with celebrated classical works. Columbus delivers jumpin' jazz in the Southern Theatre thanks to the Columbus Jazz Orchestra. If opera is your passion, turn to Opera Columbus for lavish productions.

Columbus's resident dance company BalletMet is noted for its versatility in presenting everything from full-length classics to the most recent works by contemporary choreographers.

The King Arts Complex presents lively jazz, innovative dance, and an array of provocative performances, while the Columbus Association for the Performing Arts (CAPA) brings in an eclectic mix of touring shows each season.
— *Information courtesy Experience Columbus*

Columbus Symphony Orchestra

Strawberry Cream Tart

THIS TART IS ALWAYS A FAVORITE AND A WINNER IN THE GOOD-LOOKS DEPARTMENT.

Crust:

1¾ cup all-purpose flour

½ cup confectioners' sugar

½ teaspoon salt

¾ cup cold unsalted butter, cut into ½-inch pieces

2 large eggs

Filling and Topping:

6 ounces cream cheese

½ cup confectioners' sugar

1 teaspoon vanilla bean paste

½ cup sour cream

2 quarts strawberries, hulled and halved

½ cup seedless raspberry jelly

¼ cup pistachio nuts, chopped (optional)

1. To make the crust, in a food processor, pulse the flour, sugar, and salt to blend. Add the butter and pulse until the mixture resembles coarse meal. Add the eggs and pulse until moist clumps form. Gather the dough into a ball and flatten into a disk. Wrap in plastic wrap and chill for 1 hour.

2. On a floured surface, roll out the dough to a 14-inch round. Transfer to a 9-inch tart pan with removable bottom and press into the pan. Trim the edges, leaving a ½-inch overhang. Fold the overhanging dough in and press to form high-standing double-thick sides. Pierce all over with a fork. Freeze for 20 minutes.

3. Preheat the oven to 350°F. Bake crust piercing it with a fork if it bubbles, until golden, about 30 minutes. Cool on a rack.

4. To make the filling, in a medium bowl beat together the cream cheese, sugar, and vanilla paste. Beat in the sour cream. Spread the filling in the crust. Chill until firm, about 1 hour. (The tart can be prepared to this point 1 day head. Cover and keep chilled.)

5. Remove the pan sides from the tart and slide the tart from the pan bottom onto a platter. Arrange the berries over the tart. Melt the jelly in a small saucepan over low heat; brush over the berries. Sprinkle with pistachios, if desired. (The tart can be finished 4 hours ahead. Keep chilled.)

SERVES: 8

Bananas Foster

PREPARING THIS DESSERT AFTER DINNER IN VIEW OF YOUR GUESTS MAKES FOR A GREAT SHOW.

1 Peel the bananas and cut into ½-inch slices. Brush banana slices all over with the lemon juice. Melt the sugar and butter in a 10-inch skillet over medium-high heat. Add the bananas and sauté until tender. Sprinkle with the cinnamon.

2 Remove from the heat. Add the rum and liqueur. Immediately ignite with a long match and swirl bananas and warm liquid until the flame dies out. Divide the sauce and bananas over 4 servings of ice cream.

SERVES: 4

CHEF TIPS: Bananas are ripe when the skin is yellow with brown flecks.

Use rum from the liquor store, not the diluted supermarket version.

2 ripe bananas

2 teaspoons fresh lemon juice

¼ cup brown sugar

2 tablespoons unsalted butter

⅛ teaspoon cinnamon

¼ cup white rum

2 tablespoons banana liqueur

1 pint vanilla ice cream

EASTON TOWN CENTER

Considered one of the leading examples of "new urbanism" development, Easton Town Center is a European-style pedestrian-friendly and vibrant commercial district just 10 minutes from New Albany. The 1.5-million-square-foot dining, entertainment, and retail center, with more than 200 tenants, is the heart and soul of a 1,300-acre master-planned commercial and residential community known as Easton. It is also known as a proving ground for new-to-market tenants and concepts.

When it debuted in June of 1999, Easton Town Center quickly established itself as a Midwest destination for people looking to experience an exceptionally strong and upscale mix of retail shops, fine-dining restaurants, and entertainment venues. Whether you want to eat outdoors with a fountain view, people-watch at a casual pub, enjoy a gourmet meal with that special someone, or conduct a private business meeting in an upscale dining establishment—Easton has it all.

In a typical day, visitors to Easton may surf the Internet for free at Central Ohio's largest wireless hotspot, sweat off a few pounds at a full-service 24-hour gym, catch a flick at Ohio's most popular theater, and dine on the freshest seafood available.

The community spaces at Easton have reinforced its pedestrian-friendly streetscape, with additions including a permanent outdoor children's train park and several pop-up water fountains.

With more than a million visitors each month, Easton has become an unprecedented hub for commercial activity in the region. — *Hinson Ltd.*

COURTESY EASTON / EXPERIENCE COLUMBUS

Easton Town Center

Crème Caramel Filipino Style (Leche Flan)

THIS DESSERT, WHICH IS OF SPANISH ORIGIN, IS THE PHILIPPINES' NATIONAL DESSERT. IT IS RICH, CREAMY, AND SIMPLY DELICIOUS!

1   Preheat the oven to 325°F. To a roasting pan large enough to hold a 6-cup custard mold, add hot water to come 1 inch up the side. Place this pan in the oven.

2   To make the caramel, combine the sugar and water in a 6 or 8-cup microwave-safe measuring cup. Cover tightly with microwave-safe plastic wrap and cook on high for 7 to 8 minutes, until the syrup turns deep amber (the longer it's cooked, the darker the caramel). Watch carefully, checking every 10 seconds as the caramel approaches the desired shade. Pierce the plastic with a knife and uncover carefully. Pour the caramel into the mold and tilt the mold to cover the sides as well as the base. Work quickly, as the caramel will harden.

3   To make the custard, in a medium bowl, lightly beat the eggs and egg yolks until blended but not frothy. Add the sugar and salt; whisk gently to mix. Heat the evaporated milk until it is very hot but not boiling. Slowly pour the hot milk into the eggs, whisking vigorously as you do so. Whisk in the vanilla.

4   Strain the custard into the prepared mold. Cover with foil. Put the mold in the roasting pan. Bake until a knife inserted in the center comes out clean, about 50 minutes. Remove the mold from the water and allow the custard to cool before inverting it onto a serving plate. The custard is traditionally served cold, but you may also serve it warm.

SERVES: 4

CHEF TIP: For an attractive presentation, chill the custard overnight. The custard will come out of the mold much more easily and will look perfect with the deep caramelized color on all sides.

Caramel:

1 cup sugar

¼ cup water

Custard:

3 large eggs

2 large egg yolks

¼ cup plus 2 tablespoons sugar

Pinch of salt

3 (12-ounce) cans evaporated milk

1½ teaspoons vanilla

Coconut Flan

THIS DESSERT COMBINES VIETNAMESE FLAVORS WITH WESTERN COOKING TECHNIQUES.

Caramel:

1 cup sugar

¼ cup water

Custard:

1 cup coconut milk

1 cup whole milk

¼ cup sugar

4 eggs

1 teaspoon vanilla

1 Preheat the oven to 325°F. Pour a 1-inch depth of hot water into a roasting pan large enough to hold a 6-cup custard mold. Place this pan in the oven.

2 To make the caramel, combine the sugar and water in a 6- or 8-cup microwave-safe measuring cup. Cover tightly with microwave-safe plastic wrap and cook on high for 7 to 8 minutes, until the syrup turns deep amber (the longer it's cooked, the darker the caramel). Watch carefully, checking every 10 seconds as the caramel approaches the desired shade. Pierce the plastic with a knife and uncover carefully. Pour the caramel into the mold and tilt the mold to cover the sides as well as the base. Work quickly, as the caramel will harden.

3 To make the custard, combine the coconut milk, whole milk, and sugar in a medium saucepan over low heat. Stir until the sugar dissolves completely. Remove from the heat. In a large bowl, whisk the eggs and vanilla. Gradually whisk in the hot milk, blending thoroughly.

4 Strain the custard into the prepared mold. Cover with foil. Put the mold in the roasting pan. Bake until a knife inserted in the center comes out clean, 40 to 60 minutes. Remove the mold from the water and let cool to room temperature. Cover with plastic wrap or foil and refrigerate until thoroughly chilled, at least 8 hours.

5 To serve, run a knife around the edge of the mold if the custard is not already loose. Invert a serving plate over the mold and, holding the mold and the plate firmly together, turn them over. Tap the plate on a flat surface and allow the custard to slide out onto the serving plate. Serve chilled.

SERVES: 6

CHEF TIP: For an attractive presentation, chill the custard overnight. The custard will come out of the mold much more easily and will look perfect with the deep caramelized color on all sides.

Ginger and Vanilla Crème Brûlée

THIS IS A TWIST ON THE CLASSIC CRÈME BRÛLÉE, AN ENORMOUSLY POPULAR FRENCH DESSERT.

1 Preheat the oven to 325°F. Place six ¾-cup ramekins in a roasting pan.

2 Combine the cream, sugar, and ginger in a medium, heavy saucepan. Using a small sharp knife, scrape the seeds from the vanilla bean. Add the seeds and bean to the saucepan. Stir over medium heat until the sugar dissolves and the mixture comes to a simmer. Cover, turn off the heat and let stand for 10 minutes to infuse flavors. Strain into a 6-cup measure.

3 Whisk the yolks in a medium bowl until well blended. Pour ½ cup of the cream mixture into the egg yolks while whisking quickly. This will slowly heat the yolks, reducing the chance of their curdling. While quickly whisking the cream, slowly pour the yolks into the cream. Divide the mixture among the ramekins. Pour enough hot water into the pan to come halfway up the sides of the ramekins. Carefully transfer the pan to the oven. Bake the custards until almost set in the center when the ramekins are gently shaken, about 30 minutes. Using a metal spatula or tongs, remove the ramekins from the water; let cool for 30 minutes, then cover and chill at least 3 hours and up to 2 days.

4 Sprinkle 2 teaspoons sugar evenly over each custard. Working with one custard at a time, hold a kitchen blowtorch so that the flame is 2 inches above the surface. Direct the flame so that the sugar melts and browns evenly, about 2 minutes. Refrigerate until the custards are firm again but the topping is still brittle, at least 2 hours but no longer than 4 hours. Serve crème brûlées garnished with fruit slices.

SERVES: 6

CHEF TIPS: For best results, chill the custard-filled ramekin overnight before baking.

Use a kettle to pour the simmering water into the baking pan. It's easier to pour and less likely to splash into the custards.

2 cups whipping cream

½ cup sugar

2 tablespoons chopped peeled fresh ginger

1 vanilla bean, split lengthwise (or 2 teaspoons vanilla extract)

5 large egg yolks

¼ cup confectioners' or light brown sugar

Sliced tropical fruit such as mango, papaya, or kiwi for garnish

Apple Clafoutis

A WONDERFUL VARIATION ON THE ALWAYS COMFORTING CLAFOUTIS.

1 Preheat the oven to 375°F. Generously butter a ceramic gratin dish 12 inches in diameter and 2 to 3 inches high (or two 8-inch round cake pans).

2 Combine the milk, cream, sugar, and vanilla in a medium saucepan. Bring to a boil over medium-high heat, stirring to dissolve the sugar. Reduce the heat to medium and boil gently to cook slightly, 2 to 3 minutes. Remove from the heat and set aside.

3 Place the flour in a medium bowl. Using an electric mixer, beat in the eggs one at a time, scraping the sides of the bowl often to make a smooth batter. Gradually beat in the warm milk mixture to form a smooth and thin batter. Pour the batter into the gratin dish.

4 Toss the apple slices with the brandy and arrange in layers over the batter; they will sink down as you work. Bake the clafoutis until firm to the touch in the center and lightly golden on top, 1 to 1¼ hours.

5 Let the clafoutis cool to lukewarm or room temperature. Cut into pie-like wedges and dust each serving with confectioners' sugar.

SERVES: 10

2 cups whole milk

1 cup heavy cream

1 cup granulated sugar

1½ teaspoons vanilla

⅔ cup unbleached all-purpose flour

5 large eggs

5 Granny Smith apples (or firm, ripe Anjou pears), peeled, cored and thinly sliced

2 tablespoons brandy or fruit-flavored spirit such as Calvados, Poire Williams, or Grand Marnier

Confectioners' sugar for dusting

Mexican Sundae with Tortilla Crisps

AN EASY-TO-MANAGE SUMMER DESSERT; THE SAUCE CAN BE MADE 3 DAYS AHEAD.

1 To make the sauce, in a small saucepan, whisk together the cream, hot water, and espresso powder. Bring to a simmer, stirring, over medium heat. Remove from the heat. Add vanilla and chocolate and stir until melted and smooth. Stir in the cinnamon. Set aside. (The sauce can be made 3 days ahead and kept, covered and refrigerated. Reheat it before using.)

2 To make the tortilla crisps, in a small bowl blend the butter, sugar, and cinnamon. Spread the butter mixture evenly over the tortillas. Cut each tortilla into 8 wedges (a pizza cutter works well). Place wedges on 2 baking sheets, buttered side up, without touching.

3 Preheat the oven to 400°F. Bake the tortillas until crisp, puffed, and golden, about 8 minutes. Let cool for a few minutes. (Tortilla crisps can be made a day ahead. Store in an airtight container at room temperature.)

4 Place a large scoop of ice cream in individual ice cream sundae cups. Drizzle with warm chocolate sauce. Fan out 3 tortilla crisps just inside the cups and serve immediately. (You will have some leftover tortilla crisps.)

SERVES: 8

CHEF TIP: For a quick dessert preparation after dinner, scoop the ice cream ahead of time and place individual scoops on a cookie sheet lined with wax paper. Keep frozen until ready to use.

Sauce:

½ cup heavy cream

¼ cup hot water

2½ teaspoons instant espresso powder

¼ teaspoon vanilla

8 ounces bittersweet (not unsweetened) or semisweet chocolate, chopped

¼ teaspoon cinnamon

Tortilla Crisps:

¼ cup unsalted butter, at room temperature

2 tablespoons sugar

2 teaspoons cinnamon

4 (8-inch) flour tortillas

1½ quarts premium coffee ice cream

White Chocolate Bread Pudding with White Chocolate Sauce

*B*READ PUDDING IS THE SIGNATURE DESSERT OF SOUTHERN LOUISIANA, WHERE IT IS EXTREMELY POPULAR. THIS VERSION SUBSTITUTES CHALLAH OR BRIOCHE FOR THE FRENCH CRUSTY BREAD TO GIVE THE BREAD ENOUGH CHARACTER AND RICHNESS TO HOLD UP TO THE CUSTARD MIXTURE.

1 Preheat the oven to 350°F. Butter a 13 by 9-inch glass or porcelain baking dish.

2 Cut the bread into 1-inch cubes; set aside. Combine the cream, milk, and sugar in a medium, heavy saucepan. Bring to a simmer over medium heat, stirring until the sugar dissolves. Remove from the heat. Add the white chocolate and whisk until melted and smooth.

3 Whisk the yolks and eggs in a large bowl until blended. Gradually whisk in the warm cream mixture. Add the bread pieces and stir until coated. Let stand until the bread is very soft, about 5 minutes.

4 Transfer the bread mixture to the baking dish. Cover with foil. Bake for 45 minutes. Remove the foil and bake until the pudding is golden brown and set, about 15 minutes more. Transfer to a rack and let cool slightly.

5 Meanwhile, make the sauce. Bring the cream to a boil in a small, heavy saucepan. Remove from the heat. Add the white chocolate and whisk until melted and the sauce is smooth. Set aside. Before using, reheat the sauce if necessary, stirring frequently over low heat.

6 Serve the pudding warm with the sauce and garnished with chocolate shavings and fresh berries, if desired.

SERVES: 12

CHEF TIP: Use good-quality bar chocolate like Lindt or Baker's; white chocolate chips will not work.

1 pound day-old challah or brioche loaf

3 cups whipping cream

1 cup whole milk

½ cup sugar

10 ounces white chocolate, finely chopped

8 large egg yolks

2 large eggs

White chocolate shavings and fresh berries for garnish

Sauce:

1 cup whipping cream

8 ounces white chocolate, finely chopped

Blueberry and Nectarine Crisp

PORT LENDS A SLIGHT COMPLEXITY TO THE TASTE AND COLOR OF THIS CRISP. TOP WITH VANILLA ICE CREAM.

Topping:

1 cup all-purpose flour

½ cup light brown sugar

½ cup ground pecans or walnuts

2 heaping tablespoons old-fashioned rolled oats

Pinch of nutmeg

½ cup (1 stick) unsalted butter, cut into pieces

Filling:

2 pounds large nectarines (about 6), halved, pitted, each half cut into 4 wedges

4 cups fresh blueberries

1 cup ruby port

2 tablespoons cornstarch

1 teaspoon vanilla

½ cup sugar

1   To make the topping, combine the flour, sugar, nuts, oatmeal, and nutmeg in a large bowl. Work the butter into the dry ingredients with your hands until it is crumbly. (The topping can be made ahead and kept, covered, in the refrigerator for up to a week.)

2   Preheat the oven to 375°F. Butter a 13 by 9-inch glass or porcelain baking dish.

3   To make the filling, combine the nectarines and blueberries in a large bowl. In a small bowl, stir together ¼ cup of the port, the cornstarch, and vanilla until the cornstarch dissolves.

4   Combine the remaining ¾ cup port and the sugar in a heavy saucepan. Stir over medium heat until the sugar dissolves and the mixture comes to a boil; boil for 3 minutes, whisking occasionally. Whisk in the cornstarch mixture and stir until thick and clear, about 30 seconds. Gently stir the port mixture into the fruit. Transfer the filling to the baking dish. Sprinkle the topping evenly over the fruit.

5   Bake the crisp until the nectarines are tender, the filling bubbles thickly, and the topping is crisp and brown, about 40 minutes. Let cool for 15 minutes. Serve warm.

SERVES: 8

Tiramisù with Kahlua and Amaretto

THE LIQUEURS IN THE COFFEE MIXTURE GIVE THIS TIRAMISÙ AN INTERESTING FLAVOR. HAVING LESS SUGAR THAN USUAL WILL APPEAL TO THOSE WHO ARE PUT OFF BY THE CLOYING SWEETNESS OF MANY DESSERTS.

1 Have ready an 8-inch square pan that is attractive enough to use for serving. A glass pan would be ideal to show the layering of the tiramisù.

2 In a large bowl, beat the egg yolks with the sugar. Add the mascarpone cheese and mix well. Add half of the liqueurs and beat until well blended. In a separate bowl, whip the egg whites with the salt until very stiff; gently fold them into the mascarpone mixture.

3 Pour the cold coffee and the remaining liqueurs into a shallow dish; stir briefly. Quickly soak half of the ladyfingers, carefully squeeze out excess coffee and arrange the biscuits in rows to cover the bottom of the serving dish. Cover with half of the mascarpone mixture. Repeat to make 2 layers.

4 Chill at least 4 hours. The tiramisù must be served well chilled. Sprinkle with cocoa powder just before serving.

SERVES: 8

CHEF TIPS: For best results in beating the egg whites, use a copper bowl and a chilled whisk, or use an electric mixer.

For the strong espresso coffee called for in the recipe, buy 2 cups of Starbucks Iced Espresso Grande (without ice), transfer it to a measuring cup and top it off with cold water to the 2-cup mark.

2 egg yolks

6 tablespoons sugar

10½ ounces mascarpone cheese

3 tablespoons Kahlua or other coffee liqueur

2 tablespoons amaretto

3 egg whites

Pinch of salt

2 cups strong espresso, chilled

1 (7-ounce) package ladyfinger biscuits or Italian *savoiardi*

Cocoa powder for dusting

Mormor's Meringue and Cream Torte

A TRUE MERINGUE-LOVER'S DELIGHT, THIS SWEDISH CONFECTION FROM MIA JOHANSSON-STRENCH'S FAMILY TREASURES MELTS IN YOUR MOUTH. "MORMOR" IS SWEDISH FOR GRANDMOTHER, AND IT IS OFTEN THE ELDERS WHO ARE THE MASTER BAKERS AND TEACH DAUGHTERS AND GRANDDAUGHTERS THE ART OF BAKING.

Meringue Base:

¾ cup plus 2 tablespoons sugar

3 egg whites

½ cup chopped almonds

Filling:

1½ cups whipping cream

3 egg yolks

½ cup sugar

4 (39-gram) Heath Bars*, finely chopped

Decoration:

1 cup whipped cream

2 teaspoons cocoa powder

1 cup fresh raspberries

*candy bar made of English-style toffee manufactured by Hershey's

1   Position a rack in the lower level of the oven and preheat the oven to 250°F. Line a large cookie sheet with parchment paper. Draw an 8-inch circle on the paper.

2   To make the meringue base, in a non-plastic mixing bowl combine half of the sugar (7 tablespoons) and the egg whites; beat until stiff peaks form. Fold in the remaining sugar and the almonds. Using a spatula, carefully spread the mixture within the circle on the parchment paper, keeping the sides straight and the mixture an even thickness all over. Bake for 1 hour or until dry and crisp all the way through. Let cool on a rack.

3   Meanwhile, make the filling. Whip the cream a little past the soft-peak stage but not stiff. In a separate bowl, beat the egg yolks and sugar until fluffy. Carefully stir in half of the whipped cream. Fold in the Heath Bars and the rest of the whipped cream.

4   Line a serving plate with a circle of parchment paper and set the meringue on it. (The parchment will protect the meringue base from moisture.) Make a 3-inch-tall collar with foil to fit around the meringue base and pin the collar in place. Using a rubber spatula, carefully spread the filling evenly over the meringue base. Add a foil "lid" to seal the cake tightly. Freeze for at least 6 hours. (The cake can be made ahead to this point; it will keep, frozen, for at least 6 months.)

5   Remove the foil collar. Pipe whipped cream around the base of the cake. Sprinkle with cocoa powder. Return the cake to the freezer; let the cake stand at room temperature 10 minutes before serving. Serve with fresh raspberries and a dollop of additional whipped cream, if desired.

SERVES: 8 to 10

CHEF TIP: A tidy way of chopping the Heath bar is to put it in a resealable plastic bag and pound it with a meat pounder or rolling pin.

Fresh Berry Cake with Raspberry Glaze

WHAT BETTER SUMMER DESSERT THAN A CAKE BURSTING WITH THE FLAVORS OF FRESH BERRIES!

1 Preheat the oven to 375°F. Spray an 8-inch round cake pan with nonstick cooking spray.

2 Rinse and dry the berries and toss them in a bowl with 2 tablespoons of the sugar.

3 In a medium bowl, combine ¾ cup of the sugar, the flour, ginger, baking soda, and salt; whisk thoroughly to mix. In a small bowl, lightly beat the eggs. Stir in the buttermilk and oil. Make a well in the dry ingredients, and pour in the buttermilk mixture. Stir gently until no dry flour is visible. (It is important to go easy on the mixing to ensure a tender cake.) Scrape the batter into the prepared pan. Using a slotted spoon so any juice drains, spoon the berries on top of the batter. Sprinkle the remaining 1 tablespoon sugar over the berries.

4 Bake for 35 to 40 minutes or until a toothpick inserted in the center comes out clean. Cool in the pan on a rack. Remove the cake from the pan and transfer to a serving plate. Drizzle with Raspberry Glaze.

SERVES: 8

1½ cups assorted fresh berries such as blackberries, blueberries, and raspberries*

¾ cup plus 3 tablespoons sugar

1 cup all-purpose flour

½ teaspoon ground ginger

½ teaspoon baking soda

¼ teaspoon salt

2 large eggs

½ cup low-fat buttermilk

2 tablespoons vegetable oil

Raspberry glaze (recipe below)

*Do not use strawberries as these will add too much moisture.

RASPBERRY GLAZE

1 In a small bowl or measuring cup, stir together the sugar and preserves. Add the liqueur a little at a time and stir well. Pour the glaze into a small plastic bag, cut a small hole in a corner and drizzle over the cake.

¼ cup confectioners' sugar

2 teaspoons seedless raspberry preserves

½ teaspoon raspberry liqueur

Golda's Hungarian King's Cake

THIS IS SALLY FARBER'S FAMILY RECIPE. HER GRANDMOTHER ALWAYS USED NUTS IN THE SHELL AND SHELLED THEM HERSELF. WHEN SHE BAKED, SHE WOULD MAKE ENOUGH FOR ALL THE FAMILY, WHICH CONSISTED OF THREE MARRIED DAUGHTERS AND THEIR FAMILIES. FOR SOME UNKNOWN REASON THE CAKE WOULD ALWAYS END UP WITH A PIECE OF NUT SHELL AND IT WAS ALWAYS IN THE PIECE THAT SALLY'S FATHER WAS EATING.

1 To make the cake dough, in a large bowl, cream together the butter, shortening, and sugar. Add the egg yolks, one at a time, beating until smooth after each addition. Beat in the vanilla. Sift together the flour, baking powder, and salt and gently fold into the butter mixture. The dough will be soft. Divide dough into three parts and let rest for 30 minutes (chill slightly if it is too soft to handle).

2 Meanwhile, make the lekvar filling. Combine all of the filling ingredients in a small saucepan. Stir and cover. Over low heat, heat 8 to 10 minutes to soften the prunes. Remove from the heat and let cool for a few minutes. Transfer the ingredients to a food processor and process until the filling is thick and moist. Add a tablespoon or more of water if it is too thick, and a teaspoon or so of sugar if not sweet enough. Chill slightly before using. The filling must have a thick spread-like consistency.

3 To make the sugar and nut filling, stir the pecans and sugar with just enough water to bind the mixture together.

4 Preheat the oven to 350°F. Butter a 10-inch springform pan.

5 Roll out one part of the dough until it is ½ inch thick and place it in the pan. It should come up the sides a little bit. Cover the dough with the lekvar filling, spreading it almost to the edge. Roll out the second piece of dough until it is ½ inch thick and place it over the filling. Top with the sugar and nut filling. Roll out the last piece of dough until it is ½ inch thick and place it over the filling. Beat the egg white until frothy and brush the top of the cake.

6 Bake for 30 minutes or until golden brown. Cool cake in the pan. When cooled, remove sides of pan and cut cake into wedges. Serve with sweetened whipped cream on the side, if desired.

SERVES: 12

CHEF TIP: The lekvar filling can be prepared earlier in the day and left at room temperature.

Cake:

½ cup (1 stick) unsalted butter

½ cup vegetable shortening (preferably Crisco)

1½ cups sugar

3 egg yolks

3 teaspoons vanilla

3 cups all-purpose flour

3 teaspoons baking powder

½ teaspoon kosher salt

1 egg white

Lekvar Filling:

2 cups pitted prunes

½ cup sugar

½ cup water

½ cup fresh orange juice

⅓ cup fresh lemon juice

Grated zest of 1 orange

Grated zest of 1 lemon

Sugar and Nut Filling:

2 cups ground pecans

¾ cup sugar

Black Russian Cake

THIS IS AN EXTREMELY MOIST AND DELICIOUS CAKE. THE COFFEE LIQUEUR GIVES IT AN EXCEPTIONALLY RICH AND DISTINCTIVE FLAVOR. IT IS WONDERFULLY COMPLEMENTED WHEN SERVED WITH COFFEE DRINKS AS AN AFTER-DINNER TREAT.

1 Preheat the oven to 350°F. Grease and flour a 10-inch Bundt pan.

2 In a large bowl, combine the cake mix, pudding mix, sugar, eggs, oil, vodka, liqueur, and water. Beat with an electric mixer for 4 minutes. Pour the batter into the Bundt pan. Bake for 50 minutes, or until a toothpick inserted in the center comes out clean. Cool on a rack.

3 To make the glaze, beat together the coffee liqueur and ½ cup of the confectioners' sugar.

4 Invert the cake onto a cake plate. Poke several times with a fork. Brush with the glaze, then dust with the remaining ¼ cup confectioners' sugar.

SERVES: 12

1 (18.25-ounce) package moist yellow cake mix

1 (5.9-ounce) package instant chocolate pudding mix

½ cup sugar

4 eggs

1 cup vegetable oil

¼ cup vodka

¼ cup coffee liqueur

¾ cup water

Glaze:

¼ cup coffee liqueur

¾ cup confectioners' sugar

DOTTING THE "i"

The Ohio State University Marching Band is one of the few all-brass and percussion bands in the country, and perhaps the largest of its type in the world. They developed and first tried many marching-band innovations. Among them are floating and animated formations, measured step marching, script writing, and the fast cadence with a high knee lift. Brass instruments especially designed for marching bands were also first used at the Ohio State University.

The band dotted the first *Script Ohio* "i," the march from the top of the "o" to the top of the "i", on October 10, 1936, and more than 60 years later, the honor of dotting the "i" is known throughout the world. The drum major struts out toward the top of the "i," with the sousaphone player high-stepping a couple of paces behind. As the crowd's cheering crescendoes, the drum major stops and dramatically points to the spot, and the sousaphone player assumes the post of honor, doffs his hat and bows deeply to both sides of the stadium.

Several prominent individuals, including Bob Hope and Woody Hayes, have been allowed to dot the "i". This is considered the greatest honor the band can give to any non-band person and an extremely special and rare event.
— *Diane Forrest LaHowchic (information courtesy The Ohio State University)*

Script Ohio

Sally's Orange Almond Cake

THIS CREATION OF SALLY FARBER'S WAS INSPIRED BY A WELL-KNOWN SPANISH CAKE KNOWN AS TORTA DE SANTIAGO OR GALICIAN ALMOND CAKE.

1   Preheat the oven to 350°F. Butter and flour an 8-inch springform pan.

2   In a food processor, pulse ⅓ cup of the almonds with the flour until the nuts are coarsely chopped. Remove from the processor and set aside. In the food processor, finely grind the remaining ⅔ cup almonds with ¼ cup of the sugar until the almonds have a flour consistency. Stir in the orange zest.

3   In a bowl with an electric mixer, beat the eggs until foamy. Add the remaining ½ cup sugar and the salt; beat until thick and light colored. Beat in the vanilla and almond extract. Add the almond/flour mixture and the almond/sugar mixture and stir until just incorporated. Pour the batter into the springform pan and bake for 35 to 40 minutes or until a cake tester comes out clean and the cake springs back slightly to the touch.

4   Near the end of the baking time, make the glaze. In a small saucepan combine the glaze ingredients. Bring just to a boil, stirring occasionally, so that the sugar is completely melted. Remove from the heat and keep warm.

5   Remove the cake from the oven and immediately prick the top all over with a fork. Brush the cake with about half of the warm orange glaze. Wait a couple of minutes, then brush the cake with the rest of the glaze.

6   Let the cake cool completely in the pan. (The cake can be made the day before and left in the pan at room temperature, covered with foil.) When ready to serve, remove the sides of the pan and sprinkle the cake with confectioners' sugar. Serve with whipped cream and Grand Marnier Orange Segments (recipe below), if desired.

SERVES: 8

1 cup toasted blanched almonds

⅓ cup plus 2 tablespoons cake flour

¾ cup sugar

Grated zest of 1 orange

3 large eggs

Pinch of salt

1 teaspoon vanilla

½ teaspoon almond extract

Confectioners' sugar for dusting

Orange Glaze:

¼ cup orange juice

½ cup sugar

1 tablespoon grated orange zest

GRAND MARNIER ORANGE SEGMENTS

1   In a food processor, process the zest and sugar until the zest is as fine as the sugar. Over a large bowl, cut the oranges into segments, letting the juice and the segments fall into the bowl. Squeeze the juice from the membranes. Stir in the liqueur and the sugar mixture. Cover and refrigerate overnight. Let oranges stand at room temperature for at least 30 minutes before serving.

Grated zest of 2 oranges

¼ cup sugar

8 firm navel oranges, rind and pith removed

1 tablespoon Grand Marnier or other orange liqueur

Chocolate Almond Pound Cake

THIS MOIST AND CHOCOLATE-COVERED POUND CAKE IS ADDICTIVE.

1 Preheat the oven to 350°F. Butter the sides, bottom, and tube of a 10-inch tube pan. Make a wax paper ring to line the bottom of the pan by placing the pan insert on top of wax paper and drawing around it. Butter the wax paper and place it in the bottom of the pan.

2 Sift together the flour, baking powder, and salt; set aside. Stir together the milk and vanilla; set aside.

3 In the bowl of an electric mixer, cream the butter and sugar on medium speed until light and fluffy. Beat in the eggs, one at a time. On low speed, add one-third of the flour mixture, then half of the milk mixture. Continue alternating the dry and wet ingredients, ending with the flour mixture. Mix on low speed for 2 minutes until well combined. Be careful not to over-mix.

4 Pour two-thirds of the batter into the tube pan and smooth the top with a spatula. Sift the baking soda over the chocolate syrup; stir. Stir in the almond extract. Add the chocolate mixture to the remaining batter and stir until combined, being careful not to over-mix. Pour over the batter in the pan and smooth the top. Do not stir.

5 Bake for 65 to 70 minutes, until a toothpick inserted into the cake comes out clean. Check the cake after 60 minutes. Do not let the top of the cake burn. Cool cake in pan on a rack. When the cake has completely cooled, turn it over onto a rack and remove the pan and wax paper. Turn the cake right side up onto a cake plate lined with four strips of wax paper around the edges.

6 To make the icing, in a small saucepan over very low heat, melt the semisweet and bittersweet chocolate. Be careful not to burn the chocolate. When the chocolate is almost melted, remove from the heat and stir with a small whisk until smooth. Add the butter, 1 to 2 tablespoons at a time, stirring with the whisk after each addition, until smooth. In the beginning the icing will tend to thicken, but it will thin out as you add the rest of the butter. After adding all of the butter, place the saucepan in a bowl of ice cubes. Stir with a spatula very briefly until the icing thickens a little bit. It should be of pouring consistency.

7 Pour the icing over the cake, letting it run down the sides, and sprinkle the cake with the almonds. Pull away the wax paper strips before serving.

SERVES: 12

3 cups all-purpose flour

2 teaspoons baking powder

½ teaspoon kosher salt

¾ cup whole milk

1½ teaspoons vanilla

1 cup (2 sticks) unsalted butter, softened

2 cups sugar

4 large eggs

¼ teaspoon baking soda

¾ cup chocolate syrup

¼ teaspoon almond extract

Chocolate Icing:

4 ounces semisweet chocolate

4 ounces bittersweet chocolate

1 cup (2 sticks) unsalted butter, at room temperature

¾ cup slivered almonds, lightly toasted

Black Forest Cupcakes

A LOVELY ADDITION TO AN AFTERNOON TEA CAROUSEL.

FROM MOTORCYCLES TO MATISSE

From motorcycles to Matisse, there's a museum in Columbus to satisfy any enthusiast. The Columbus Museum of Art houses an outstanding permanent collection of late-nineteenth- and early-twentieth-century American and European modern art and regularly hosts traveling exhibitions on such luminaries as Degas, Monet, and Picasso. The Ohio State University's Wexner Center for the Arts presents some of the best in contemporary visual, performing, and film arts. Explore the African-American experience through interactive exhibits, galleries, and kids' activities at the King Arts Complex.

For fun with a scientific spin, check out COSI Columbus—the Center of Science and Industry—downtown on the banks of the Scioto River. Offering a range of interactive activities, this hands-on science center entertains and educates, encouraging visitors to soar into space and dive deep into the ocean, among other adventures. For a bit of flower power, visit the Franklin Park Conservatory. Dating back to 1895, this amazing facility displays more than 400 species of tropical plants, orchid and bonsai collections, and special exhibits such as striking glass sculptures by artist Dale Chihuly.

The Motorcycle Hall of Fame Museum, east of Columbus in Pickerington, is the leading caretaker of American motorcycling's history and heritage. Home to an impressive collection of motorcycles, it regularly hosts temporary exhibits that pay tribute to popular motorcycling culture.
— *Information courtesy Experience Columbus*

1 Preheat the oven to 350°F. Line 2 mini muffin pans with paper liners.

2 In a medium saucepan, bring 2 inches of water to a simmer; remove from the heat. Cut the butter into 1-inch pieces and put into a heatproof bowl with the chocolate chips. Set the bowl over the hot water and stir until melted and smooth. Let cool slightly. Whisk in the eggs and liqueur. Stir in the sugar and flour until blended. Stir in the pecans and cherries.

3 Spoon the batter into the liners, filling them three-quarters full. Place a pecan half on top of each cupcake. Bake until a toothpick inserted into the center comes out clean, 16 to 18 minutes. Let cool 2 to 3 minutes in the muffin pans, then transfer the cupcake to a rack to cool completely.

YIELD: 24 mini cupcakes

CHEF TIP: Can be stored in an airtight container for up to 3 days or frozen for up to 1 month.

½ cup (1 stick) unsalted butter

½ cup semisweet chocolate chips (3 ounces)

2 large eggs

1 tablespoon cherry liqueur

¾ cup sugar

½ cup all-purpose flour

¼ cup chopped pecans

¼ cup chopped dried cherries

24 large pecan halves

Wexner Center for the Arts

Chocolate and Port Gâteau with Chocolate Icing

THIS IS A VERY RICH DESSERT. IT IS WONDERFUL SERVED WITH FRESH RASPBERRIES.

1 In a medium saucepan, bring the port to a boil. Remove from the heat. Add the butter and chocolate chips and stir with a whisk until melted and smooth. Beat in the egg yolks and sugar. Add the flour and stir until combined. Chill the mixture in the saucepan until slightly warm, about 15 minutes.

2 Preheat the oven to 325°F. Grease a 9-inch tart pan with removable bottom.

3 Beat the egg whites with the salt until they stand in stiff (but not dry) peaks. Gently fold into the port mixture. Do not over-mix. Pour the batter into the pan and level the top with a spatula. Bake for 30 minutes or until a toothpick inserted in the center comes out with a small amount of moist cake but not batter.

4 To make the icing, combine the chocolate with the cream and coffee powder in a saucepan over low heat. When the chocolate is completely melted, stir with a whisk until smooth. Let sit for about 10 minutes to thicken a bit.

5 Place a cake rack over a sheet of wax paper. Remove the rim from the cake pan and slide the pan onto the rack. Pour the icing over it, smoothing it with a metal spatula and letting the icing run down the sides.

SERVES: 8

½ cup tawny port

½ cup (1 stick) unsalted butter

3 ounces semisweet chocolate chips

3 eggs, separated

1 cup sugar

¾ cup all-purpose flour

⅛ teaspoon salt

Chocolate Icing:

8 ounces semisweet chocolate, chopped

½ cup whipping cream

1 teaspoon instant coffee powder

Flourless Chocolate Torte
with Toffee and Amaretto Cream

THE BROKEN SHEETS OF GOLDEN TOFFEE ATOP THE DARK CHOCOLATE TORTE AND A DOLLOP OF STARK WHITE CREAM TO THE SIDE MAKE A DRAMATIC PRESENTATION OF THIS VERY POPULAR DESSERT.

1 Preheat the oven to 350°F. Grease the bottom and sides of a 9-inch springform pan and line the bottom with parchment paper.

2 In a medium bowl, beat the egg yolks with the sugar until thick and creamy. Beat in the cocoa powder and melted chocolate.

3 In a separate bowl, beat the egg whites until soft peaks form. Fold into the chocolate mixture. Pour into the prepared pan and smooth the surface with a rubber spatula.

4 Bake until the cake has risen slightly, the edges are just beginning to set, and a thin glazed crust (like a brownie) has formed on the surface, 30 to 35 minutes. Cool in the pan on a rack.

5 Meanwhile, make the toffee. Melt the superfine sugar in a heavy saucepan over high heat, shaking the saucepan so that the sugar browns evenly. Bring to a boil and cook until golden. Pour onto a sheet of greased foil. Let cool until set. Break into large pieces.

6 To make the amaretto cream, combine the cream, amaretto, and confectioners' sugar and whip until thick and fluffy. Chill well before serving.

7 Remove the sides of the springform pan and remove the parchment paper. Transfer the cake to a serving plate. Garnish with pieces of toffee and serve with amaretto cream.

SERVES: 12 to 14

CHEF TIP: You may replace the amaretto with Cointreau or Kahlua.

6 eggs, separated

½ cup superfine sugar

3½ tablespoons sifted cocoa powder

8 ounces dark chocolate, melted

Toffee:

½ cup superfine sugar

Amaretto Cream:

1 cup whipping cream

2 teaspoons amaretto

2 teaspoons confectioners' sugar

Index

Note: A page number in italic indicates a sidebar.

adobong manok, 180
almonds
  baked brie, 65
  biscotti, 212
  chocolate pound cake, 237
  orange almond cake, 236
  Oriental coleslaw, 117
  paste, 211
  saffron rice pilaf with raisins, 149
  tapenade (olive purée), with brandy, 49
  wedges, with Cointreau, 210–11
amaretto
  flourless chocolate torte with toffee, 239
  tiramisù, with Kahlua, 231
appetizers
  beef, skewered, 81–82
  black bean, olive, and pepper spread, 53
  brie, baked
    with caramel sauce, 65
    with Kahlua sauce, 65
  bruschetta, 54
  calamari, 72
  cheese, baked
    with caramel sauce, 65
    with Kahlua sauce, 65
  cheese dip
    feta and herbs, 52
    swiss and cream cheese, 51
  cheese puffs, 64
  cheese spread, with basil and spinach, 48
  chicken, skewered, 81–82
  chicken bites, with cashew coating, 77
  chicken wings, spicy, 80
  crab cakes, with lemon dill sauce, 73
  crostini
    with curried shrimp, 57
    with portobello mushrooms and
      herbs, 56
  eggs, deviled, with jalapeño, 65
  flatbread with goat cheese, onions, and
    rosemary, 55
  hummus, garbanzo bean and
    cauliflower, 50
  mushrooms, stuffed with crab and
    cheese, 66
  nuts, spiced, 47
  omelet, potato, 68–69
  popovers, blue cheese, 63
  pork
    kabobs, 83
    potstickers, 78–79
    skewered, 81–82
    with red pepper, 84
  potato omelet, 68–69
  potstickers, 78–79

appetizers, continued
  puff pastry
    with honey mustard and prosciutto, 62
    with pepperoni and Asiago, 60
    with pesto, 59
    with spinach and artichoke, 61
  rémoulade, 70
  roulade of smoked salmon and trout, on
    pumpernickel, 58
  satay, 81–82
  shrimp
    rémoulade, 70
    spicy, 71
  spring rolls, 76
  summer rolls, Vietnamese, 74–75
  tapenade, with almonds and brandy, 49
  tomatoes, roasted, with goat cheese, 67
  tortilla chips, 53
  tortilla Española, 68–69
apple cider, mulled, 42
apples
  clafoutis, 227
  salad
    with creamy beets, 116
    with spinach, cranberries, and
      cashews, 110
apricots, dipping sauce, 77
artichoke, puff pastry rolls, with spinach, 61
arugula, salad, with figs and warm shallot
  vinaigrette, 114
asparagus
  berry glazed, 132
  roasted, with goat cheese and bacon, 131
  salad, with red peppers, 109
  soup
    cauliflower, 98
    creamy, 93
avocadoes
  milkshake, 29
  salad, Tex-Mex, 122
  salad, with beef, 126

bacon
  asparagus with goat cheese and
    bacon, 131
  French green bean "kindling", 136
  sautéed collard greens, 134
  warm spinach salad, 113
bananas
  Foster, 223
  salad, with pineapple, kiwi, and
    mango, 90
beans
  black, dip, with olives and peppers, 53
  French green
    "kindling", 136
    with mushrooms, 135
  garbanzo see chickpeas

beans, continued
  green
    dry curry, 137
    minestrone, 101
    salad, with carrots and noodles, 120
  white, minestrone, 101
beef
  barbecued, Korean style, 191–92
  curry, 193
  filled phyllo pastry, 195
  flank steak
    stuffed with prosciutto and spinach, 189
    with Far East seasonings, 188
    with papaya-kiwi marinade, 187
  round steak, rolled and stuffed, 190
  salad
    Tex-Mex, 122
    with avocadoes, 126
  satay, 81–82
  stew, Malaysian style, 194
  tenderloin
    grilled, with Oriental seasonings, 186
    with mustard peppercorn sauce, 185
  veal
    fried, topped with vegetables, 196
    shanks, braised, 197
beets
  roasted, with thyme and orange, 133
  salad
    creamy, with apples, 116
    with pears and bitter greens, 111
beverages
  Bellini, 33
  daiquiri, strawberry, virgin, 32
  kir royale, 32
  lassi, mango, 31
  margarita, 33
  milkshake, avocado, 29
  mimosa, 34
  punch
    cranberry pineapple, 39
    cranberry slush, 37
    cranberry wassail, 41
    fruit slush, 38
    iced tea with bourbon, 30
    mulled apple cider, 42
    sea breeze, 37
    spiced hot, 42
    tea and spices (Cajun-style), 38
  sangría, 35
    strawberry and peach, 35
    white, 36
  tea
    ginger, 40
    green cardamom chai, 41
    iced, 30
    lemongrass, 30
  tropical fruit sparkler, 36

biscotti
  almond, 212
  dried cranberry, 213
blackberries, berry cake with raspberry
  glaze, 233
Black Russian cake, 235
blueberries
  berry cake with raspberry glaze, 233
  crisp, with nectarine, 230
bourbon
  iced tea, 30
  sweet potato purée with bourbon and
    buttered pecans, 143
braciole di manzo alla calabrese, 190
brandy
  apple clafloutis, 227
  sangría, 35
  tapenade (olive purée), 49
bread pudding, white chocolate, with
  white chocolate sauce, 229
briouat bil kefta, 195
broccoli, with ginger, 133
bruschetta, 54
bulgogi, 191–92

cabbage
  minestrone, 101
  Oriental coleslaw, 117
  pork potstickers, 78–79
  salad, with caraway, 117
cakes, *see also* desserts
  berry, with raspberry glaze, 233
  chocolate
    almond pound, 237
    and port, with chocolate icing, 239
    cupcakes with cherry liqueur
      (Black Forest), 238
    flourless torte with toffee and
      amaretto cream, 240
    with vodka and coffee liqueur
      (Black Russian), 235
  orange almond, 236
  white, with prune and nut layers
    (Hungarian King's), 234
calamari, spicy, 72
Calvados, apple clafloutis, 227
cantaloupes, garnish for asparagus soup, 93
carrots
  minestrone, 101
  roasted, with other root vegetables, 152
  salad, with green beans and noodles, 120
cashews
  chicken bites with cashew coasting, 77
  salad, with cranberries and spinach, 110
  spiced nuts mix, 47
cauliflower
  hummus, 50
  soup, 98
celery
  chopped salad with Russian dressing, 121
  minestrone, 101
champagne
  Bellini, 33
  kir royale, 32
  mimosa, 34

char sui, 200
cheese
  asparagus with goat cheese and bacon, 131
  baked
    pasta supreme, 164
    with caramel sauce, 65
    with Kahlua sauce, 65
  beet, pear, and bitter leaf salad, 111
  bruschetta, 54
  caramelized onion and tomato
    galette, 155
  crostini
    curried shrimp, 57
    with portobello mushroom and
      herbs, 56
  dip, feta and herb, 52
  flatbread pizza with caramelized onions
    and rosemary, 55
  goat cheese and potato pie, 156
  Greek shrimp with feta, 166
  grilled chicken Caesar salad, 124
  lemon and roasted garlic risotto, 151
  macaroni with five cheeses, 154
  oven-roasted tomatoes, 67
  peach salad, 115
  pepperoni and Asiago pinwheels, 60
  pesto, 54
  pesto pinwheels, 59
  popovers, with blue cheese, 63
  potato Parmesan au gratin, 144
  puffs, with Gruyère and Parmesan, 64
  roasted potatoes with herbs and
    Parmesan, 142
  rolled stuffed beef, Calabrian style, 190
  smoked ham and vegetable quiche, 158
  spinach and artichoke puff pastry rolls, 61
  spinach salad with cranberry vinaigrette
    and walnuts, 112
  spread
    baked Swiss and cream cheese, 51
    with basil and spinach, 48
  stuffed mushrooms, 66
cherries, chocolate cupcakes, 237
chicken
  adobo (with soy and vinegar), 180
  bites, with cashew coating, 77
  drummettes, 80
  grilled
    Caesar salad, 124
    with creamy mustard sauce, 173
    with herbs, 174
    with plum sauce, 175
  Mediterranean (with prunes and
    olives), 182
  salad, Chinese, 125
  satay, 81–82
  sautéed
    with curried pear sauce, 179
    with paprika and vegetables
      (Paprikash), 180
    with potatoes and other vegetables
      (Clemenceau), 178
  stir-fried
    with snow peas, 177
    with vegetables (Kung Pao), 176

chickpeas, with spinach, 146
chocolate
  cake
    almond pound, 237
    Black Russian, 235
    with port, 238
  cupcakes, with cherry liqueur, 237
  madeleines, 217
  tart, raspberry-topped, with pecan
    crust, 221
  torte, flourless, with toffee and amaretto
    cream, 239
  truffles, with Kahlua, 220
  white, bread pudding with white
    chocolate sauce, 229
chocolate chips, cookies, with mint, 216
chowder, corn, 102
cider, mulled apple, 42
clafoutis, apple, 227
clams, seafood stew, 172
cocktails
  Bellini, 33
  grand mimosa, 34
  iced tea with bourbon, 30
  kir royale, 32
  margarita, 33
  mimosa, 34
coconut
  flan, 225
  satay, 81
  soup, with pineapple, and fruit
    salad, 90
Cointreau
  almond wedges, 210–11
  sangría, 36
coleslaw, Oriental, 117
collard greens, sautéed, 134
Columbus, Ohio
  arts and recreation, *207, 210, 221*
  Battelle, *90*
  Easton Town Center, *223*
  health care, *207*
  High Street, *215*
  museums, *237*
  North Market, *188*
  notable citizens, *92*
  performing arts, *221*
  schools, *207*
  school sports, *210*
  science and technology, *90*
  workforce, *207*
cookies, *see also* desserts; squares
  biscotti
    almond, 212
    dried cranberry, 213
  brown sugar ginger crisps, 214
  madeleines, Grand Marnier, 217
  mint chocolate chip, 216
  oatmeal, crispy thin, 215
  peach currant rugelach, 218
  vanilla cream wafers, 209
cooking clubs
  how to establish, 17–19
  meetings, 17–18
  organizational tips, 19–20

Cooking with Friends
  description, 13
  developing this book, 15–16
  editorial and executive board, *15*
  history, 14
  members, *12,* 13
  sample menus, 21–24
corn
  chowder, 102
  pudding (side dish), 135
  soup, with crab, 103
  Tex-Mex salad, 122
couscous
  with olives and roasted tomatoes, 147
  with shrimp salad, 123
crab
  cakes with lemon dill sauce, 73
  soup, with corn, 103
  stuffed mushrooms, 66
cranberries
  dried
    biscotti, 213
    vinaigrette, with shallots, 112
  grilled chicken Caesar salad, 124
  salad, with spinach and cashews, 110
cranberry juice
  punch, with pineapple juice, 39
  slush, 37
  wassail, 41
crème brûlée, ginger and vanilla, 226
crème caramel, Filipino style, 224
crème de cassis, kir royale, 32
crisp, blueberry and nectarine, 230
crostini
  curried shrimp, 57
  portobello mushroom and herbs, 56
cucumbers
  chopped salad with Russian
    dressing, 121
  gazpacho, 91
  mayonnaise, 170
  relish, 82
  soup
    chilled, 89
    with pork and noodles, 104
cupcakes, chocolate and cherry, 237
currant peach rugelach, 218

daiquiri, strawberry, virgin, 32
desserts, *see also* cakes; cookies; squares
  apple clafoutis, 227
  bananas Foster, 223
  bread pudding, white chocolate, with
    white chocolate sauce, 229
  crème brûlée, ginger and vanilla, 226
  crisp, blueberry and nectarine, 230
  flan
    coconut, 225
    crème caramel, Filipino style, 224
  ice cream sundae, with chocolate-
    espresso sauce, and tortilla chips, 228
  tart
    chocolate, raspberry-topped, with
      pecan crust, 221
    strawberry cream, 222

desserts, *continued*
  tiramisù, with Kahlua and amaretto, 231
  torte, meringue and cream, 232
  truffles, chocolate and Kahlua, 220
dill, soup, 92
dips and spreads, *see also* dressings and sauces
  black bean, olive, and pepper, 53
  cheese
    baked Swiss and cream cheese, 51
    feta and herb, 52
    with basil and spinach, 48
  hummus, garbanzo bean and
    cauliflower, 50
  tapenade (olive purée), with almonds
    and brandy, 49
dressings and sauces, *see also* dips and
    spreads
  apricot dipping sauce, 77
  Asian pear dipping sauce, 192
  balsamic vinaigrette, 153
  browned butter caper sauce, 171
  Caesar salad dressing, 124
  Cantonese marinade, 200
  Chinese, for roasted peppers, 139
  chutney vinaigrette, 110
  coffee and chocolate sauce for
    ice cream, 228
  cranberry shallot vinaigrette, 112
  creamy mustard dressing, 113
  creamy mustard sauce, 173
  cucumber mayonnaise, 170
  curried pear, 179
  herb vinaigrette, 111, 152
  hoisin-chili dipping sauce, 75
  hoisin-sherry marinade, 186
  lemon aïoli, 72
  lemon dill, 73
  lime and garlic dressing, 123
  mustard peppercorn sauce, 185
  oil, tomato, and onion, for beef, 190
  Oriental sesame, 120
  Oriental vinaigrette, 112, 117
  papaya-kiwi marinade, 187
  parsley mustard vinaigrette, 126
  peanut sauce, spicy, 81
  rémoulade, 70
  Russian dressing, 121
  saffron, 69
  shallot honey vinaigrette, 115
  shallot sauce, 203
  shallot vinaigrette, warm, 114
  soy and sesame, 125
  soy dipping sauce, 78
  soy, honey, and garlic marinade, 188
  soy, lemon, and olive oil, 118
  spicy lime sauce, 198
  turkey marinade, 183
  white chocolate sauce, 229
dumplings, 180

eggplant, soup, with tomatoes, 95
eggs
  deviled, with jalapeño, 65
  Spanish omelet, 68–69
espinacas con garbanzos, 146

fagotins des haricots verts, 136
figs, salad, with arugula and warm shallot
  vinaigrette, 114
fish
  salmon
    baked, with capers, 169
    poached, with cucumber
      mayonnaise, 170
  seafood stew, 172
  smoked salmon and trout roulade, 58
  sole, sautéed, with browned butter caper
    sauce, 171
flan
  coconut, 225
  crème brûlée, ginger and vanilla, 226
  crème caramel, Filipino style, 224
flatbread, pizza, with goat cheese,
  caramelized onions and rosemary, 55
Foodbank, Mid-Ohio, *18*
fruit
  apple clafoutis, 227
  bananas Foster, 223
  berry cake with raspberry glaze, 233
  crisp, blueberry and nectarine, 230
  orange almond cake, 236
  raspberry-topped tart, 221
  salad, with pineapple coconut soup, 90
  soup, 90
  strawberry cream tart, 222
fruit punches
  cranberry pineapple, 39
  cranberry slush, 37
  fruit slush, 38
  sea breeze, 37
  tropical fruit sparkler, 36
fruit sparkler, 36

garbanzo beans, hummus, 50
garlic
  pesto, 54
  roasted, 151
gazpacho, white, 91
ginger
  crisps, with brown sugar, 214
  tea, 40
glazes
  berry, for asparagus, 132
  coffee, for Black Russian cake, 235
  orange, for cake, 236
  raspberry, for cake, 233
  rum, for ham, 204
Goi Cuon, 74–75
gougères (cheese puffs), 64
grains, quinoa salad, 118
Grand Marnier
  apple clafloutis, 227
  chocolate truffles, 220
  grand mimosa, 34
  madeleines, 220
  margarita, 33
  orange segments, 236
grand mimosa, 34
greens
  beet and pear salad, 111
  peach salad, 115

greens, *continued*
    sautéed collard greens, 134
    with Oriental vinaigrette, 112

ham
    baked pasta supreme, 164
    honey mustard and prosciutto palmiers, 62
    pork medallions, 201
    rum-glazed, 204
    smoked, with vegetables, quiche, 158
    stuffed in flank steak, 189
honey, vinaigrette, with shallots, 115
hummus, garbanzo bean and
    cauliflower, 50
Hungarian king's cake, 234

ice cream, Mexican sundae, 228
iced tea, with bourbon and juices, 30
insalata di asparagi e peperoni rossi, 109

Jansson's Temptation, 144

kabobs
    beef, chicken, or pork appetizers, 81–82
    pork, Moorish, 83
    pork, with peppers
Kaeng Poo Kab Kao Phod, 103
Kahlua
    chocolate truffles, 220
    sauce, with baked brie, 65
    tiramisù, with amaretto, 231
kir royale, 32
kiwi
    papaya-kiwi marinade, 187
    salad, with pineapple, banana, and
        mango, 90

lamb
    filled phyllo pastry, 195
    rack of, herb-crusted, 184
lassi, mango, 31
leche flan, 224
leeks
    braised, Greek style, with tomatoes, 137
    soup
        dilled, 92
        with asparagus, 93
lemon aïoli, 72
lemongrass
    defined, 30
    tea, 30
lemon rice, 148
    risotto, with roasted garlic, 151
lemon squares, 219
lentils, soup (Masoor Dal), 99
lettuce, asparagus and red pepper
    salad, 109
lumpia Shanghai, 76

madeleines, Grand Marnier, 217
main dishes
    beef
        curried, 193
        flank steak
            grilled with Far East seasonings, 188

main dishes, *continued*
    beef, *continued*
        flank steak, *continued*
            stuffed, 189
            with papaya kiwi marinade, 187
        meat-filled phyllo pastry, 195
        round steak, stuffed, 190
        sirloin, barbecued, with Asian pear
            dipping sauce, 191–92
        stew, 194
        tenderloin
            with mustard peppercorn sauce, 185
            with Oriental seasonings, 186
        veal
            braised shanks, 197
            sautéed with vegetables, 196
    chicken
        grilled
            with plum sauce, 175
            with Provençal sauce, 174
        paillards with creamy mustard sauce, 173
        sautéed
            with curried pear sauce, 179
            with potatoes and other vegetables
                Clemenceau), 178
        stir-fried
            with snow peas, 177
            with vegetables (Kung Pao), 176
        with garlic, prunes, and olives (Pollo
            Mediterraneo), 182
        with paprika (Hungarian Paprikash), 180
        with soy sauce and vinegar (Adobong
            Manok), 181
    ham, rum-glazed, 204
    lamb
        meat-filled phyllo pastry, 195
        rack, herb-crusted, 184
    noodles, Thai fried (pad Thai), 168
    pasta
        angel hair with citrus and mint, 163
        baked, with prosciutto and cheeses, 164
    pork
        ribs, barbecued with spicy lime
            sauce, 198
        stir-fried with tofu, 199
        tenderloin
            Cantonese style, 200
            grilled, spicy, 204
            in baguette, 202
            medallions in crème fraîche, 201
            with shallot sauce, 203
    salmon
        poached, with cucumber mayonnaise, 170
        with capers, 169
    scallops, baked, with garlic and shallots, 165
    seafood stew, 172
    shrimp
        stewed (étoufée), 167
        with feta, 166
    sole, sautéed, with caper sauce, 171
    tofu, stir-fried with beef, 199
    turkey, deep-fried, 183
    veal
        braised shanks (osso buco), 197
        sautéed with vegetables, 196

mangoes
    lassi, 31
    salad, with pineapple, banana, and kiwi, 90
    salsa, 84
ma-po tofu, 199
margarita, 33
marinades *see* dressings and sauces
masoor dal, 99
mayonnaise, cucumber, 170
meringue, torte, with raspberries and
    cream, 232
Mexican truffles, 220
Mid-Ohio Foodbank, *18*
milkshake, avocado, 29
mimosa, 34
minestrone, 101
mint
    chocolate chip cookies, 216
    pea and spinach soup, 96
mushrooms
    baked pasta supreme, 164
    pork potstickers, 78–79
    portobello, crostini with cheese and
        herbs, 56
    roasted, soup, 100
    sautéed, 138
    stuffed, with seafood, 66
    vegetable kabobs, 153
    with French beans, 135
mussels, seafood stew, 172

nectarines, crisp, with blueberries, 230
New Albany, Ohio
    Abercrombie & Fitch company, *52*
    architecture, *27*
    arts and culture, *129, 142, 148*
    Arts Council, *142*
    businesses, *161, 184*
    Chamber of Commerce, *178*
    children's dance and theatre, *87, 156*
    children's playground, *19, 40*
    children's Safety Town, *19, 40*
    children with special needs, *20*
    Classic Invitational Grand Prix
        & Family Day, *45, 57*
    Columbus Coalition Against Family
        Violence, *57*
    Columbus Symphony Orchestra
        concert, *132*
    Community Events Board, *174*
    Community Foundation events, *68*
    Community Performing Arts
        Center, *148*
    community stewardship, *45*
    Cooking with Friends *see* Cooking with
        Friends
    downtown, *165*
    Ealy homestead, *34*
    fitness, *107, 126*
    golf, *110*
    herb gardening, *102*
    history, *31, 34, 39*
    Homeless Families Foundation, *78*
    hospital, *202*
    library, *87, 99, 165*

New Albany, Ohio, *continued*
   lifestyle, *27, 107*
   location, *161*
   Music at Market Square, *138*
   notable citizens, *92*
   parks and recreation, *117*
   schools, *87, 89*
   school sports, *115, 123*
   sports, *107, 110, 115, 123, 126*
   street names, *39*
   surrounding area, *207*
   tennis, *123*
   village center, *161*
   walking trails, *126*
   Wexner Community Park, *40*
   Women's Network, *49*
noodles *see* pasta
nuts
   almonds
      baked brie, 65
      biscotti, 212
      chocolate pound cake, 237
      orange almond cake, 236
      Oriental coleslaw, 117
      paste, 211
      saffron rice pilaf with raisins, 149
      tapenade (olive purée), with brandy, 49
      wedges, with Cointreau, 210–11
   cashews
      chicken bites with cashew coating, 77
      spinach, cranberry, and cashew salad, 110
   mixed, spiced, 47
   peanuts, spicy sauce, 81
   pecans
      baked brie, 65
      chicken bites with pecan coating, 77
      chocolate cupcakes with cherry liqueur, 237
      grilled chicken Caesar salad, 124
      Hungarian king's cake, 234
      pie crust, 221
      sweet potato purée with bourbon and buttered pecans, 143
   pistachio nuts, strawberry cream tart, 222
   walnuts
      beet, pear, and bitter leaf salad, 111
      spinach salad with cranberry vinaigrette and goat cheese, 112

oatmeal cookies, crispy thin, 215
olives
   black
      spread, with black beans and peppers, 53
      with couscous and roasted tomatoes, 147
   green
      chicken Mediterranean, 182
      chopped salad with Russian dressing, 121
      tapenade, with almonds and brandy, 49
omelet, potato, Spanish, 68–69
onions
   caramelized
      and tomato galette, 155
      flatbread pizza with goat cheese and rosemary, 55

onions, *continued*
   roasted, with other root vegetables, 152
   soup
      bisque, 94
      minestrone, 101
      vichyssoise, 97
      with asparagus, 93
oranges
   glaze, 236
   in Grand Marnier, 236
osso buco, 197

pad Thai, 168
palmiers, *see also* pinwheels
   honey mustard and prosciutto, 62
papaya, marinade, with kiwi, 187
parsnips
   roasted, with other root vegetables, 152
   soup, with asparagus, 93
pasta
   angel hair, with citrus and mint, 163
   baked
      macaroni with five cheeses, 154
      with prosciutto, cheese, and vegetables, 164
   farfalle, with roasted peppers, 140
   salad
      Oriental coleslaw, 117
      with carrots and green beans, 120
   soup, with pork and cucumber, 104
   stir-fried, shrimp pad Thai, 168
pastry
   meat-filled, 195
   paté brisée, 157
   pie dough, 155, 158
   smoked ham and vegetable quiche, 158
peaches
   peach currant rugelach, 218
   salad, 115
peanuts, sauce, spicy, 81
pears, salad, with beets and bitter greens, 111
peas, *see also* snow peas
   soup, with spinach, 96
pecans
   baked brie, 65
   buttered, sweet potato purée with bourbon, 143
   chicken bites with pecan coating, 77
   chocolate cupcakes with cherry liqueur, 237
   grilled chicken Caesar salad, 124
   Hungarian king's cake, 234
   pie crust, 221
   spiced nuts mix, 47
pepperoni and Asiago pinwheels, 60
peppers
   kabobs
      with other vegetables, 153
      with pork, 84
   roasted
      and potatoes with rosemary, 141
      Chinese style, 139
      with pasta, 140
   salad, with asparagus, 109
   spread, with black beans and olives, 53

pesto, 54
   pinwheels, 59
pickles and relishes, cucumber, 82
pies
   dough, 155, 158
   goat cheese and potato, 156
   pecan crust, 221
Pinchos Morunos, 83
pineapple juice, punch, with cranberry juice, 39
pineapples
   salad, with banana, kiwi, and mango, 90
   soup, with coconut, and fruit salad, 90
pinwheels, *see also* palmiers
   pepperoni and Asiago, 60
   pesto, 59
   spinach and artichoke, 61
pistachio nuts, strawberry cream tart, 222
pizza, goat cheese, caramelized onions, and rosemary, 55
Poire Williams, apple clafloutis, 227
pollo Mediterranean, 182
popovers, blue cheese, 63
poriyal, 137
pork, *see also* bacon; ham
   kabobs, 83
   mini skewers, with mango salsa, 84
   potstickers, 78–79
   satay, 81–82
   soup, with cucumber and noodles, 104
   spareribs, barbecued, with spicy lime sauce, 198
   stir-fried, with tofu (ma-po tofu), 199
   tenderloin
      baked
         in baguette, 202
         medallions with crème fraîche, 201
         with shallot sauce, 203
      grilled
         or roasted (Cantonese), 200
         spicy, 204
port, chocolate cake, 238
potatoes, *see also* sweet potatoes
   au gratin, 144
   filled phyllo pastry, 195
   minestrone, 101
   omelet (Spanish), 68–69
   pie, with goat cheese, 156
   roasted
      and peppers with rosemary, 141
      with herbs and Parmesan, 142
   vegetable kabobs, 153
potstickers, 78–79
prasa, 137
prosciutto
   baked pasta supreme, 164
   palmiers, with honey mustard, 62
   stuffed flank steak, 189
prunes
   chicken Mediterranean, 182
   Hungarian king's cake, 234
pudding, bread, white chocolate, 229
puff pastry
   honey mustard and prosciutto palmiers, 62
   Morrocan meat-filled phyllo pastry, 195

puff pastry, *continued*
    pepperoni and Asiago pinwheels, 60
    pesto pinwheels, 59
    spinach and artichoke rolls, 61
punches
    cranberry pineapple, 39
    cranberry slush, 37
    cranberry wassail, 41
    fruit slush, 38
    iced tea with bourbon, 30
    mulled apple cider, 42
    sangría, 35
        strawberry and peach, 35
        white, 36
    sea breeze, 37
    spiced hot, 42
    tea with rum and spices, 38

quiche, smoked ham and vegetable, 158
quinoa salad, 118

raisins, saffron rice pilaf with almonds, 149
raspberries
    berry cake with raspberry glaze, 233
    glaze, 233
    meringue and cream torte, 232
    topping for chocolate tart, 221
rémoulade, shrimp, 70
rendang, 194
rice
    lemon and roasted garlic risotto, 151
    lemon-flavored, 148
    pilaf, with saffron, almonds, and
        raisins, 149
    wild and brown, casserole, 150
risotto, lemon and roasted garlic, 151
Rödbetssallad, 116
roulade, smoked salmon and trout, on
    pumpernickel, 58
rugelach, 218
rum
    bananas Foster, 223
    glaze for ham, 204
    spiced punch, 38
rutabagas, roasted, with other root
    vegetables, 152

saffron sauce, 69
salads, *see also* side dishes and vegetables
    apple and beet (Rödbetssallad), 116
    arugula and figs, 114
    asparagus and red pepper, 109
    avocado and beef, 126
    beef and avocado, 126
    beef and vegetables, 122
    beet and apple (Rödbetssallad), 116
    beet, pear, and bitter leaf, 111
    cabbage and caraway, 118
    Caesar, with chicken, 124
    carrot, with green beans and
        noodles, 120
    cashew and cranberry, 110
    chicken
        Caesar, 124
        Chinese, 125

salads, *continued*
    chopped, with Russian dressing, 121
    coleslaw, 117
    couscous and shrimp, 123
    cranberry and cashew, 110
    figs and arugula, 114
    green bean, with carrot and noodles, 120
    greens
        with beets and pears, 111
        with Oriental vinaigrette, 112
        with peaches, 115
    lettuce wraps, chicken, 125
    peach and greens, 115
    pear, beet, and bitter leaf, 111
    quinoa, 118, 119
    red pepper and asparagus, 109
    shrimp and couscous, 123
    shrimp and vegetables, 121
    spinach
        warm, 113
        with cranberry vinaigrette, walnuts,
          and cheese, 112
    steak and vegetables, 122
    vegetables and shrimp, 121
    vegetables and steak, 122
salmon
    baked, with capers, 169
    poached, with cucumber
        mayonnaise, 170
    seafood stew, 172
    smoked, roulade, with trout, 58
salsa, mango, 84
sangría, 35
    strawberry and peach, 35
    white, 36
satay, beef, chicken, or pork, 81–82
sauces *see* dressings and sauces
scallops, baked, with garlic and
    shallots, 165
sea bass, seafood stew, 172
sea breeze punch, 37
seafood
    crab
        cakes, 73
        soup, with corn, 103
        stuffed mushrooms, 66
    scallops, baked, with garlic and
        shallots, 165
    shrimp
        curried, on crostini, 57
        Greek style, with feta, 166
        piquant, 71
        rémoulade, 70
        salad
          with couscous, 123
          with vegetables and Russian
            dressing, 121
        stewed (étoufée), 167
        stir-fried, with snow peas, 145
        with fried noodles (pad Thai), 168
    stew, 172
shallots
    baked scallops with garlic, 165
    pork tenderloin, with shallot
        sauce, 203

vegetable kabobs, 153
vinaigrette
    warm, 114
    with cranberry, 112
    with honey, 115
shrimp
    curried, on crostini, 57
    Greek style, with feta, 166
    lumpia Shanghai, 76
    piquant, 71
    rémoulade, 70
    salad
        with couscous, 123
        with vegetables and Russian
          dressing, 121
    seafood stew, 172
    stewed (étoufée), 167
    stir-fried, with snow peas, 145
    Vietnamese summer rolls, 74
    with fried noodles (pad Thai), 168
side dishes and vegetables, *see also* salads
    asparagus
        berry glazed, 132
        roasted, with goat cheese and
          bacon, 131
    beans
        French green
          "kindling", 136
          with mushrooms, 135
        green, dry curried, 137
    beets, roasted, with thyme and orange, 133
    broccoli, with ginger, 133
    cheese pie, with potatoes, 156–57
    chickpeas with spinach, 146
    collard greens, sautéed, 134
    corn pudding, 135
    couscous, with olives and roasted
        tomatoes, 147
    ham and vegetable quiche, 158
    leeks, with tomatoes, Greek style, 137
    macaroni with five cheeses, 154
    mushrooms, sautéed, 138
    olives, with couscous and roasted
        tomatoes, 147
    onions, caramelized, and tomatoes
        (galette), 155
    pasta, with roasted peppers, 140
    peppers
        roasted, 139
          with pasta, 140
          with potatoes and rosemary, 141
    potatoes
        pie, with goat cheese, 156–57
        roasted
          with herbs and cheese, 142
          with peppers and rosemary, 141
        with cheese, 144
    rice
        lemon, 148
        lemon and roasted garlic risotto, 151
        saffron pilaf, with almond and
          raisins, 149
        wild and brown, casserole, 150
    snow peas, with shrimp, 145
    spinach with chickpeas, 146

side dishes and vegetables, *continued*
  squash and zucchini, 144
  sweet potatoes, puréed, with bourbon
    and pecans, 143
  tomatoes
    with caramelized onions (galette), 155
    with couscous and olives, 147
    with leeks, Greek style, 137
  vegetable kabobs, with balsamic
    vinegar, 153
  vegetable quiche, with ham, 158
  vegetables, roasted, with herb
    vinaigrette, 152
  zucchini and squash, 144
snow peas, *see also* peas
  stir-fried
    with chicken, 177
    with shrimp, 145
sole, sautéed, with browned butter caper
  sauce, 171
soups
  asparagus, 93
  cauliflower, 98
  corn and crab, 103
  corn chowder, 102
  crab and corn, 103
  cucumber
    chilled, 89
    with pork and noodles, 104
  eggplant and tomato gratin, 95
  fruit, summer tropical, 90
  gazpacho, white, 91
  lentil (Masoor Dal), 99
  minestrone, 101
  mushroom, roasted, 100
  onion bisque, 94
  pork and cucumber with
    noodles, 104
  spinach and sweet pea, 96
  sweet pea and spinach, 96
  sweet potato, 97
  tomato and eggplant gratin, 95
  vegetable, 101
    dilled, 92
  vichyssoise, 97
soy, dipping sauce, 78
spaetzle dumplings, 180
Spanish potato omelet, 68–69
spices, Cajun mix, 72
spinach
  cheese spread, with basil, 48
  puff pastry rolls, with artichoke, 61
  salad
    cranberry cashew, 110
    warm, with creamy mustard
     dressing, 113
    with walnuts and goat cheese, 112
  soup, with peas, 96
  stuffed flank steak, 189
  with chickpeas, 146
spreads *see* dips and spreads
spring rolls, 76
squares, *see also* cookies; desserts
  almond wedges with Cointreau, 210–11
  lemon, 219

squash
  soup, dilled, 92
  summer, with zucchini, 144
squid, calamari, spicy, 72
strawberries, cream tart, 222
summer rolls, 74–75
summer squash, with zucchini, 144
sweet potatoes
  puréed, with bourbon and buttered
    pecans, 143
  roasted, with other root vegetables, 152
  soup, with onions, 97

tapenade (olive purée), with almonds and
  brandy, 49
tarte au fromage de chèvre et aux pommes
  de terre, 156
tarts
  chocolate, raspberry-topped, with pecan
    crust, 221
  goat cheese and potato pie, 156
  strawberry cream, 222
tea
  chai, green cardamom, 41
  ginger, 40
  iced, with bourbon and juices, 30
  lemongrass, 30
tequila, margarita, 33
tiramisù, with Kahlua and amaretto, 231
toffee, flourless chocolate torte with
  amaretto cream, 239
tofu
  stir-fried
    with pork (ma-po tofu), 199
    with snow peas, 177
tomatoes
  braised, Greek style, with leeks, 137
  chopped salad with Russian dressing, 121
  galette, with caramelized onions, 155
  minestrone, 101
  oven-roasted, with goat cheese, 67
  soup, with eggplant, 95
  with couscous and olives, 147
tortes
  chocolate, flourless, with toffee and
    amaretto cream, 239
  meringue and cream, with
    raspberries, 232
tortilla Española, 68–69
tortillas
  chips, 53
  crisps, 228
  with Mexican sundae, 228
tropical fruit sparkler, 36
trout, roulade, with smoked salmon, 58
tuna, seafood stew, 172
turkey, deep-fried, 183

veal
  fried (braciola), topped with
    vegetables, 196
  shanks, braised (osso buco), 197
vegetables, *see also* side dishes and
  vegetables; *specific vegetable*
  kabobs, with balsamic vinaigrette, 153

vegetables, *continued*
  mélange of roasted root vegetables with
    herb vinaigrette, 152
  on veal braciola, 196
  potstickers, 78–79
  roasted, 152
  smoked ham and vegetable quiche, 158
  soup, 101
  spring rolls, 76
  stir-fried, with chicken Kung Pao, 176
  summer rolls, 74–75
vichyssoise, 97
Vietnamese summer rolls, 74–75
vinaigrettes
  balsamic, 153
  chutney, 110
  cranberry shallot, 112
  herb, 111, 152, 153
  Oriental, 112, 117
  parsley mustard, 126
  shallot
    warm, 114
    with honey, 115
vodka
  chocolate cake with vodka and coffee
    liqueur (Black Russian), 235
  Russian dressing, 121
  sea breeze punch, 37

wafers, vanilla cream, 209
walnuts
  spiced nuts mix, 47
  spinach salad with cranberry vinaigrette
    and goat cheese, 112
wassail, cranberry, 41
wine
  red, sangría, 35
  white
    sangría, 35–36
    sea breeze punch, 37

zucchini
  minestrone, 101
  soup, dilled, 92
  vegetable kabobs, 153
  with summer squash, 144

Cookbook Order Form

PLEASE SEND A COMPLETED ORDER FORM AND PAYMENT TO:

New Albany Cooking with Friends

PO Box 741, New Albany, Ohio 43054

Fax Number: (614) 939-4611

cookwithfriends@insight.rr.com   www.nacookingwithfriends.com

Qty   Total

_____   *New Albany Cooking with Friends: A Signature Collection* @ $29.95 each   _____

6.75% tax for Ohio residents   _____

Postage and handling (within US and to Canada):
$12.00 for 1 book plus $2.00 for each additional book (up to 5 books*)   _____

Grand Total   _____

Name_____

Address_____

City_____   State_____ Zip code_____

Telephone_____   Email_____

Payment (please circle one):   check (payable to New Albany Cooking with Friends)   Visa   Mastercard

Card number_____   Expiration date_____

Name of cardholder_____   Signature_____

*For shipping and handling information for more than 5 books, please contact us at cookwithfriends@insight.rr.com

Proceeds from *A Signature Collection* will support Mid-Ohio FoodBank,
New Albany Special Connections, and New Albany Safey Town and Adventure Playground.

THANK YOU FOR YOUR ORDER